To the Limit of Endurance

Number Nine:
C. A. Brannen Series

To the Limit of Endurance

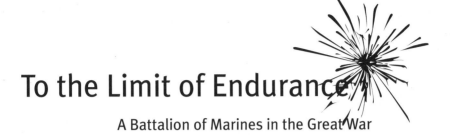

A Battalion of Marines in the Great War

Peter F. Owen

Texas A&M University Press
College Station

Library of Congress Cataloging-in-Publication Data

Owen, Peter F.
To the limit of endurance : a battalion of Marines
in the Great War / Peter F. Owen — 1st ed.
p. cm. — (C.A. Brannen series ; no. 9)
Includes bibliographical references and index.
ISBN-13: 978-1-58544-599-8 (cloth : alk. paper)
ISBN-10: 1-58544-599-1 (cloth : alk. paper)
1. United States. Marine Corps. Marines, 6th
Battalion, 2nd. 2. World War, 1914–1918—Regimental histories—United States. 3. World War,
1914–1918—Campaigns—France. 4. World War,
1914–1918—Campaigns—Belgium. I. Title.
D570.3486th.O94 2007
940.4'5973—dc22
2007003206

Contents

Illustrations

A gallery of photographs follows page 52 and page 130

Preface

IN AUGUST 1917 MAJ. THOMAS HOLCOMB assembled a new battalion of marines at Quantico, Virginia. Ten months later he would lead his men into combat. As Holcomb assessed the problem of preparing his command for the Western Front, he may well have believed he had everything he required: superb manpower, modern weaponry, sound doctrine, and, especially, plenty of time. But when the men of the 2nd Battalion, 6th Marines (2/6) waded into the wheat fields near Belleau Wood in June 1918, they were nonetheless woefully unprepared. The roots of 2/6's shortcomings, the effects of the battalion's misguided preparations on its performance in combat, and the course of its adaptation to the realities of the Western Front are the subjects of this study.

The current transformation of warfare has encouraged historical interest in how armies adapted to change during the First World War. A number of recent historians have analyzed elements of combat effectiveness within the American Expeditionary Forces. Paul Braim, Edward M. Coffman, Mark E. Grotelueschen, Douglas V. Johnson, Stephen J. Lofgren, Allan Millett, Williamson Murray, Rod Paschall, James Rainey, Donald Smythe, and David Trask have all addressed the difficulties the AEF encountered coming to grips with a new type of warfare. These scholars have addressed factors such as inexperience, rapid expansion, incoherent doctrine, insufficient training, and occasional bad leadership.[1]

By focusing on a single battalion, this study provides an enlightening perspective on training, performance, and adaptation that suggests broader conclusions relevant to the study of the AEF and of transformation during war. In the Great War the infantry battalion fought at the sharp end of combat, living and dying according to its tactics and training. A battalion commander directed his men from the front, and his personal leadership affected every soldier. Importantly, the grim effects of attrition were most pronounced within an infantry battalion. Confining the study to a single battalion facilitates dissection and analysis of these factors.

It is important to place this battalion's experience in context. Only twenty-four U.S. divisions participated in what the AEF termed "active combat." These divisions fielded 288 infantry battalions, of which the Marine Corps supplied only 6. The remaining battalions of the AEF were separately categorized according to their division: five divisions were Regular Army, eleven National Guard, and eight National Army. As a marine battalion, 2/6 benefited from service considerations distinct from those associated with these three components of the U.S. Army. Yet in many important ways, the marine battalions more closely resembled their best Regular Army counterparts than either of these professional organizations resembled the National Guard or National Army battalions.[2]

Marine battalions adopted the organization, tactics, equipment, and even dress of the AEF, while the quality of marine recruits and the backgrounds of marine officers and noncommissioned officers (NCOs) had pronounced effects on performance. The marines of 2/6 benefited from officers and NCOs as experienced as any in the AEF. The Marine Corps enjoyed a qualitative edge when selecting its recruits, all of whom consistently completed an uncompromising basic training. The First World War was a defining experience for the Corps, which earned a lasting reputation on the battlefields of France. While these service considerations may suggest lessons of note peculiar to the Marine Corps, 2/6 arguably represents the best that the AEF could be in 1918. Since by many yardsticks this battalion came as close to an ideal organization as any, and because it saw as much brutal and varied fighting as any, the odyssey of 2/6 provides an important case study on the readiness and resilience of all American infantry in the First World War.

Despite its qualitative manpower advantage, 2/6 suffered from the same doctrinal malaise that affected all American fighting units. The Marine Corps had not adequately prepared its officers for the Western Front, and the AEF was hardly ready to remedy these deficiencies. The AEF had yet to develop a relevant tactical doctrine, causing the 2nd Division, in which 2/6 served, to adopt French trench-warfare tactics. Initially, the officers of 2/6 lacked the requisite experience to master the subtle nuances integral to these combat tactics. The AEF exacerbated the problem by burdening the battalion with an unwieldy task organization. As it developed, these tactics proved unsuitable for the type of fighting the marines would see at Belleau Wood and Soissons.

Few U.S. battalions trained as long as 2/6 did before entering combat. Fewer still enjoyed a respite that enabled them to adapt their tactics to the conditions they encountered. The majority conducted two to three months of training before entering combat, then fought one or possibly two major engagements prior to the armistice. In contrast 2/6 trained for ten months, then fought, bled, rebuilt, and fought again several times over. The 2nd Division conducted an intense period of retraining after its initial actions, an opportunity enjoyed by only a handful of divisions. In 2/6 each battle brought fresh lessons and hard-won experience, though decimating the battalion's ranks. Attrition bled the unit so severely that it retarded the maturation of its combat effectiveness.

In these initial battles the battalion prevailed despite its inappropriate tactics because it could sustain tremendous casualties without losing unit cohesion. After these actions the surviving company and platoon commanders had experienced enough fighting to implement the fundamental principles that underlay the French tactics. The battalion retrained after Soissons and adopted a single method of attack that provided a fair formula for success. Concurrent improvements at higher and supporting echelons ensured that 2/6 fought under more favorable circumstances.

Nonetheless, by this point attrition and the unsteady leadership of a new battalion commander threatened to undermine the unit's maturation. In its initial engagements 2/6 had attacked as a spirited band of brothers that could absorb blow after bloody blow yet still fight on as a cohesive unit. By the armistice the battalion functioned as a coldly efficient but brittle machine, one that achieved a single, stunning success in each engagement but shattered its cohesion in the process.

These observations beg the following questions: How good were the leadership, discipline, and morale in 2/6? Were its doctrine, training, organization, and equipment well-suited to the Western Front? Which factors determined the battalion's performance and casualties in each combat operation? How did the unit adapt to its experiences?

I selected this particular battalion for several reasons, not the least of which being that I commanded a platoon in 2/6 in 1987. Of more academic concern, a survey of firsthand sources available revealed a disproportionately high number of excellent accounts by marines of 2/6. In addition, several officers in 2/6, most notably Thomas Holcomb, Clifton B. Cates, and Graves B. Erskine, held very senior positions in the Marine Corps during and after the Second World War. This study thus may prove useful to some future researcher assessing the influence of the World War I experience on the Marine Corps's development between the wars.

Of the official primary sources available, the most useful were the "Muster Roll of the United States Marine Corps," reports submitted by each company monthly; the U.S. Marine Corps Personal Papers and Oral History Collections; Record Group 117.4.2, "Correspondence between Officers of the American Expeditionary Forces and the American Battlefield Monuments Commission," and Record Group 127, A1, Entry 120, "Records Relating to Marine Participation in World War I," from the National Archives and Records Administration; and the U.S. Army's nine-volume *Records of the 2nd Division* and the accompanying *Translations of War Diaries of German Units Opposed to the 2nd Division.* Official published histories included the American Battlefield Monuments Commission compilation *American Armies and Battlefields in Europe;* Edwin N. McClellan, *The United States Marine Corps in the World War; History of the Sixth Regiment United States Marines; History of the Sixth Machine Gun Battalion;* and Oliver L. Spaulding and John W. Wright, *The Second Division, American Expeditionary Forces in France, 1917–1919.* Two tactical publications proved crucial to this study: the Army War College *Manual for Commanders of Infantry Platoons* and the AEF pamphlet *Offensive Operations of Small Units.* Also consulted were official military personnel files from the National Military Personnel Records Center.

A few stylistic comments deserve explanation. Battalion unit designations are abbreviated according to current Marine Corps convention; accordingly, "2nd Battalion, 6th Marines" is written "2/6" and read "Two Six." Marine rifle companies during the First World War were numbered (for example, "78th Company") and redesignated with letters upon joining the AEF (for example, "Company E"). For consistency, I have maintained the numerical marine designation.

I must acknowledge the generous and indispensable assistance of numerous people. First of these are my editors, Mary Lenn Dixon, Thomas Lemmons, and Kevin Brock, and the staff of the Texas A&M University Press for their patient guidance and assistance. Dr. Donald F. Bittner and Lt. Col. John Hemleben provided superb counsel and guidance during my initial graduate research at the Marine Corps University. Brig. Gen. Edwin H. Simmons, USMC (Ret.), director emeritus of the Marine Corps History and Museums Division, availed himself for an enlightening interview. Danny J. Crawford of the division's Research Section lent critical assistance as did J. Michael Miller at the Marine Corps University Archives. Key Marine Corps documents within the National Archives would have escaped my search without the diligent efforts of archivist Trevor Plante. I was especially fortunate to correspond with and interview several relatives of members of 2/6: Jeannette Barber, great-niece of 1st Sgt. Simon D. Barber; J. P. Brannen, son of Cpl. Carl Brannen; John C. Green, son of Capt. Kirt Green; George C. MacGillivray, himself a marine veteran of Guadalcanal, son of Corporal MacGillivray; William W. Sellers, son of Capt. James McB. Sellers; and Lucien H. Vandoren, son of Capt. Lucien H. Vandoren. Marine veteran, historian, and author George Clark never tired of responding to my calls for help. Col. Robert Abbott, Dr. John Cann of the Marine Corps University, Cmdr. Steve Owen, Lt. Col. John Swift, and Col. James Seaton all provided invaluable comment on the manuscript. My friend Alain Romelot of Charly-sur-Marne guided me around the battlefields of Belleau Wood and Soissons. I must acknowledge my lifelong friend Col. Joe Dowdy, who prodded me in 1989, off the coast of Lebanon, to undertake this project. Most especially I must thank my wife, Katie, who has sacrificed more than any other to help me see this book to completion.

To the Limit of Endurance

1 The First to Fight

WHEN CONGRESS DECLARED WAR on Germany in April 1917, the Marine Corps was better prepared to fight than the rest of the country, but nonetheless was not ready to take the field immediately. With a strength of 17,400, the commandant, Maj. Gen. George Barnett, could boast a nucleus of disciplined fighting men already in uniform.[1] Crisp, efficient, and experienced in small wars throughout Latin America, the marines had little doubt their fighting ability would soon be tested in the world war.

Yet experience gained in sea duty, expeditionary service, and occasional combat in Latin America and Asia against poorly organized, trained, and armed irregulars would offer limited benefit to marines thrust into the cauldron of the Western Front. Of course, a number of qualities honed in expeditionary duty would prove indispensable: individual and small-unit discipline, rifle marksmanship, a corps of professional noncommissioned officers, and most of all, an esprit de corps. But the officers' woeful, albeit understandable, ignorance of progressive innovations in warfare and of tactics above the company level would carry a bloody price.

In a pattern that has been often repeated since, a quickening tempo of worldwide expeditions had frustrated the efforts of the Marine Corps to transform itself. In the thirty-six months prior to the American declaration of war, the sea-going companies and garrisons of the corps had been committed to expeditionary forays. Marines had landed in Vera Cruz, Haiti, and Santo Domingo. They had maintained a perpetual commitment to legation guards in Peking and Nicaragua. Finally, they had performed traditional service in marine barracks and aboard U.S. Navy vessels. All of these tasks had further fragmented General Barnett's unrealized vision of a 5,000-man expeditionary Advance Base Force. The Advance Base Force would have fielded a brigade of infantry, artillery, and support troops perpetually ready to sail with the fleet. Yet due to its worldwide commitments, the Corps entered the First World War with no such force; in fact, it possessed only a few scattered companies available for immediate service.[2]

Adamant that the Marine Corps would not sit on the sideline for the duration of the war, Barnett petitioned Secretary of the Navy Josephus Daniels for a meeting with Secretary of War Newton D. Baker. The general offered Baker a regiment of marines for service with the AEF immediately and promised a second regiment to follow soon after. Accepting Baker's precondition to conform to army standards of equipage, uniform, drill, and tactical doctrine, Daniels and Barnett left Baker's office with the promise that the first regiment, the 5th Marines, would accompany the 1st Infantry Division to France. Barnett built the 5th Marines using almost all of his immediately available prewar regulars, scraping together companies from ships and stations along the East Coast and the Caribbean and flushing out their rosters with the few hundred marines then in recruit training. Before the 5th Marines had sailed for France, recruiting began to build a second regiment out of whole cloth: the 6th Marines.[3]

The Recruits

Because the 5th Marines had snatched up most of the marines available, the Corps amassed the majority of the 6th Marine Regiment with men who had enlisted after the declaration of war. As it turned out, this was no handicap. In the spring of 1917, recruiting sergeants found that they could pick and choose from a number of qualified candidates, rejecting all but the most fit. Oddly, in a nation where only one out of thirty men aged eighteen to twenty-four years old were enrolled in college, the Marine Corps found itself deluged with fit, educated collegians.[4]

Recruiters capitalized on exuberant public support following the declaration of war. When the University of Minnesota held a euphoric patriotic rally, 2nd Lt. Carleton S. Wallace, the former captain of its track team, swaggered among the exultant students in his dress blue uniform. Upward of five hundred undergraduates enlisted en masse, with the blessing and applause of the university faculty.[5]

It is safe to say that many of these educated recruits could have obtained commissions in the army or the National Guard. Had these men entered the army, few would have wound up in the infantry. Over the protests of commanders overseas, the army's classification system directed all but unskilled laborers into specialist fields.[6] Because marine volunteers were beyond the reach of the army's personnel bureaucracy, and because specialists comprised a relatively tiny minority in the Corps, marine infantrymen tended to have a great deal more education and vocational training than their army counterparts.

A quick look at a few of these men is instructive of the caliber of marine recruits. One obvious officer candidate, Cadet Carl Andrew Brannen, resigned from Texas A&M University when war came and joined what he described as the "mass exodus" to enlist. At eighteen, Brannen felt that his age designated him as "the most appropriate one" to represent his family in uniform. Discarding a temptation to join the air corps, the young man chose the marines because he liked the recruiting posters.[7]

In another case, Levi Hemrick had dreamt of visiting France all his life. Intelligent, conscientious, and at times philosophical, Hemrick enjoyed a draft exemption as the principal of a three-teacher school in Dekalb County, Georgia. Although he held few illusions about life as a marine, he felt the tug of duty and reasoned a trip to France at least offered a potential chance to see Paris. Hemrick found a milk truck headed to Atlanta and hopped aboard to seek the recruiting office.[8]

Melvin L. Krulewitch had earned a Bachelor of Arts degree in 1916 from Colombia University. The twenty-one-year-old had wrestled, rowed competitively, and thrown the shot put in college. The cousin of a naval captain, Krulewitch pictured marines as gallant "khaki-clad figures springing from the bow of a motor sailor, leaping on the beautiful, silvery sand, with the palm trees growing around there in Central America." Reality hit him abruptly. His fellow recruits left him aghast. "Many of them needed a bath," he later recalled, surmising, "The Marine Corps Recruiting Station on East 23rd Street was used for gathering up, shall we say, the leavings of the Bowery and all kinds of people of that sort." Krulewitch's fellow recruits notwithstanding, the recruiters generally selected only literate, healthy, and physically fit young men, self-starters who responded to the Marine Corps's "First to Fight" call.[9]

Born on Chicago's South Side, John Joseph Kelly had grown up quick-fisted. The fourth son of Irish immigrants, Kelly made up for his five-foot-five, 112-pound build with irrepressible humor and never-say-die toughness. Somewhat of a romantic, he had run off with a traveling circus at sixteen. He returned home two years later to discover that his eldest brother was a captain in the National Guard, another was flying in the Air Corps, and the third was in army intelligence. Kelly felt obligated to do one better and sought out the marines.

Don Paradis was working his way up the ladder at the Detroit City Gas Company. The company had given him a new Model T Ford, which he used to make his rounds investigating customer billing complaints. Paradis was a big man, and at twenty-one years of age, he had common sense to match his size. Management appreciated the way the young man kept their customers happy, and his future with the gas company looked bright. But Paradis took the developing U-boat menace personally and began making the rounds of the recruiting offices. He found the army recruiting office filthy, smoky, and crowded with drunks. The navy office was worse. Dejected, he headed home only to happen upon some marine recruiters who had pitched a tent in Grand Circus Park. They promised him that he would be in France in four to six months. "That promise, and those clean, snappy uniforms did the trick."[10]

Throughout the spring and summer of 1917, many thousands more found their way to recruiting stations in the big cities. As this vast, untapped sea of men came rushing to arms, the Marine Corps had little difficulty finding adequate recruits. The "First to Fight" poster campaign became one of the most successful recruiting drives in history. By war's end the Marine Corps would have rejected three applicants for every man enlisted.[11] Those accepted were typically fit and eager, the cream of the first crop of volunteers. Trains whisked those enlisting east of the Mississippi to Port Royal, South Carolina. A quick barge ride across the sound deposited them on a humid, flea-bitten sand spit of misery: Parris Island.

Parris Island

The primary mission of the Marine Corps recruit depots has never been to teach combat skills. At Parris Island (and in 1917 at Mare Island on San Francisco Bay) the Marine Corps transformed civilians into marines and boys into men. The job has been not so much to instruct techniques as to instill discipline. Drill instructors have used nearly unvarying methods over the years, most of them unpleasant, to foster an immediate, instinctive obedience to orders.

Training at Parris Island in the summer of 1917 was often harsh because it was so primitive rather than through any brutal design. Most recruits slept under canvas. Those who had bedding found it infested with vermin. A metal pail served as each man's laundry. Drill sergeants inspected each recruit's freshly cleaned clothing daily (often tossing wet uniforms into the company street for real or imagined dirt). The depot had not yet built a proper chow hall, and Don Paradis recalled sitting on the ground while sand dusted his food as he ate. Levi Hemrick loathed breakfast: "foul-smelling eggs, spuds boiled in their jackets, fried fat-back, and black coffee." Recruits debated whether the Marine Corps served such ghastly food deliberately, as part of the general toughening process, or because of wartime short-ages. But they unanimously agreed that it tasted awful.[12]

Lacking facilities to house the influx of recruits, the Corps used labor parties to build new buildings on the island, physically tough-ening the privates of 1917 as they constructed barracks in which most would never sleep. Hoisting I-beams in thirty-man teams built strength and teamwork. Private Krulewitch remembered unloading so many bricks that the rough edges sandpapered the skin off his hands. Companies marched from their bivouacs to the beach to fill pails with oyster shells, then staggered back in agony one mile to the company street. The crushed shells were dumped in the street to cover the soft sand.

Recruits who had grown up in the squalor of America's slums and dirt-poor farms were occasionally ambivalent to the physical labor, harsh quarters, and unsavory rations. Nonetheless, the harsh regimen of drill and physical training profoundly impressed every recruit. In 1917 the Marine Corps divided a recruit's ten-week stay at Parris Is-land into roughly equal amounts of drill, rifle marksmanship, and working parties.[13] This regimen greatly surpassed what most First World War armies devoted to recruit training in both time and in-tensity.

Drill enjoyed primacy in Parris Island's curriculum, and with good reason. Popularly known as "torture under arms," rifle drill instilled unwavering discipline and an unequivocal understanding that the Marine Corps tolerated nothing short of swift, precise, and complete obedience to commands. Brannen, a former Texas A&M cadet, ob-served, "My drill master was satisfied with nothing short of perfec-tion."[14]

Drill served more than just instilling discipline. In 1917 "close or-der" and "open order" drill served as rudimentary tactical doctrines. In a manner that would not have looked out of place in the Civil War, the Marine Corps expected its battalions to fight as precision units, marching in the same formations and to the same commands on the battlefield as on the drill field. If the Corps could be condemned for clinging to outdated tactics, it must be remembered that the European armies of 1914 had abandoned such methods only after suffering through months of colossal casualties.

Marines learned bayonet fighting through the most painful drill of all. Pvt. Melvin Krulewitch called it torture, "because you had to squat down in a peculiar position and hold that nine-pound rifle out and take the most fantastic positions from which you couldn't move. It would be a crippling position. And then the crazy things they taught you: parry, bayonet thrust, parry saber thrust, parry cavalry attack."[15] He was right. There would not be many opportunities in France to parry cavalry sabers. Some of these drills were crazy things to teach men headed to the Western Front, but every exercise painfully performed with precision welded the recruit's bond of discipline more tightly.

If drill was the catechism of the Marine Corps, then rifle qualification was a sacrament. In a war where many army replacements would arrive at the front without having fired a weapon, marine marksmanship would astound both allies and adversaries. More than any other attribute, rifle marksmanship set the U.S. Marine apart from other fighting men. Superbly accurate and firing a powerful .30-caliber round, the 1903 Springfield was a rifleman's rifle. The Corps knew how to teach men to shoot and refused to cut corners. After three weeks of tedious instruction and practice, recruits found themselves scoring hits from the thousand-yard line.[16]

Throughout the days of hard labor, drill, and rifle practice, the recruits exercised at every opportunity. Paradis remembered six o'clock reveille was rudely followed by a twenty-minute jog about the parade deck. He found the frequent conditioning hikes even tougher. The heavy field pack carried in those days hung from two thin web shoulder straps that cut into a man's shoulders. On the hottest days some recruits finished only by "sheer grit and determination."[17]

Most painful of all, rifle calisthenics, or "butts and muzzles," forced recruits through unnatural contortions with their nine-pound rifles. Krulewitch could still chant the drill decades later: "Front and center, up on shoulders, low swing, muzzle forward, lunges, right lunges, left lunges." Another marine lamented his experience in a letter home. "Designed to make either a MAN or a lunatic out of you. I have heard big men sobbing and crying through gritted teeth. I have done it myself."[18]

Despite their moans and lamentations, nearly all marines recognized, even boasted, of the transformation their drill sergeant had wrought. Levi Hemrick claimed that he "took on from fifteen to twenty-five pounds, most of it going into broadening of the shoulders, hardening of arm and leg muscles." The former schoolmaster felt justifiably proud of his appearance: "The sun's heat and the outdoor exercise added a healthy rugged tone to our facial complexion and strengthened the lines that led to the mouth and chin. Both the head and body posture went through a change that indicated development of physical power, firmness, determination and boldness; a fighting man's image." Marine recruit training in the Great War was effective, albeit anachronistic. The Corps consistently developed all of its recruits to its rigid standards. Since the army struggled with expansion, poor personnel management, equipment shortfalls, epidemics, weather, disorganization, and an absence of definitive guidance, "Training of the U.S. Army . . . was shallow, inappropriate, and spotty." In contrast, marines left Parris Island physically and mentally tough and harshly disciplined. They could shoot well. They marched magnificently. If they were unready for the Western Front, they were bright, eager, and superbly prepared to learn.[19]

Unbeknown to the new marines, their leaders were far less prepared to train them.

The New Lieutenants

The recruits shipped to Parris and Mare Islands would fill the platoons of the 6th Marines. Finding lieutenants to lead these platoons presented a more troubling dilemma. The Marine Corps had no officer candidate school in 1917 and no recruiting organization to find and screen potential officers. Marine officers had been commissioned for a number of years from the Naval Academy or from the enlisted ranks, but neither of these traditional sources could meet the demands of the expanding Corps. The navy, suffering growing pains of its own, had invested too much engineering and seamanship training on its midshipmen to squander them on the marines. The Corps itself was swearing in many top NCOs as lieutenants.[20] However, should the commandant commission too many of his sergeants, the relative quality of both his officer and NCO ranks would inevitably suffer.

General Barnett took a bold step. Writing personally to the deans of the country's top universities and military schools, he offered to commission around ten seniors from each on the dean's recommendation alone. Caught in a manpower crisis, he gambled that a reputation of good character would compensate for a lack of military screening and indoctrination. By October 1917 Barnett had commissioned 506 lieutenants directly from civilian life.[21] To his credit, many of these men proved themselves as some of the top platoon leaders in Marine Corps history.

One of the best of these was a football player and Phi Beta Kappa student in his senior year at the University of Chicago, James Mc-Brayer Sellers. Sellers had graduated from Wentworth Military Academy in Lexington, Missouri. Attending Wentworth was a Sellers family tradition—he had been born on campus during his father's tour as superintendent, and his brother served on the staff. When Wentworth received the commandant's letter, his brother advised him to pounce on the opportunity. "I did not know what the outfit was," Sellers later confessed. "I thought it was something like the Coast Guard or the Merchant Marine." The young man walked down to the recruiting station in Chicago and liked what he heard. His classmate and football captain, Red Jackson, was game too. The Corps wanted them to depart immediately, but a month of classes and final examinations were all that stood between them and their diplomas. Well, they reasoned, there was a war on after all. The two pleaded their case to the dean, who acquiesced, swept up in the patriotism of the moment. "You go on in, and I will get you your diploma," he assured them. The classes and exams were dispensed with, and within days, Sellers was riding eastward with his degree and a commission as a second lieutenant.[22]

The Marine Corps shortly assembled 345 shiny new lieutenants like Sellers at a rifle range in Winthrop, Maryland. The new officers congregated here for instruction and, hopefully, qualification with the Springfield rifle. Sellers qualified on both the army and navy rifle courses, though he found the navy course much tougher; it included firing from the standing position at the five-hundred-yard line. Fulfilling the commandant's promise to adopt army regulations did not translate into suspending the Corps's high standards of marksmanship. Having won shooting trophies at Wentworth Military Academy, Sellers was one of only two candidates who fired expert on the navy course.[23]

While at Winthrop, Sellers first met many of the future lieutenants with whom he would serve in France. Twenty-three-year-old Clifton B. Cates had earned his Bachelor of Law from the University of Tennessee in 1916. A baseball and football player, Cates would earn a remarkable reputation in combat and emerge as one of the standout marine officers of the war. Carl Brannen would remember him as "the most optimistic person I ever saw."[24]

Another Tennessee man, twenty-two-year-old Johnny Overton, the Yale track captain and a Skull and Bones member, had set records in middle- and long-distance running his senior year. Born in Nashville, the son of the president of Alabama Fuel and Iron Company, Johnny had intended to follow his father in coal mining or iron manufacturing.[25]

One twenty-year-old lieutenant was not at all happy with his decision to join the Marine Corps. Graves B. Erskine had served along the Mexican border with the Louisiana National Guard and felt that entitled him to have an opinion on how the Corps ought to be run. So far, this outfit was moving far too slowly to suit him. Erskine had left Louisiana State University to fight, not to sit around Winthrop, Maryland. "I'm going to Canada to join the Black Watch," he declared to those in earshot and submitted his resignation. Lt. Col. Paul Rixey summoned the impertinent upstart, patiently lectured him on how things worked in *this* Marine Corps, and tore up the resignation letter.

Erskine soon made friends with Lt. William Arthur Worton. Unlike most of the Winthrop bunch, Worton had received his commission through a peculiar footnote to Marine Corps history, the 1st Marine Company of the Massachusetts Naval Militia. Enjoying a similar status to members of the National Guard, the sixty-five Massachusetts Marines drilled aboard the battleship USS *Kearsarge* each weekend and put to sea for two weeks each summer. Quite the blue-blooded company, it was supervised by an inspector-instructor from the regular Marine Corps named Capt. Frederick H. Delano, a relative of the Roosevelt family. At sixteen Worton had enlisted as a private. By the time he entered Boston Latin School at age nineteen, the young man held a commission from the governor of Massachusetts as a marine officer. After America declared war, the Department of the Navy federalized the 1st Marine Company and distributed its marines throughout the Corps.[26]

After three weeks of rifle marksmanship at Winthrop, the fresh lieutenants reported to the new Officer Training School at Quantico, Virginia. Along with similar courses held at Marine Barracks Washington, D.C., and Parris Island, the Officer Training School fell far short of expectations. Instead of preparing to command rifle platoons, the disgusted young officers piddled away their days learning semaphore and drilling. The Marine Corps made some effort to train them for combat, though, the students throwing dummy grenades and learning a little extended-order drill. But most officers completed the course knowing little more of tactics than their greenest private. In Cates's estimation, "Half of it wasn't worth a hoorah."[27]

The Corps pulled virtually all of the platoon commanders destined for the 6th Marines out of Cates's Officer Training School class two months before graduation in order for them to command the marines expected imminently from Parris Island. According to James Sellers, the staff at the school selected the best officers in the class for service with the 6th Marines.[28] If true, the regiment would have culled no more than 135 out of the class of 345—roughly the top 40 percent. Once again the Marine Corps's inability to provide training and experience mandated reliance on a qualitative measure of innate ability. These lieutenants would have to master their duties while on the job. Untrained and unfamiliar with the ways of the Corps, the eager new officers were ripe for molding in the hands of their new battalion commander.

The Commander

Maj. Thomas Holcomb's seventeen years ashore and afloat spanned an era in which an officer's actions in a few moments under fire could spawn a legendary reputation. Renowned officers such as Johnnie "The Hard" Hughes, "Hiking Hiram" Bearss, and Smedley "Old Gimlet Eye" Butler enjoyed a modest celebrity status in the Corps. Perhaps it says as much about Holcomb as it does about his contemporaries that he had won no nickname. A native of New Castle, Delaware, Holcomb spent much of his early career quietly guarding naval installations in the Philippine Islands against a possible reemergence of Emilio Aguinaldo's insurrection. He later served a number of years in Peking, deterring any Boxer-like uprising that might once again imperil the Legation Quarter. Neither emergency came to pass, and Holcomb's name stayed out of the headlines.

In 1910 Holcomb extended his tour in Peking to study Chinese full time. This extension in such a coveted assignment reveals that he had already been identified as an officer of exceptional potential. Although having earned only a high school degree, Holcomb valued education far more keenly than did the majority of his contemporaries. The Marine Corps kept him at his studies for four years, recognizing his intellect and the importance China might play in the near future.

Not merely an academic, Holcomb demanded the same high standards of discipline and toughness as any marine officer. During his time in Asia, he had earned a minor reputation as a competitive shooter, firing on the Marine Corps Rifle Team on six occasions before 1912. Holcomb had little use for a marine who could not shoot. One of his platoon commanders stated years later that the major accepted only experts and sharpshooters into his battalion; mere marksmen were not allowed.[29]

In 1914 the commandant brought Holcomb to Washington as his inspector of target practice. This was Holcomb's first stateside shore duty in twelve years. A politically astute officer, he served for a period as General Barnett's aide, taking pains to ensure the Marine Corps stayed in good graces with patrons such as Assistant Secretary of the Navy Franklin D. Roosevelt. In 1917 Holcomb was a newly married major looking forward to the birth of his first child. On August 14 he took command of the 2nd Battalion of Col. Albertus Catlin's 6th Marine Regiment.[30]

Holcomb's officers remember him as a strict yet compassionate leader, a "deep, deep thinker" who held strong views on the role of an officer. Arthur Worton recalled that the major lectured him one time on the magnitude of his duties as an instructor: Holcomb viewed an officer as a teacher, his men as students. "For the few minutes that you're in battle, that's nothing; you're always a school teacher in the Marine Corps. If you're not a good one, then you're not a good marine." Lieutenant Cates was unimpressed with Holcomb—at first: "When we first joined the battalion we didn't think too much of him. We thought he was a little too uppity. We soon changed our opinion. After Soissons, he was tops with everyone."[31]

Holcomb whisked his officers off to training schools whenever possible, even taking commanders from their platoons at the front. Lieutenants could expect frequent, personal instruction from their battalion commander on proper conduct. Graves Erskine thought he would show off as a busy beaver one morning at Quantico by shoveling snow. Decidedly unimpressed, Holcomb brought him up short: "Let me tell you something, young man. You are a commissioned officer. You get paid to use your brain and not your hands. Now put that shovel away and get an orderly to do it."[32]

The major had old corps ideas about discipline as well and how enlisted marines should behave. But a good marine could expect a fair shake and a second chance, when warranted. Two privates with otherwise spotless records came before the major one day on charges. The camp guard had caught them devouring ice cream they had lifted from a Quantico druggist. The two sheepish men reported to Holcomb, fearing a court-martial or worse. He gave them holy

hell, despite their platoon commander's attestation to their previous good service and a plea for clemency, and sent the two off to the
brig to sweat it out overnight. When they reappeared before him in
the morning, Holcomb let them off with a stern warning, provided
that they reimburse the druggist. He took care to attribute his le-
niency to their platoon commander's favorable remarks, then dis-
missed them. In doing so Holcomb had not only preserved the clean
records of two promising marines but also had shrewdly reinforced
the lieutenant's stature and authority within the platoon.[33]

Such a bond between officers and men is crucial to combat effectiveness. Building his battalion from the ground up, Holcomb had to
quickly assemble a collection of raw recruits, green lieutenants, and
a sprinkling of old Corps regulars. There would be time for tactics
later. Before the scholar-commander could open school, he had to
first build a thousand individual marines into a spirited team.

The Battalion

The new base at Quantico did not impress marines reporting aboard
in the summer of 1917. Unpaved streets of mud and the scent of fresh-
cut lumber betrayed the last-minute efforts of the Corps to construct
a base for expeditionary troops. The clatter of construction and the
pounding of hammers never ceased. As trains dumped off recruits
at the railhead, senior NCOs formed them into rifle companies and
marched them to wooden barracks smelling of green pine. Marines
bound for France drew forest green winter uniforms for the first
time, underlining the hasty, urgent assemblage of wartime units: new
green uniforms, freshly cut lumber, and raw, untrained manpower.

Having just landed after a short boat ride from the Winthrop rifle
range, James Sellers jotted down his first impression of the emerging
camp:

> The place here looks just like pictures of mining towns I have
> seen. There is one small street which constitutes the original
> town. This street leads right up from the pier. There are rows
> and rows of unpainted wooden shacks, sprung up almost lit-
> erally overnight. The small streets between are all cut up with
> rainwash, and we stumble over what is left of a former small
> forest, roots and stumps, and sewer excavations. South of the
> town is another city of tents from which come the sound of
> bugles, roll calls and the barking of dogs. And there is a dance
> hall where they charge 20c for a dance with one of the painted

ladies brought to town for the purpose. Between nearly every two tents, there are dummies for bayonet practice, and at all hours of the day enlisted men can be seen slaughtering these dummy Germans.[34]

As fast as the carpenters built new barracks, they filled with new marines. The small battalion headquarters included a commander, executive officer, adjutant, quartermaster, and sergeant major. In France most battalion commanders would scrounge up an additional lieutenant and assign him the duties of intelligence or scout officer. According to army tables of organization, the battalion would need more than thirty officers and one thousand men to fill its authorized ranks.

A captain commanded each of the four companies, with a first sergeant assigned as his senior NCO. The army's system of letter-named companies imposed later in France would be universally ignored in the Marine Corps. Each marine company retained its unique numerical designation. In 2/6 the companies numbered 78th, 79th, 80th, and 96th. Most companies received five lieutenants, an executive officer and four platoon commanders. Each platoon rated a gunnery sergeant as platoon sergeant and six sergeants to lead each of the eight-man squads.

Holcomb and his few regulars found themselves engulfed by wartime volunteers. Ninety-three percent of the regiment's men had seen less than twelve months' service.[35] As trainloads of raw manpower disgorged from the railhead, the handful of old salts hastily organized and equipped the four rifle companies.

Capt. Robert E. Messersmith, supposedly a "tough hombre," commanded the 78th Company. Messersmith had served as a Coast Guard cadet in 1909 before his commissioning. He had fought in skirmishes in Nicaragua, including the capture of rebel forts at Coyotepe and Barranca in October 1912.[36]

Messersmith posted 2nd Lt. Amos Shinkle as his company executive officer over 1st Lt. Julius C. Coggswell. A squeaky-voiced lieutenant from Charleston, South Carolina, Coggswell did not make much of an impression at first. Sellers described him in a letter as "well meaning but very kiddish and irresponsible, and more or less of a joke in the company." Shinkle, however, impressed Messersmith as a self-reliant man who had overcome humble origins through bullheaded determination. One of the few prior NCOs among the lieutenants, Shinkle had never finished grammar school and had worked as a common laborer and carpenter from the age of thirteen to support his family. He had enlisted in 1913 and had served as an enlisted marine assigned to the presidential yacht. Shinkle had passed the officer's examination in 1917, which included algebra, geometry, and plane trigonometry, through determined self-study.[37]

Lt. James Sellers, the Wentworth Military Academy graduate who had distinguished himself on the rifle range at Winthrop, commanded one of Messersmith's platoons. Lt. James Pickens Adams, who had played football for Clemson, led another platoon and helped Sellers coach the company football team. Sellers noticed that Adams had a tendency to lower his head and drive through obstacles rather than expending precious brainpower figuring out an easier way.[38]

Nearly two-thirds of Messersmith's men had enlisted in the mass exodus from the University of Minnesota. They had ridden to Mare Island together, endured boot camp together, and crossed the country together.[39] The old regulars and remaining wartime volunteers like Johnnie Kelly, the pint-sized Chicagoan, found themselves surrounded by collegiate men-turned-marines.

In order to present a uniform appearance on parade, Messersmith organized his four platoons by height. A diminutive gunnery sergeant named Charles Lyman seemed small in front of the tall marines of Sellers's 1st Platoon. The lieutenant thought that "any one of them could physically have broken [Lyman] in two," but nobody doubted who ran the platoon. Lyman had left Philadelphia years earlier and had become accustomed to a certain way of soldiering that no world war was going to upset. He napped in the platoon office after lunch each day, and God help the private who disturbed him. Far from resenting the inexperience of the raw lieutenant, Lyman took a fatherly interest in his eager platoon commander. Sellers in turn quickly learned to trust his gunnery sergeant's words of advice.[40]

Capt. Randolph T. Zane reported from the marine barracks at Pearl Harbor and took command of the 79th Company. Zane was married to the daughter of the governor of California. Although Holcomb may have appreciated Zane's political connection, he learned to prize the captain's leadership far more. Lieutenants Worton and Erskine, the well-mannered Bostonian and the Louisiana upstart, reported to Zane. "Calm as a cucumber," recalled Erskine. But "if you didn't come from the Naval Academy you didn't stand very high with him." "An extremely capable student of war," thought Worton. "A wonderful captain for a young officer to serve under." Zane "looked after his company after we got to France, and was *respected* by the men of his command," recalled an NCO in Erskine's platoon.[41]

Second Lt. John A. West, a husky All-American fullback from the University of Michigan, joined the 79th Company as a platoon commander, as did a hell-raising young graduate of Indiana's Culver Military Academy, Charles I. Murray. Track star Carl Wallace, whose mere presence had stampeded students from the University of Minnesota, also commanded a 79th Company platoon.[42]

Zane had the extreme good fortune to have 1st Sgt. Bernard L. Fritz assigned to his company. One of the most remarkable NCOs to ever serve in the Marine Corps, Fritz had studied at the university in Heidelberg, Germany, before returning to the United States to become a Jesuit priest. Following a different call, he gave up his vestments and enlisted as a marine private. By the time he joined the 79th Company, Fritz had nearly twenty years of service. He had fought at Veracruz along the way and had refused a commission despite his obvious qualification. "I'm a first sergeant, and I enjoy being a first sergeant," he explained to Worton. Originally from Casker, Minnesota, Fritz had a reputation as a tough disciplinarian. He recited regulations as he had learned to quote scripture. Towering over the company, the sergeant enjoyed the immediate, unanimous respect of every marine.[43]

In sharp contrast to Fritz, Sgt. Richard Mazereeuw stood out from his peers for sheer vulgarity. Tall, thin, and irrepressibly Irish, Mazereeuw had a filthy, unmistakable mouth, which made him a minor celebrity within the 79th Company. He smoked a long-stem pipe incessantly yet could set a superb example of military correctness when the mood struck him.[44]

The 79th Company's privates included Oscar Rankin, a "pious peaceful man" and a former minister. He would often lead prayer meetings in the company mess tent. Rankin partnered up with Pvt. Thomas Gragard. Two brothers who had enlisted together, Sidney and Glenn Hill, also wound up in the 79th Company.[45]

Capt. Franklin B. Garrett sought to build his 80th Company into a handpicked force. He sorted through the trainloads of new marines, weeding out men he determined to be unfit for expeditionary service. Grover O'Kelley, "a fine, Christian man, from Birmingham, Alabama," and his boot-camp buddy Don Paradis easily met Garrett's standards. The company commander promoted the pair to corporal in September and to sergeant a month later. Lieutenants in the 80th

Company included Thomas S. Whiting, a Virginia Military Institute graduate, and two graduates of Culver Military Academy, Cecil B. Raleigh and Charles H. Ulmer. A bright young Georgetown lawyer named Lucien H. Vandoren would join them before embarkation, and a third Culver graduate, John G. Schneider of St. Joseph, Missouri, would report in France.[46]

Capt. Donald F. Duncan commanded the 96th Company. He also hailed from St. Joseph and had graduated from Culver; his family knew that of young Lieutenant Schneider. A bachelor, Duncan had served in the Canal Zone in Panama and guarded naval prisons in Portsmouth, New Hampshire, and Puget Sound, Washington. He had spent two uneventful years on Guam just prior to joining the 6th Marines. Duncan was beloved by his marines, in whom he encouraged a rough-and-tumble spirit. First Lt. James F. Robertson, an émigré from South Africa, was the 96th Company's executive officer. "A big, rough and ready man. . . . [A] fine marine, but the men hated his guts. He was a hard boiled rascal," remembered Cates.[47]

Duncan gave Lieutenant Cates command of the 96th Company's 4th Platoon. To Cates's delight, he found himself teamed with charismatic Gy. Sgt. (Gunnery Sergeant) Fred Stockham. As the platoon sergeant, Stockham quickly won his lieutenant's admiration as well as the respect of his marines. "When the going was hard, and your tail was dragging, it was Sergeant Stockham who was there with a word of encouragement or a pat on the back that pulled you through," recalled one marine. When mail call disappointed a young marine, the gunny would reassure him with his upbeat sayings, "'No news is good news,' or, 'That letter can arrive tomorrow.'"[48] Orphaned as a young boy, Stockham had enlisted in 1903. After serving with Holcomb in the Legation Guard in Peking, Stockham left the Corps in 1907 to join the Newark (New Jersey) Fire Department. Returning to the ranks in 1912, he fought at Leon, Nicaragua. When the United States entered the Great War, Stockham was a recruiting sergeant in St. Louis, Missouri.

Captain Duncan's hometown friend, Sgt. Aloysius Sheridan, was likewise assigned to the 96th Company. Duncan no doubt exerted some influence to get his friend into his command, but if their was any jealousy over Sheridan's relationship with his captain, there is no record of it.[49]

In late summer a middle-aged lieutenant by the name of Evans Spalding reported to the 96th Company. Spalding came from money and had traveled the world a bit. His father ran the Boston and Maine

Railroad, providing the son with the finances to dabble about looking for adventure. He had served in a volunteer ambulance unit in France and made sure his new comrades knew all about it. Spalding had "*savoir faire*," according to Worton, and evidently did not take all of this Marine Corps discipline too seriously. Holcomb hated him.[50]

Holcomb knew his battalion would soon depart for France. The 5th Marines had sailed while many of his men were just arriving at Parris Island. Johnnie-the-Hard Hughes's 1st Battalion, 6th Marines, only days older than Holcomb's battalion, followed in mid-September.[51] But Holcomb could count himself lucky to have a core of old-school regulars leading his companies. His lieutenants appeared fit, spirited, and eager to learn. Likewise he could hardly have asked for a more disciplined, high-spirited bunch of privates. The battalion commander needed only a modern tactical doctrine and the time to train his marines to execute it. Tragically, he would have neither.

"Machine Like Musketry": Training at Quantico, August 1917–January 1918

The failure of the Marine Corps to provide a coherent tactical doctrine would undermine Holcomb's efforts to train 2/6. In 1917 rifle marksmanship dominated American tactical thought, and Lt. Col. Harry Lee was the rifle's first prophet. The executive officer of the 6th Marines, Lee had written an article in the fledgling *Marine Corps Gazette* that espoused the tactical doctrine of the Corps. Based on the U.S. Army's *Field Service Regulations of 1914* and *Infantry Drill Regulations of 1911,* Lee's article reveals at a glance the outdated tactical thought that misguided marine instruction in 1917.[52]

Lee's "Musketry Training" envisioned the company attack as an exercise in precision drill, emphasizing absolute, centralized control. He flatly stated his object that "the action may be machine like." Small-unit leaders did not learn principles to apply to dissimilar situations; they learned a complicated drill by rote and functioned within it automatically.

In Lee's ideal infantry attack, the company deployed on line from a rendezvous point. Company commanders designated sectors of fire, rates of fire, range estimation, and other fire commands to the lieutenants, who in turn relayed the commands to squad leaders, who relayed them to the riflemen. During the conduct of fire, the captain would issue commands to send forward replacements or ammunition and to change the method of fire. Once "fire superiority" was achieved, he would commence rushes.[53]

Anticipating that battlefield noise would drown out shouted commands, Lee wrote out a complicated system of whistle and hand-and-arm signals. For example, for the signal "What range are you using?" he instructed: "Extend the arm toward the person addressed, one hand open, palm to the front, resting on the other hand, fist closed." Other signals directed the riflemen to rush by company, by section, by squad, and by individual. Signals from battalion commanders and higher were to be relayed by semaphore (hence the classes Cates had attended in Officer Training School). An attack consummated when the marines charged the enemy position, during which phase Lee admonished all to "look to their target, in order that, on arrival at the position, their bayonets may pierce that at which they have been firing during the advance."[54]

The entire system of centralized command and control hoped to overcome the fog of war by creating an orderly linear battlefield. Marching and shooting as a well-drilled team, a disciplined force of well-trained riflemen would rush and blast their way through a similarly arrayed but poorly disciplined force of inferior marksmen. Predicated on the principle of fire superiority, this doctrine demanded that the attacking force neutralize the defender with accurate, sustained rifle fire. Lee's instructions were doomed to fail when applied by unsupported infantry attacking concrete-reinforced machine gun positions. The inflexible tactics would leave bewildered small-unit leaders unprepared to capitalize on fleeting opportunities. Unable to achieve fire superiority, devastated by the defensive fire of water-cooled machine guns, and deaf and blind to commands from surviving leaders, marines would be forced to improvise in a Marine Corps that had excoriated individual initiative for the sake of discipline.

Lee's article lagged behind army doctrine in published regulations. The *Infantry Drill Regulations* emphasized individual initiative over rigid formations. Soldiers were expected to rush from covered position to covered position, not dash madly and erect. Small-unit leaders especially were told: "It is impossible to establish fixed forms or to give general instructions that will cover all cases. Officers and noncommissioned officers must be so trained that they can apply suitable means and methods to each case as it arises." Despite these progressive concepts, the *Infantry Drill Regulations* "remained comfortably American in its emphasis on initiative, but it ignored the drastic changes in technology," according to one recent historian. Notwithstanding Lee's article, marine officers were expected to be proficient in the *Infantry Drill Regulations,* and their tactical views generally mirrored those of the mainstream Regular Army. Professional soldiers of the prewar army prided themselves on their marksmanship as much as any marine.[55]

European officers of 1914 would have felt comfortable teaching Lee's method of musketry. But during three years of war, European armies had adapted to the realities of modern warfare. Reinforced machine gun positions, sited to cut down attackers with interlocking fields of fire, dominated the No Man's Land between enemy lines. It took artillery, not mere riflemen, to achieve fire superiority over such positions. To conserve manpower, the Germans had pulled many defensive positions back to the reverse slope, hidden from artillery forward observers. By 1917 German development of storm-troop infiltration techniques neared full implementation.[56]

The Marine Corps had not lived these three years with its head in the sand. Commandant Barnett had shipped officers to the Western Front as observers. These observers, and army officers on similar missions, brought back the techniques of trench warfare. Yet they did not revolutionize tactical doctrine. Consumed by expeditionary duty and focused on developing the Advance Base Force, the Corps had little inclination and fewer resources to revamp infantry regulations. Furthermore, both army and marine officers believed that a decision on the Western Front could only be achieved by an end to the trench-warfare stalemate and a return to an ill-defined concept of "open warfare." It was in this vaguely understood arena, out of the trenches, in which Americans vowed their peerless riflemen would realize victory.[57]

Holcomb pressed his battalion through what training he could. The men formed for physical training each morning at precisely 7:00 A.M. New marines sadly found that they had not left butts and muzzles behind at the recruit depot. They bayoneted straw dummies, threw dummy grenades, and drilled hour after hour. Accustomed to perfection, the old regulars honed the battalion to parade-like sharpness. "Precision was the password," remembered Lieutenant Erskine.[58] But the companies allocated most of their dwindling number of training days to polishing an implausible doctrine.

If the marines' precision marching lacked relevance to the Western Front, it nonetheless made for a grand parade. On September 5, 1917, the 6th Marines boarded trains at Quantico Station early in the dawn. The regiment marched down Pennsylvania Avenue in a "Preparedness Parade" led by President Wilson and returned late in the evening, dehydrated and sore from a long day of waiting and marching. Still clad in summer khakis, Corporal Paradis thought he looked less than warlike: "We were a skinny, undressed outfit in that parade."[59]

The men in the ranks had begun to suspect that preparedness for parades did not amount to being ready to fight. Years later, after surviving five major offensives, Paradis would note with hindsight that they should have learned how to dig foxholes. It is one thing to dig a hole in the ground but another to dig fast, narrow, and deep while under fire. Lieutenant Sellers agreed: "Practically all we did was drill and dig trenches. We did not have any real combat training, map reading, or other important requirements for survival in the field." Arthur Worton also thought the lieutenants ought to have devoted some time to map reading and the use of terrain.[60]

Holcomb too sensed the battalion had much to learn. Toward the end of September, he began to put companies through mock trench fighting.[61] Absent formal guidance and experienced instructors, these exercises provided little practical benefit. They did demonstrate the battalion commander's justifiable concern for his unit's unprepared state and the willingness of his men to apply themselves to what opportunities arose.

The major began quizzing his officers on French and British field manuals. He took the information in these guides seriously and expected his officers to follow suit—as young Lieutenant Cates discovered one day. Cates had not done the reading on field engineering prior to officers school.

> Holcomb: "How many entrances should a dugout have?"
> Cates: "Well, at least one."
> Holcomb was not amused. "That's a hell of a bright answer!"
>   he barked.[62]

The two officers were sizing each other up, and thus far neither was decidedly impressed with the other.

Over the winter, veteran officers from Canada came to Quantico to lend a hand. These men had survived horrific combat at places such as Vimy Ridge. "My eyes have been opened up a great deal," Lieutenant Sellers wrote home. Although after an inspection Holcomb received a commendatory letter, complimenting him on the battalion's superb discipline, appearance, and spirit, the Marine Corps could not provide the field training the companies needed, including cooperation with artillery, penetrations and envelopments, gas warfare, and a hundred other life-or-death tasks the marines would perform the following summer.[63]

The Lewis Gun Experiment

Maj. Edward B. Cole commanded the 1st Machine Gun Battalion.[64] His gunners fired the excellent Lewis machine gun, one of the best modern weapons available. The Marine Corps had purchased the weapons after its observers had seen the American-designed Lewis prove itself in battle with the British Expeditionary Force. Light enough for one man to carry, the Lewis could be taken forward alongside advancing riflemen. The accurate and dependable weapon promised to deliver a heavy punch during the critical assault phase.

Initially the Marine Corps issued the machine guns exclusively to Cole's command. But in order to place firepower in the infantry battalion's hip pocket, each battalion formed a machine-gun platoon. Major Cole's machine gunners, many of whom had attended a school at the Lewis gun factory in Utica, New York, instructed 2/6's gunners. A prehistoric lieutenant named Thomas J. Curtis, with twenty years' enlisted time and a "fondness for using big words wrongly," ran the classes. Sellers heard him remonstrate his students, "Name those parts proper and chronological, and don't be ambiguous."[65]

After a week of such instruction, the Marine Corps pronounced that each company would have its own eight-gun platoon. The erstwhile students now became the duty experts and instructed the battalion's four new machine-gun platoons. But before the incorporation of Lewis guns got far along, a critical shortage of the weapons in the Air Corps forced the marines to relinquish all their guns. The machine gunners of 2/6 reverted to riflemen. A critical augmentation to the battalion's firepower had been lost. It would not be made good.[66]

Humor Is Out of Place

Quantico turned cold by the end of September, but not all of the marines had been issued forest green wool uniforms. Holcomb was not about to have his men fall out wearing two different-color uniforms, no matter how deeply the cold bit through their thin summer khakis. The battalion formed for physical training each frosty morning, shivering together, privates and majors alike.

This astounded the aristocratic Lieutenant Spalding. He was a grown man, not a twenty-year-old cub. He had been to France—why he was practically a veteran—and was not about to freeze when he had a perfectly fitted regulation set of forest greens to keep him warm. One especially bitter morning, Spalding donned his winter service trousers and prescribed field shirt before marching down the company street with the 96th Company.

As Holcomb sat astride his horse, scrutinizing the ranks, he espied the solitary green figure in a mass of khaki. The major exploded. "Mr. Spalding!" he yelled, spurring over to the 96th Company. "Mr. Spalding! Where did you get those breeches?" The nonplused lieutenant turned, saluted, and replied, "Brooks Brothers, Major, Brooks Brothers." Holcomb barely managed to keep his cool. "I'll give you five minutes to get out of them and get back here."

"He has no sense of humor, no sense of humor," Spalding wailed as he dashed off.[67]

To young Lieutenant Worton fell a task for which the Massachusetts Naval Militia had never prepared him. Quantico had become a boomtown, with a rough frontier look and temptations to match. Following the thousands of marines and construction workers came ladies who knew how to part a man from his pay. The women set up shop at the Potomac Inn and in a few small houses, and the men and the money soon followed.

The marine base encircled Quantico town, pinning it against the Potomac River. The base commander felt that it was more or less a Marine Corps town. He summoned Worton, whose lot had come up as the officer of the day, and instructed the young lieutenant to march into town with the military police and run the women out.

Worton's great prostitute round up started at ten in the morning on a Tuesday, when few customers would be around. Presenting a no-nonsense appearance in his pressed khakis with sword, Worton dutifully marched his guard into Quantico. It was a small town, and in no time the MPs had one hundred ladies lined up on the platform. Worton purchased one-way tickets to Washington with Corps funds. He noted approvingly that his marines were polite and deferential and that they maintained a professional bearing in their interaction with the working girls. A few of the older NCOs did seem a bit familiar to some of the ladies, and one sergeant in particular whispered at length to one of his charges, but the authority of the officer of the day seemed intact.

The train soon arrived, and Lieutenant Worton began to breathe more easily. He began to congratulate himself for escaping embarrassment during this potentially undignified task. Then, alarmingly, six of the women left the line and strode directly toward him. Worton froze. Filled with dread, the young gentleman stood flat-footed as the ladies surrounded him. Each one then planted a warm, full kiss on the flabbergasted officer before stepping aboard the train. To the delight of the NCOs, they called out loudly to Worton, "Goodbye, sweetheart!"[68]

Final Days

Worton and 2/6 would depart from the same platform soon. The 1st Battalion had sailed in September. When the regimental headquarters company and the 73rd Machine Gun Company left on October 16, speculation of an imminent departure gripped the men. Only Holcomb's 2/6 and Berton Sibley's 3/6 remained at Quantico. Pre-embarkation inspections and final gear issue seemed to confirm what everyone suspected: 2/6 would leave next, and soon. Holcomb's companies were up to strength. His men had drawn their combat issue. He had completed about all the training Quantico offered. The major had one last matter to attend to before he would be ready.

Mrs. Holcomb had not yet given birth. Major Holcomb knew what awaited him and his men on the Western Front, and he could estimate the odds against his safe return as well as the next man. Presumably he felt that if he ever was going to lay eyes on his child, he had better do so before going off to war. As a recent aide to the commandant, Holcomb undoubtedly still held some influence at Marine Corps headquarters. One can only conjecture who whispered what to whom, but without a doubt the order of embarkation was reversed. Sibley's 3/6 sailed for France first, on October 24. As the train carrying Sibley's marines pulled away from Quantico, Holcomb's battalion snapped to present arms while a band played "The Star Spangled Banner."

The image of Holcomb's battalion seeing off Sibley's reveals a forgotten, human side of the old Marine Corps. Amid all the complexity and confusion involved in transporting a brigade of marines to France, despite all the heady urgency of wartime, the Corps interchanged the departures of two battalions so one major could see his child born. In Europe a war of attrition was being fought, and there the human element was being supplanted by statistics. The contribution of the puny U.S. Marine Corps could be eaten up in a few days' "wastage" on the Western Front. Perhaps after a few bloodbaths had decimated the battalion several times over, the faces of the men would lose significance and become numbers in a ledger. But in October 1917 the Corps had not shaken off the closely knit bonds of the prewar years, and its officers still considered themselves part of an exclusive fraternity, even an extended family.

Whether or not Holcomb urged his superiors to switch the orders, or merely kept silent, the decision uncomfortably smacks of cronyism. No doubt there were men in both battalions who had good reasons to wait on the next ship, just as there were other men in both battalions eager to get the great move started. Still, on the balance one battalion was pretty much the same as the next. In the calculus of 1917, enabling one father to see his firstborn child was still as strong a reason as any to shuffle troop movements.

A few weeks after 3/6 sailed, Bea Holcomb gave birth to a healthy boy.[69] The major's men took advantage of the reprieve. Many enjoyed furloughs over Thanksgiving and Christmas. As they filtered back to Quantico, the winter grew miserably wet and severe. If anything, training accelerated. The Canadian officers and a few Scots supervised construction of an authentic trench line, and the companies became reasonably adept at trench warfare. As the new year arrived, daily rumors tortured the anxious leathernecks.

In mid-January 1918 the word came. The night before embarkation, Lt. Charles Murray decided it was an occasion for a lot of drinking. Cates, Erskine, West, and the bachelor company commanders, Duncan and Messersmith, were up for a hell raising, and the drinking commenced. Somewhere along the way they discovered that if one tossed a .45-caliber pistol round into the stove, it exploded. Inevitably that struck all hands as just the thing to do the night before sailing off to war, and more rounds were scrounged up.

Once again Arthur Worton had the duty, and he found himself trying to maintain his dignity as he trotted through the snow to the officers quarters, sword banging against his thigh. "Gentleman!" he declared as he entered, "This must stop!"

It stopped only long enough for the four lieutenants to overpower Worton, lash him to the bulkhead, and nail his shoes to the floor. The lieutenants poured liquor down his throat as the two captains beamed with pride. But before they could force much booze into Worton, the sergeant of the guard showed up looking for his duty officer. This took the wind out of everybody's sails. The four officers could truss up old Worton, but nobody messed with the sergeant of the guard. The party subsided, Worton recovered, and he took his revenge a few hours later when he roused four tender-headed lieutenants for a five o'clock reveille.[70]

On January 19 the marines of 2/6 at long last heaved full packs onto their shoulders, crunched through a newly fallen snow, and boarded the train. Huddled in their forest greens and overcoats, the men endured a cold ride north to Philadelphia, where they filed aboard the troopship USS *Henderson* one thousand strong. After a short stop in New York to join a convoy, the battalion was underway for France, the war, and the American Expeditionary Forces.

2 The American Expeditionary Forces

ON FEBRUARY 8, 1918, MAJOR HOLCOMB and his marines filed down the gangway of the USS *Henderson* at the port of Saint-Nazaire and into a war far different from the one America had entered ten months previously. Germany had gambled that the same unrestricted submarine campaign that brought the United States into the war would prevent a large American army from taking the field in Europe. As indicated by the safe arrival of ships such as the *Henderson,* Germany's U-boat fleet had failed to stop the flow of Allied ships across the Atlantic. If the war progressed deep into 1918, German troops would face significant numbers of American divisions on the Western Front.

Although the U-boats had not prevented the American Expeditionary Forces from reaching French soil, Germany's peace with Russia, the Treaty of Brest-Litovsk, had freed reinforcements for the Western Front. German general Erich Ludendorff saw here a final, though closing, window of opportunity to win the war. His title as "first quartermaster general" did not adequately describe the authority he wielded as the right hand man to the chief of the General Staff, Field Marshall Paul von Hindenburg. Ludendorff retained operational control of all Germany's armies, and his strategy for 1918 would seek a decision in the west before U.S. power reached a strength to prove decisive. For both sides, the campaign would be a race against the clock.

Pershing's Army

Gen. John J. Pershing, commander in chief of the AEF, had to accomplish two conflicting objectives. Most immediately he had to train and equip American soldiers in sufficient numbers to help defeat Imperial Germany. Of only slightly less importance to the Wilson administration, he also needed to field these troops as an independent army, one that would make an undeniably crucial influence upon the course of the war. The contribution of this victorious American army would make the president of the United States an equal partner

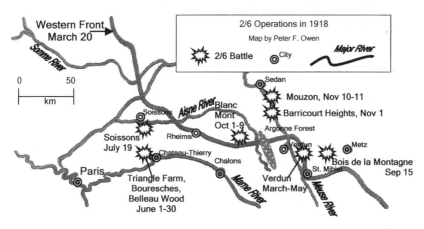

with other Allied heads of state at postwar negotiations. This was no trifling matter for President Wilson, for his Fourteen Points conflicted with the war aims of the Allies. In order for Wilson to achieve his policy objectives at the negotiating table, the AEF would need to make an incontestably decisive contribution to Germany's defeat.[1]

Central to Pershing's vision for the AEF would be a uniquely American tactical doctrine, expressed only as a foggy concept called "open warfare." As opposed to trench warfare, which had brought the Europeans only stalemate and horrifying casualties, open warfare would seek a decisive battle of maneuver. U.S. officers felt the innate qualities of rifle marksmanship and independent character would give Americans the edge in this arena. Unfortunately the AEF had no document that adequately explained this concept and how it was to be applied by the American battalions on the Western Front.[2]

The War Department's *Field Service Regulations* constituted the cornerstone of American doctrine. The book addressed large-formation maneuvers, such as approach marches, patrolling, and manning outposts. Yet nowhere in its pages could a soldier find any reference to "open warfare." Perhaps the most progressive example of American doctrine was the *Manual for Noncommissioned Officers and Privates of Infantry*. According to a recent historian, the manual "displays, with a clarity that is somewhat absent in the higher level manuals, the essence of the concept of open warfare as it had evolved from its distinctly American roots. That notwithstanding, it displays reflections of a more mechanical day of warfare." Both the *Field Service Regulations* and the *Manual for Noncommissioned Officers and Privates of Infantry* failed to incorporate many aspects of combat that had already proved elemental in the European war. Had Pershing's army mastered the tactics in these two books, his soldiers would merely have been on par with the European armies of 1914. Night combat, camouflage, trench warfare, cooperation with artillery, and the use of machine guns all received perfunctory attention, yet these were the bread-and-butter tactics of armies on the Western Front. The defensive role of machine guns was neglected entirely. The War Department and the AEF had failed not only to explain Pershing's concept of open warfare but also to offer any sort of doctrine relevant to the current conflict.[3]

Pershing's divisions could not afford to wait for open-warfare doctrine to catch up. Each division instead attempted to complete three-month training cycles that, with French assistance and instruction, decently prepared them for trench fighting. Only one, the 1st Infantry Division, completed the cycle from start to finish. The experience of the 2nd Division, which Holcomb's battalion now joined, typifies the experience of most AEF units. Although the remainder of the division had preceded 2/6 to France, many of these battalions had been detailed to guard duty or working parties. A few fortunate units had trained alongside the French, though this experience roughly compared to what 2/6 had accomplished at Quantico. The arrival of 2/6 coincided with the commencement of the first month of real training for the 2nd Division.

Arms and Equipment

The individual marine rifleman was reasonably well clothed and equipped by 1918 standards. The 6th Marine Regiment directed the following for service at the front: helmet, overcoat, sweater, service coat and breeches, flannel olive drab shirt, woolen undershirt and drawers, gloves, canvas leggings or wrap puttees, field shoes, both English and French gas masks, and metal identification discs. In the haversack marines bundled three pairs of socks, one more set of woolen underwear, an extra shirt, a razor, a comb, soap, a towel, a toothbrush, an overseas cap, and two days' reserve rations. Wrapped around the haversack was a blanket and either a poncho or slicker. Some men carried extra equipment such as wire cutters, picks, trench knives, and trench boots.[4]

The wool, forest green service uniform kept marines warm even when damp, though it proved stifling in hot weather. By June most enlisted marines would replace their tattered, lousy forest greens with army olive drab. Enlisted marines retained their special identity only by prominently displaying the Marine Corps emblem on their overseas caps. According to Lt. Arthur Worton, all hands also wore the metal eagle, globe and anchor device on the right pocket of their army blouse. A few industrious fellows retained their marine buttons and sewed them on the army blouses as well.[5]

The cotton field equipment was sturdy enough, though the shoulder straps of the haversack cut painfully into a man's shoulders on the march. The bayonet, mess kit, and shovel all hung on the outside for easy access. A first-aid bandage and a single canteen hung from the ammunition belt. Contrary to current practice, marines in 1918 were expected to drink sparingly. The U.S. Army's *Field Service Regulations* stated, "Under ordinary conditions a canteen of water should last one man a day's march."[6] With a basic load of one hundred rounds of rifle ammunition, a marine equipped as described above hefted a load weighing more than sixty pounds.

The primary hand grenade supplied to marines was the French F1. This was a "pineapple-type" fragmentation grenade. By 1918 the F1 grenade had a modern, pull-type fuse that burned for five seconds before detonation.[7] The U.S. Army developed a web grenade carrier during the First World War, but few if any made it into the hands of marines. Accordingly, marines stuffed their grenades into the cargo pockets of their blouses.

Four marines in each platoon went into battle with Vivien-Bessiers grenade launchers affixed to the muzzles of their Springfield rifles. These French weapons shot a powerful fragmentation grenade two hundred yards. The rifle grenadier launched the weapon by placing the butt of his rifle on the ground, inserting a grenade and rotating it so it locked into the launcher. He then held the muzzle at an angle that corresponded to the estimated range and fired a standard ball round through the grenade. This launched the grenade and ignited the fuse. The grenade's seventy-five-yard fragmentation radius compensated for the launcher's imprecise aim. The arc of the trajectory especially suited this weapon to firing over the head of friendly troops.[8]

Having surrendered the superb Lewis machine guns, marines were disgusted to discover they would have to stagger into the fight armed with the cumbersome, temperamental Chauchat automatic rifle. Lieutenant Sellers recalled: "They looked like they were made out of cigar boxes and tin cans, and we had an awful time making the men carry them. It was almost as dangerous for the man shooting one as it was for anyone out in front being shot at." Lieutenant

Cates agreed: "[The Chauchat was] a pain in the neck. Lock it in a vice, lock it in and fire it at 100 yards and you'd have a dispersion of 20–25 feet. Very heavy. My platoon had 19 clip bags. We had to rotate them on the march, the lieutenants taking their turn same as everyone. Those bags weighed 50–60 pounds." Heavy, inaccurate, and unreliable, the Chauchat nevertheless constituted the battalion's only organic direct-fire weapon heavier than the Springfield rifle.[9]

While the AEF failed to furnish adequate firepower to its soldiers and marines, the men were fed well when the food could reach them. Many ate better than they had at home. Each company had a mess sergeant and two cooks, who rolled a kitchen behind the column. With fires lit on the march, the cooks baked fresh bread and brewed a stew called "slum gullion," or just "slum." Another popular staple was the "trench doughnut," consisting of bread dipped in a milk-and-sugar batter, then deep fried in boiling grease. Lieutenant Worton, who later served in the Second World War as a general officer, observed, "Food was, in some ways, better than what we had in the Pacific."[10]

Of course, at the front the quality and frequency of meals eroded considerably. The first sergeant detailed additional marines to assist the cooks and carry the chow up to the forward positions. This duty had its own hazards. If the Germans spied the chow detail using the same route at the same hour each day, they would drop a few shells in to intercept. Often the stew got cold before the runners arrived, and the grease turned a sickly white. When the runners could not get forward at all, marines ate canned "monkey meat" and hard bread. If fires could be lit, the men fried the meat in their mess kits, then softened the hard bread by crumbling it in the grease and sprinkling sugar over the whole mess. Luxuries purchased from the YMCA included candles, jam, cookies, and most prized, cigarettes.[11]

The 2nd Division
On the long ride from Saint-Nazaire to the battalion training area, the cars carrying 2/6 paused at a small depot to allow the marines to stretch their legs. This halt unfortunately afforded the opportunity for some boys in the 80th Company to succumb to an age-old temptation plaguing soldiers on the march. After sliding open the car door, the stiff and tired leathernecks discovered a barrel of white wine on the train platform. "There was no discussion," recalled Pvt. Levi Hemrick. "No orders were given for none were needed, because everybody was of the same mind." In seconds the wine barrel was

rolled across the platform and ensconced inside the boxcar. As the train eased out of the station, forty marines snapped open their aluminum canteen cups. As they sampled the sweet wine, all agreed that train travel in the AEF was not so bad after all.

A warning that the train would be searched at the next stop did not faze the tipsy marines. A few hands quickly emptied the car's garbage can. With commendable teamwork, the men hefted the heavy cask on their shoulders and poured the wine into the metal can. With the car still hurtling through the countryside, they slid open the door and heaved the empty barrel outside. At the next town a cursory inspection by company officers, who may not have been too eager to discover any wrongdoing in their ranks, reported only forty marines riveted to a card game being played out on the lid of a garbage can.

The platoon escaped the wrath of the French police but paid for their misdeed nonetheless. As the train climbed into the mountainous Vosges region that night, the marines shivered under blankets on the hardwood floor. Forty heads pounded mercilessly from the orgy of drinking. The cold car reeked of vomit, urine, and the stale, putrid perspiration of the filthy drunk. Another day and night of riding and misery lay ahead. Sore, shivering, and grateful to be off the train at last, the marines emerged from their car and took in the frosty hills of their first billet overseas.[12]

AEF General Headquarters was assembling the U.S. 2nd Division in the Vosges area in eastern France. With 28,000 men, a U.S. division at full strength fielded twice the manpower of a French, British, or German division. In theory such an organization could maintain combat efficiency for twice as long as its Allied counterparts before casualties required it to rest and refit. The core fighting strength of U.S. divisions was its two infantry brigades, each fielding two infantry regiments of three battalions each. The 5th and 6th Marine Regiments and the 6th Machine Gun Battalion comprised the 4th Marine Brigade; army doughboys comprised the remainder of the 2nd Division. The army's 9th and 23rd Infantry Regiments and the 5th Machine Gun Battalion constituted the 3rd Infantry Brigade, the division's other infantry brigade.[13]

Pershing's interest in open warfare notwithstanding, the AEF trained and organized its battalions for trench warfare. These were rifle battalions, long on manpower, short on heavy infantry weapons, and lacking a suitable command-and-control system. Holcomb did not have a large staff. Maj. Franklin B. Garrett, the original 80th Company commander, would serve as Holcomb's second in com-

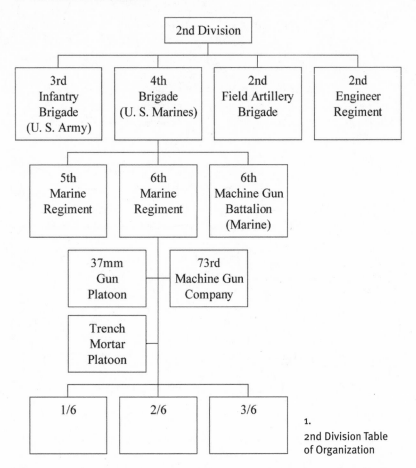

1.

2nd Division Table of Organization

mand. Lt. Pere Wilmer, who served as Holcomb's adjutant, handled the bulk of both operational and administrative staff work. Holcomb selected Lt. Carleton Wallace to lead the scout section of twenty-five marines and appointed the mustang Lieutenant Shinkle as battalion quartermaster. Sgt. Maj. Charles Ingram assisted Holcomb in leading the battalion. This puny staff could hardly plan and coordinate operations for such a huge organization, much less integrate supporting arms. In the 2nd Division detailed planning would be conducted at brigade level or higher, with battalion commanders reduced to the role of executors.[14]

In combat each company augmented the headquarters staff with a sergeant and two privates as runners, often labeled "the suicide

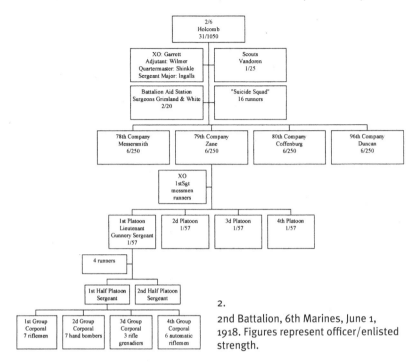

2.

2nd Battalion, 6th Marines, June 1, 1918. Figures represent officer/enlisted strength.

squad." Another sergeant and four privates served as the battalion's runners to regiment. Major Holcomb and Sergeant Major Ingram personally trained these men, upon whom so much would depend.[15]

Medical personnel in marine organizations were detailed from the U.S. Navy. Two surgeons, naval lieutenants Gordon Grimland and George White, and about twenty hospital corpsmen served in the battalion aid station. The surgeon, assistant surgeon, chief pharmacist's mate, and five to seven hospital corpsmen operated this station, and two to four corpsmen joined each rifle company. Members of the regimental band served as litter bearers.[16]

Each of Holcomb's four 250-man companies had four cumbersome, 57-man platoons. To ease command and control, platoons were reorganized in battle into two "half-platoons," creating smaller organizations that were less cumbersome to direct on the battlefield; these were led by sergeants. Corporals led four squad-sized elements called "groups" that composed each half-platoon: an 8-man rifle group, an 8-man "hand bomber" group, a 4-man rifle grenadier group carrying two rifle grenade launchers, and a 7-man automatic rifle group carrying two Chauchat automatic rifles.[17]

Holcomb had no heavy weapons at his command; he would depend upon higher echelons to furnish firepower greater than his Chauchats. The 4th Brigade fielded six machine-gun companies, each of which rated sixteen Hotchkiss machine guns.[18] A heavy air-cooled gun, the Hotchkiss could sustain only a twenty-five-round-per-minute rate of fire. Nonetheless, marine machine gunners considered it an excellent weapon because of its reliability, 3,800-yard effective range, and superior fire-control equipment.

Each regiment also had a Stokes mortar platoon and a 37-mm gun platoon. One officer in 2/6 described the Stokes as "a fine little gun for short range work [at] one hundred to eight hundred yards." It took just two weeks to train a crew.[19] The 37-mm field gun, also referred to as a "one-pounder" due to the weight of its projectile, was the only infantry weapon with the punch to penetrate a fortified machine-gun position. Marines found these elephantine weapons impossibly heavy but depended upon their reliably lethal fire. Because these weapons were centrally controlled at higher echelons, battalion commanders like Holcomb were frustrated by their inability to control their fire, a situation that could severely reduce their ability to influence the fight.

Further removing heavier weapons from the control of the infantry, the 4th Brigade issued a memorandum on command and control of machine guns that confused the relationship between machine-gun companies and the battalions they supported. The memo implied that machine gunners would take orders only through their own chain of command. Machine guns were under the tactical control of the regimental machine-gun officer, though Holcomb had the authority to give orders to the machine-gun officer in his sector. But the major's company commanders had no authority over machine gunners. This muddled directive only added to the complex procedures Holcomb would face when he needed fire support.[20]

German Defensive Tactics

The 2nd Division would face a formidable pattern of defense that the German Army had more or less institutionalized by 1918. This elastic defense in depth sought to economize Germany's dwindling manpower by relying upon machine guns and artillery to repulse Allied attacks. Rather than holding every inch of ground without regard to casualties, the German high command instructed its infantry to give ground stubbornly, then counterattack when the enemy had overextended himself.

In the German concept of elastic defense, an Allied battalion in the attack would first encounter the outpost zone. Here defending machine gunners occupied mutually supporting reinforced-concrete blockhouses with their excellent Maxim guns trained along interlocking fields of fire. Of great importance to the German scheme, artillery observers occupied fortified posts wherever the ground afforded clear lines of observation into the outpost zone and beyond. Usually 500–1,000 yards deep, the outpost zone served to protect the main defenses from reconnaissance and to disrupt the enemy's formation.

Assaulting troops who successfully negotiated the outpost zone next ran up against the main line of resistance. Consisting of three successive trenches and protected by belts of barbed wire, the main position was dug behind the crest of hills and ridges wherever possible to protect it from direct observation and flat-trajectory guns. Frontline defenders shifted laterally, to the rear, and even forward into shell holes to avoid any Allied barrage. When the attacking infantry closed, these frontline troops manned additional concrete machine-gun emplacements and rifle embrasures in the main line of resistance to devastate enemy formations as they struggled through the wire. If the attack was stopped here, the frontline battalion would counterattack in squad and platoon strength to capture or kill survivors in the outpost zone. The German infantryman's preferred weapons in both defense and counterattack were the light, portable Maxim and the hand grenade. When used in swift, violent tandem, these two weapons too often overwhelmed disorganized and disoriented Allied infantry.

Notwithstanding this formidable counterstroke, the Germans recognized that a strong, well-supported Allied attack could penetrate their main line of resistance. Here is where the elastic defense took its name. German commanders were encouraged to resist at the main line, then fall back into the battle zone. The farther an Allied battalion advanced into the defenses, the further its momentum and cohesion withered. Concurrently, German resistance grew stiffer and tougher.

Up to one and a half miles deep, the battle zone was the ground where the Germans planned to decisively defeat an Allied attack. Additional concrete machine-gun emplacements dotted the terrain. Reserve battalions lurked deep underground in dugouts, from which they emerged to counterattack, usually in company strength, according to the direction of the frontline battalion commander.

Behind the battle zone, a second series of trenches, the "artillery protective line," served as a final barrier to contain penetrations. From beyond this line German artillery would continue to pummel the attacking infantry while Allied artillery was increasingly left out of range. To defeat major offensives, entire divisions stood ready to throw their weight into the counterattack.[21]

The marines of 2/6 would attack into some variation of this defense in every major engagement. While the ability of the Germans to withstand the marines' attacks would vary considerably as numbers, manpower, ammunition, and morale deteriorated, their defense in depth always presented a formidable, deadly challenge. When Holcomb and his marines arrived in France, no Allied army had yet to realize a decisive breakthrough.

Training for Trench Fighting, February 11–March 16, 1918

The marines of 2/6 remembered the bitterly cold month at Bourmont as a period of toughening. Freezing rain storms soaked their wool uniforms and turned the roads and fields to bone-chilling mush. Rising daily at 6:00 A.M., the leathernecks gobbled a hot breakfast by candlelight, stuffed bacon sandwiches in their packs, filled their canteens with hot coffee, and plodded off under sixty-pound packs to the practice trenches. Companies often marched up to twenty miles daily just hiking to and from the training grounds. One of the 78th Company's platoon commanders, Lieutenant Sellers, recalled of this time the "rough training consisting of practice hikes, more trench digging, bomb throwing, and occasionally standing by all night in trenches. The weather worked against us, and there was a great deal of mud." When not training, the marines tried to warm up and dry out in their miserable billets. The battalion headquarters and 80th and 96th Companies billeted in the small town of Blevaincourt, while the 78th and 79th Companies billeted nearby in Robecourt. Quartered in drafty barns, the marines huddled around tiny iron stoves and slept on dirty straw, four blankets for two men. Showers were cold and taken only on Sundays. Marines became ingenious and audacious at stealing wood, dismantling entire sheds in the dead of night.[22]

Shortly after arriving in the Vosges, Lieutenant Cates described a tough day in the practice trenches in a letter home: "Men found they had grown soft at sea, and their shoulders protested the bite of the thin web straps, burdened with the unaccustomed weight of steel helmets, gas masks, and one hundred rounds of rifle ammunition. Instead of finding a warm place to roll up in their blankets, the marines worked through the night, digging, stringing wire, and standing watch. The dawn and a false promise of warmth were welcomed, and spirits restored on the hike back as the men realized they had stood the test all right after all, with only a few blisters and sore muscles." A month later Cates was more upbeat, writing that the 96th Company had enjoyed "the best day's training that we have had." The marines had thrown live grenades and fired rifle grenades, Chauchats, and pistols. He noted his men were "not so scared of [grenades] now."[23]

Some days were more miserable than others, and it took a great deal of suffering to accomplish even a modest daily regimen. Perhaps the most hated weather of infantrymen is a soggy mixture of rain and snow. At such times the slush soaks through boots, socks, and uniforms; saturates firewood; and drowns all hopes of drying out. Through one such storm, Holcomb's marines trudged off in the early morning for another long day on the ranges. The hike was longer than usual, for the column was headed for a distant grenade range. Lest any marine have kept his feet dry, the men sloshed knee deep through a rain-swollen stream to emerge shivering onto the range.

Capt. Bailey Coffenburg, who had taken command of the 80th Company, detailed Sergeant Paradis's squad as a working party. Paradis and his bunch found that they had to assemble each grenade, screwing volatile detonators into perhaps six hundred weapons. Between the volatility of grenades of the period and the dreary start to the day thus far, Paradis braced himself for an ugly moment. Hour after hour his shivering marines tediously inserted the detonators, taking care not to scrape or jostle the fuse.

By 4:30 P.M., Paradis breathed more easily. The last grenade had been thrown, and he looked forward to getting his cold muscles moving on the hike back to the billets. But a summons by Major Holcomb forebode one more dirty job.

Along with two lieutenants and a dozen other NCOs, Paradis reported to Holcomb. According to local regulations, explained the major, the unit throwing grenades had to police the range for unexploded ordnance. As the rest of the battalion shuffled away, Paradis and the unlucky band formed on line and gingerly stepped into the field, squinting through the fading light for the tiny grenades. They found quite a few, which a French officer plucked off the ground and placed in a box carried by two NCOs. "Major Holcomb was not very happy about the deal," recalled Paradis. "But he took his place in line."[24] It is significant that Holcomb assigned only officers and NCOs to this detail. The unspoken message was loud and clear: when there was a dirty, dangerous job to do in 2/6, leaders would be out in front.

No hour was allowed to go to waste now. Catching up on time misspent at Quantico, Holcomb crammed every available hour of each marine's day with marching, exercises, or field firing. Although a determined minority of privates managed to find the energy to venture off after a late dinner in search of wine, most could barely muster the energy to wring out their sodden uniforms and boots in front of their wood-burning stoves before collapsing onto a straw mattress. While the troops had an hour or two each evening to recuperate, Holcomb allowed his sergeants and junior officers no such relief. NCO school began upon return to camp, and officers had additional instruction after supper.[25]

A Promising French Attack Doctrine

Holcomb had his officers studying two French manuals translated by the army that provided the tactical doctrine used in the 2nd Division: a short, well-written pamphlet entitled *Instructions for the Offensive Combat of Small Units* and a detailed handbook, *Manual for Commanders of Infantry Platoons*. These two publications offered an innovative doctrine for trench combat. The *Manual* presented a recipe for infantry assaults surprisingly similar to the widely lauded German stormtroop tactics.[26]

With fifty-seven marines and a front of fifty to seventy-five yards, lieutenants found themselves hard-pressed to control their huge platoons. To ease their burden, their commands were task organized into two "demi-platoons" or "half-platoons"—one half-platoon commanded by the lieutenant and the other by his gunnery sergeant. The platoon attacked in four skirmish lines, or "waves." Automatic riflemen and designated hand grenadiers attacked in the first and third waves in order to maximize firepower to the front. Rifle grenadiers formed in the second and fourth waves to fire overhead of the first wave. Platoons advanced by alternating rushes of each half-platoon. Riflemen in the first wave fired one five-round clip between rushes. Upon hitting enemy positions, the half-platoon was to overwhelm the enemy by fire and movement.[27]

The attackers combined the effects of the organic infantry weapons to place the enemy on the horns of a dilemma: "The automatic

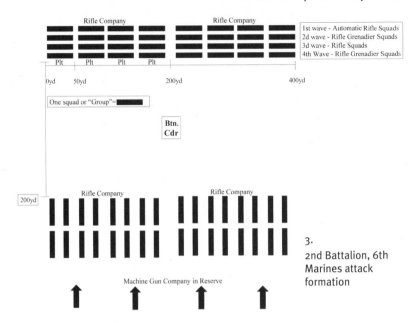

3.
2nd Battalion, 6th
Marines attack
formation

rifles and the rifles take care of whatever rises above the ground, and thus oblige the defenders to conceal themselves, while the hand and rifle grenades take care of whatever is hiding below the ground."[28]

When the half-platoon hit resistance too heavy to overcome, the attacking marines took cover and returned fire, depending on an adjacent half-platoon to take the enemy in the flank. Upon reaching strong points, the company commander directed supporting platoons through gaps to take such positions from the rear, though only those that threatened the general progress of the attack were reduced. Assault and support platoons pressed on until reaching the enemy's main line. At this point the company commander sent out contact patrols along his front to fix the next enemy position while platoon commanders consolidated their defenses in expectation of the counterattack German tactics emphasized.[29]

Artillery achieved three tasks during the assault: it countered enemy batteries, destroyed defensive positions, and "accompanied the attacking infantry." This last step created a walking curtain of shrapnel eighty yards to the immediate front of the leading wave.[30] Such barrages suppressed the enemy until the attacking infantry arrived on top of him, obscured the attackers from observation, and acted as a moving control measure to guide the infantry forward abreast of units to its flanks. Obviously, such a barrage was enormously dif-

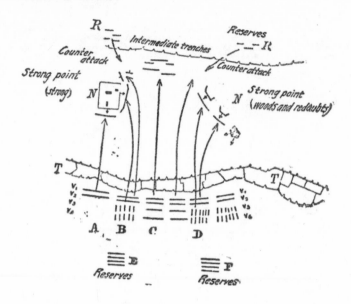

4.

Diagram of a Company Attack from the *Manual for Commanders of Infantry Platoons*. Letters A through F denote attacking platoons. N denotes enemy strongpoints in the enemy main battle area. R denotes enemy reserves. T denotes the enemy first trench line.

ficult to orchestrate, and its timetable could be upset unless nearly everything went right.

The critical weakness of French doctrine was the inability of communications technology to provide the battalion commander with reliable command and control. Repeated experience had taught the French that only close cooperation between infantry and artillery could succeed in breaking entrenched positions. Poor communications forced attackers to rely on scheduled fires and on-call missions. Infantry assaults on well-organized positions only succeeded when most everything proceeded according to plan. Not surprisingly, such success occurred with bitter infrequency.[31]

The doctrine the 2nd Division had adopted relied heavily on three conditions. First, the lead wave must follow closely on the heels of the walking barrage. Without the protection of this artillery bombardment, the infantry would suffer from withering machine-gun fire. Second, the attacker had to have a reasonably accurate understanding of the enemy disposition and terrain in front of him; the battalion's command-and-control process was not nimble enough to rapidly respond to unforeseen circumstances. Third, the very low ratio of officers to troops in the infantry battalions placed a premium on leadership from the NCOs.

Thus the *Manual for Commanders of Infantry Platoons* placed tremendous emphasis on small-unit leadership. A 2nd Division training memorandum proclaimed: "Attack can no longer be considered as a mere rigid program to be executed without initiative on the part of subordinates. Command must be vigorously executed, and troops led with great energy from corporals up to the highest commanders."[32]

The *Manual* further admonished NCOs and company-grade officers to seek out and exploit opportunities. Company commanders were expected to press forward with reconnaissance without waiting for instruction. Support company commanders had the authority to commit themselves to a perceived enemy weakness in order to maintain momentum: "If the results of this reconnaissance and a personal estimation of the situation by commanders of the units show that the occasion is favorable, these commanders themselves (captains, etc.) must take it as a strict duty to exploit the success obtained by appropriate action."[33]

The 4th Marine Brigade quickly assimilated those tangible elements of French doctrine that corresponded to qualities already well developed within its ranks. Its battalions enthusiastically marched back and forth across the muddy fields around Bourmont until they could execute French attacks with parade-ground smartness. But the exploitation of opportunities and close cooperation with artillery that the doctrine demanded were concepts easy to articulate but enormously difficult to practice under fire. Moreover, Holcomb's battalion appears to have focused on perfecting merely the procedure of these tactics. Archival evidence suggests that 2/6 was not grasping the more conceptual qualities of flexibility, initiative, and judgment required to exploit enemy weakness and seize opportunities.

In early March, 2/6 participated in a regimental-size attack exercise. Holcomb's order scripted the assault as precisely as a parade. The bulk of the three-and-a-half-page order details control measures that delineate the formations and movements for the subordinate units. The battalion's mission statement is omitted, and tasks to the companies amount to little more than "take the trench in front of us."[34] This attack order illustrates how the marines had trained to the letter of their doctrine but had not even begun to explore the decentralized, initiative-based tactics more suited to the chaos of combat.

Upon reflection after a life spent in uniform, Clifton Cates suggested that the training in the Vosges had fallen short of the proficiency envisioned in the tactics manuals. He conceded that most training days consisted of merely "forced marches and a little more extended order drill. In fact, we didn't have any fire and movement at all. It was pitiful, but no one was to blame—just the way it was at that time."[35]

That the battalion could have begun to implement such innovative tactics in the short training time allotted is doubtful. The intricacies of the French trench doctrine were too complex and required too expansive an experience base for 2/6 to master. The war would not wait for the marines to catch up. Shortly after this exercise, the battalion entrained for its baptism of fire at Verdun, at that time a quiet sector used by the French to rest veterans and train recruits. Holcomb's men would finish training by trial and error.

School Crazy

The American Army in 1918 was "school crazy," according to Lt. Arthur Worton of the 79th Company. That suited Major Holcomb, whom Worton described as "a great believer in schools." In February Franklin Garrett, now a major, returned from the Staff Officers College to serve as Holcomb's second in command. Leaving the battalion in Garrett's hands, Holcomb set off to attend a course himself, this one taught by the U.S. I Corps Schools at Gondrecourt.[36]

Lieutenant Worton and three other lieutenants, one from each company, attended the month-long course with Holcomb. Majors, captains, and lieutenants were mingled into one class, army and marine. Although Pershing had intended for American officers to take over the instruction, French and British instructors were conducting much of the training when Holcomb and Worton attended. Perhaps because of the Allied flavor to the training, Holcomb surprisingly "didn't like it worth a damn." Worton was more sanguine: "I didn't have the schooling that I needed, nor did the other officers."[37]

Worton's recollection of this training reveals a professional tension between the Allied instructors and the American students: "[The French officers] didn't think that even our company officers understood the methods of warfare and maneuverability of troops. Well, to a certain extent, they were possibly correct. [Marine officers] didn't know the use of terrain. Nor did I know the use of terrain. And the French were past masters of the use of terrain." Worton was impressed with the sergeant major from the Coldstream Guards who drilled the class. Each officer took a turn leading a company on maneuvers with live ammunition fired overhead. "When we'd fall in, if we didn't do things properly, he'd address us by name, 'I don't presume that's proper in the U.S. Army, I know it's not in the British Army. I presume you stand at attention.'" Some majors [no doubt meaning Holcomb] "didn't want to take nonsense from this fellow."[38]

After the course, Holcomb returned to his battalion. Worton was attached to a French infantry company near Verdun to see how a veteran unit practiced what he had learned in the school. The lieutenant was flabbergasted at the lack of fighting spirit among the *poilus*.[39] On one night, while returning from a raid on a German trench, Worton spotted an enemy patrol. He reached for his pistol, but Lieutenant Drot, the English-speaking officer he was bird-dogging, grabbed him.

> "Don't shoot," Drot rebuked Worton.
> "Well, those are Germans," retorted Worton.
> "Sure, but they've been over catching a Frenchman, we've been over to get a German. We got our German, they may have their Frenchman, but don't start a row, we'll all get killed. You Americans haven't been in this war long enough to understand. You carry out your orders, but you don't do anything more."[40]

Worton returned to the 79th Company comfortable with his understanding of French trench-warfare techniques but decidedly uncomfortable with French esprit de corps. The burden being laid upon the AEF to salvage a desperate situation on the Western Front was rapidly becoming apparent to the marines of 2/6.

Quiet Sector

What Worton and his fellow marines did not know was that the French Army had come close to collapse in 1917. Mutiny had been widespread, and in many divisions entire regiments had refused to return to the front. While harsh measures coupled with the energetic leadership of Gen. Henri-Philippe Pétain had restored order, Allied confidence in the French was shaken.[41]

On March 21, 1918, Ludendorff launched his offensive at the British Army along the Somme. Spearheaded by storm troops using innovative infiltration and combined-arms techniques, and supported by equally important developments in artillery tactics, the Germans cracked the British line. Ludendorff followed this success with a second offensive near Lys on April 9.[42]

During this calamity, the U.S. 2nd Division defended a quiet sector near the old battlefield at Verdun. This gave the doughboys and marines some combat experience while freeing experienced Allied divisions to contain Ludendorff's first two offensives. The effect of this crisis on 2/6 was that the intended one-month stay in this sector was extended by another month, curtailing the number of training days Holcomb's marines would have to practice the open-warfare skills upon which so much depended.

The battalion hiked from its frigid billets in the Vosges to the rail depot on March 17. After detraining southeast of Verdun, 2/6 arrived at Camp Massa the following day. Burdened by their heavy winter kit, veterans recalled the March 18 hike to Camp Massa as "the first and probably the most strenuous of the five or six really memorable hikes of the battalion." From March 19 to 28, 2/6 remained in reserve, furnishing trench-digging details to the other battalions of the regiment. The leathernecks underwent occasional light shellfire but suffered no casualties. They also fumbled through their first gas alarm. A 79th Company marine recorded, "The constant whirring of the aeroplanes overhead, and the bang of the anti-aircraft guns, soon made the troops feel like veterans." In a sobering omen, litter bearers occasionally trudged past, evacuating wounded French soldiers.[43]

Soon it was 2/6's turn to move up. The battalion relieved 3/6 on the night of March 28–29, occupying a frontline position embracing the shattered towns of Mesnil, Bonzee, and Mont-sous-le Cote. A shattering bombardment revealed that the Germans had detected the relief. Leading the 79th Company forward, Captain Zane kept his cool and maneuvered around the barrage. Upon reaching the company's strongpoint at Bonzee, Zane swiftly placed Lieutenant Erskine and Lieutenant West with their platoons up front, with Lieutenant Stockwell's platoon in support. All of the marines wriggled underground to escape the bombardment, finding their dugouts claustrophobically cramped. To the amazement of all hands, the company had completed the relief without suffering any casualties. Nearby the 78th Company found that "Space was so limited it was necessary for two men to sleep in a single bunk, only 24 inches wide."[44]

The defensive positions the marines occupied were a series of squad and platoon emplacements at intervals of 50–150 yards. Each of these positions was organized for all around defense. Most were arrayed around machine guns covering specific sectors of no man's land so that the entire front could be enfiladed in a crossfire. Approximately 50–200 meters behind the front line, a support trench provided defense in depth.[45]

The battalion's marines gained valuable experience on survival at the front, learning to construct trenches, to maintain dispersion, and about how to bring up supplies under fire. Lieutenant Cates recalled, "Every time one man would move up in that quiet sector the enemy would snipe at him with an Austrian 88." This seasoning accustomed the men to combat, and they surged with confidence. On April 17 Cates wrote home: "It is a grand and glorious feeling to hear the shells whizzing over, that is, if you are in a bomb proof dugout. The men have about gotten use to it and are not gun shy now."[46]

The men also grew confident operating in no man's land. Patrols generally were one of two types, wiring parties or reconnaissance missions, and usually consisted of not less than twenty-five marines under an officer. One trade the men had learned well at Quantico was how to set up barbed wire. In the Verdun sector marines learned to take advantage of pitch-dark nights to repair wire by touch—and to do it quietly. They learned to cut lanes through their own wire in patient silence at night and to rush out these lanes efficiently in daylight. Reconnaissance patrolling was almost exclusively conducted by the battalion scouts under Lieutenant Wallace, though Lieutenant Cates would occasionally crawl out by himself two hundred yards and just listen. One night "all hell broke loose," and Cates was badly cut up struggling back through the wire. He returned wiser but with his irrepressible aggressiveness intact.[47]

Eventually the marines gained the grim but important seasoning that comes with losing comrades. In an intense artillery duel on Easter morning, April 5, more than three hundred shells hit Cates's position. Pvts. James Metcalf and Edward Grober were killed by mustard gas, with Pvts. Earl Anderson and Lambert Hehl injured. A few nights later the battalion scout platoon got itself tangled in the enemy's wire. Before the scouts could extricate themselves, someone tripped a booby trap. The resulting detonation severely wounded Lieutenant Wallace and Pvt. Kenneth Whittaker. To take over for Wallace, Holcomb brought in a razor-sharp replacement lieutenant from the 80th Company named Lucien H. Vandoren. Vandoren, a native of Washington, D.C., had placed first in his Georgetown law class in 1917. He would prove indispensable in the coming battles.[48]

During such crises as befell Wallace's patrol, battalion officers learned to command despite chaos and uncertainty and to safeguard communications. Shellfire cut telephone lines fifteen or twenty times a day. Colonel Catlin, the regimental commander, believed the Germans overheard phone conversations when the front lines were only one hundred yards apart through the use of powerful induction coils. Pyrotechnics provided an alternate means of communications in an emergency. A white-star rocket signaled a request for a ten-minute barrage. The barrage could be extended through additional rockets or by telephone. Red rockets signaled rounds falling short. During an enemy attack, the barrage began in front of the friendly trench, then advanced toward the enemy trench one hundred yards at a time, clearing the intervening ground.[49]

The 2nd Division headquarters was not considered ready to assume its own sector, so the American regiments fell under French command there. Catlin received orders from the commanding general of the French 33rd Division, who retained tactical responsibility for the sector. The 2nd Division's field artillery brigade had not completed its training, so French artillery supported the regiment. Whether due to the marines' inexperience or due to a French practice of limiting their subordinates discretion in tactics, the French commander issued standing orders to the 6th Marines that included explicit instructions not only on how to conduct the relief but also where Catlin was expected to dispose his platoons and the counterattack plans for each.[50]

The 80th Company moved into the sector assigned by the French commander on April 17. Private Hemrick described the move up "by way of a hillside communication trench that has been there for years. It is more like a wide, deep, hillside gully than a man-made trench. Its bottom oozes with mud and contains almost knee deep potholes filled with churned-up mud and water. The banks are seeping wet from winter thaws and early spring rains." The trench was six feet deep, with a firing step and loopholes on the German side. The marines in the company being relieved were blasting away with everything they had, and the 80th Company joined in. Hemrick suspected that the other unit had initiated the firefight as a show for he and his comrades. Hemrick was especially chagrined when he learned after the shooting ebbed that the 80th Company's Sgt. Barnard Rowan, of Philadelphia, had been killed in the exchange of fire.[51]

In such moments hospital corpsmen quickly learned that the most handy tool for their work was the bandage scissors. Most tucked a pair in their right puttee, from where they could quickly grab it and cut through uniforms and web gear to expose a wound. Thomas leg splints, which placed fractured femurs in traction, reducing pain and shock, were considered "a godsend."[52]

After receiving aid from the company corpsmen, casualties were carried or assisted through preestablished evacuation lanes 500–2,000 yards back to the battalion aid station, where the battalion surgeon reassessed the injury and injected anti-tetanus serum. The corpsmen often provided sweet coffee or chocolate to a wounded marine while he awaited the ambulance that would transport him two to three miles behind the front to a field hospital, the lowest echelon in the medical organization that could conduct surgeries.[53]

Despite fleas, lice, rats, and the difficulties associated with observing field-sanitation practices in combat, the 4th Brigade suffered comparatively low losses to disease. Wounded outnumbered ill casualties approximately six to one.[54] This low ratio was striking when compared to the American experience in the Spanish-American War and reflects both a commendable degree of small-unit discipline and a core of dedicated, professional medical personnel.

Commanders rightly regarded small-unit discipline as a matter of life and death and pounced on any indication that it might be undermined. The 80th Company suffered an accidental casualty while in the front line in May, and throughout the 6th Marines, at least one man was killed and two wounded from careless weapons handling. Colonel Catlin, irked by the needless losses and suspicious that some such injuries may not be accidental, determined to nip the problem in the bud. He directed his commanders in the future to treat such injuries as self-inflicted wounds, punishable by general court-martial, unless the commander could clearly show that no misconduct was involved.[55]

Holcomb's insistence on smartness and tight discipline was not always well received. The 78th Company had relieved an apathetic French unit that had left the trenches in a slovenly manner. Ammunition, including live grenades, was left carelessly in the nooks and crannies of the fortifications and among the wood and chicken-wire bunks. Holcomb found this entirely unacceptable and laid into Lieutenant Sellers, in whose sector much of the debris lay. The company leaders bristled from the sharp rebuke. After the major had marched out of earshot, Sellers was shocked to hear Gunnery Sergeant Lyman refer to Holcomb with "the most vile expression I had ever heard."[56]

Sergeant Mazereeuw, the 79th Company's famously profane Irishman, fell from grace after hitting the bottle one time too many. Captain Zane busted him to private. Pious Oscar Rankin was now a corporal and a squad leader in Lieutenant Erskine's 2nd Platoon. Perhaps with a reference from First Sergeant Fritz about humbling those who exalt themselves, Zane placed the vulgar old salt in Rankin's squad. Mazereeuw's comeuppance not only served to maintain the high standards of discipline in the Corps but also suggests that veteran marines like Zane and Fritz were beginning to trust the leadership of wartime volunteers like Rankin.[57]

For the rest of April and the first ten days of May, Holcomb's companies rotated between rest camps and the front. The battalion defended a miserable sector from April 25 to May 3 near Ronvaux, "where we found old, water soaked dugouts, some of them fifty feet deep," according to Lieutenant Sellers. Food here was "poorer than usual" due to the exposed position. The 78th Company lost Pvt. Ray Crow, and the 96th Company lost Pvt. Willard Clark to shellfire. Lieutenant Cates's marines spent days and nights pumping water out of the frigid dugouts, and no fires were allowed. On April 25, suspecting a raid, the 96th Company stood to under shelling all night. Artillery, flares, and automatic weapons covered no man's land. Cates recorded that he got just two hours' sleep during this miserable sixty-two-hour period.[58]

Gas and the Fear of Gas

At Quantico, Scot and Canadian officers had put the fear of gas into the marines, telling the Americans, "One sniff of mustard gas, you'll die." To prevent that, in March and April 1918 every marine carried not one but two masks: the British c.e. Box Respirator and the French M2. The M2 was merely a linen bag with goggles strapped across the wearer's face. Instead of intake valves, it filtered gas through layers of cloth impregnated with chemicals. The more modern British respirator also protected the face with a goggled mask but eliminated gasses through a charcoal filter in the carrier strapped to the wearer's chest. Filtered air flowed through a rubber hose, which the user held in his mouth. A spring clasp held the nostrils shut. Although the stifling masks impaired one's vision and made conversation nearly impossible, they worked.[59]

Out with his platoon on a trench-digging mission, Lieutenant Sellers heard a wailing screech pierce the night air. In a flash he had his marines strapping on their masks. Anxiously, they waited to see if their masks performed as advertised. All digging ceased. The marines peered nervously through the foggy mask lenses. Every ear strained to hear over the rasping of forty rubber tubes. Sellers heard the wail again—and relaxed. To his relief, and embarrassment, he had mistaken the braying of an old army mule for the gas alarm.[60]

Sellers had been on edge with good reason. On April 13, German artillery had bombarded 1/6's 74th Company with a mixture of mustard, phosgene, and high explosives. In an overwhelming example of the lethality of chemical warfare, 295 marines suffered burns from the gas, of whom 18 perished. The regimental gas officer, Lt. Henry Chandler, reported that the casualties were especially severe due to insufficient alarm devices and inadequate dugouts. Many of the marines had prematurely removed their respirators; many more had no means of changing out of their impregnated uniforms. Chandler recommended that each battalion stockpile enough clothing for 5 percent of its strength to prepare for future emergencies.[61]

In response the 2nd Division issued new general orders for defense against gas attacks. The division required marines and soldiers within two miles of the front to carry both the English respirator at the ready across their chest and the French M2 gas mask affixed to their right hip. Frontline units inspected masks and gas alarms every day. Any detail of ten men posted its own gas sentry.[62]

As this strike grimly reveals, fears of gas attacks were well founded. By the armistice, 18 percent of all marine casualties would be gas related. While the fatality rate was just 2 percent compared to 26 percent from all other causes, survivors rarely fully recovered. The average gas casualty spent sixty days hospitalized. Veterans after the war suffered pulmonary fibrosis, which led to emphysema and tuberculosis.[63]

Marines encountered mustard, or "Yperite," most frequently. Whether masked or not, a marine exposed to mustard almost immediately felt burning in areas of the body wet from perspiration: under the armpits, in the crotch and lungs, and around the eyes. Exposed skin burned soon thereafter. The best mitigating measures were to move to an uncontaminated area, remove clothing, and bathe with a heavy soap. None of these measures were practical for marines under fire.[64]

During its final period in the line in this sector in the first eleven days of May, Holcomb's marines relieved a French battalion and defended another sector encompassing the deserted villages of Watronville, Tresaveaux, and Rondveaux. The Americans found this area in far better shape than the soggy trenches they had left at Ronvaux. Enemy activity was restricted to artillery, air, and heavy sniper fire, the latter attributed to the hilly ground, which afforded German sharpshooters excellent vantage points over the Allied positions. Total losses during this period were "about one percent."[65]

Reflecting on this initial frontline duty after the war, Private Hemrick wrote, "We had to learn an awful lot of things under fire that could have very well been taught back in a training camp." He also characterized the intermittent fighting astutely: "More like friendly rivals training with live ammunition than angry enemies in a fight to kill each other. It was like giving a fellow a chance to learn his trade and how bad it could be, without killing him."[66]

The battalion's turn in the trenches had introduced the marines to modern warfare. The leathernecks had gained useful experience in defensive operations, growing leaner and hardening to the dangers and privations of combat. Most importantly, the men learned to function as a cohesive unit under combat conditions. Unfortunately, the eight quiet weeks spent defending a static sector afforded no opportunity to hone the offensive skills the battalion would require in the heavy actions to come.

Mechanical Perfection in Open Warfare, May 13–31, 1918

Holcomb's final opportunity to prepare for significant combat arrived in mid-May. After another long ride, 2/6 debarked in the early evening of May 12 and immediately stepped off on a twenty-mile march to the village of Changy, arriving at 1:30 in the morning of May 13. Instead of receiving a well-deserved rest, the men awoke to an early reveille and orders to ensure weapons were spotless and equipment and uniforms shipshape. At the battalion's formation, the marines were startled to find that they would be inspected by none other than General Pershing himself.[67]

When the general began his inspection of the battalion, First Sergeant Fritz watched from the rear of the 79th Company with keen interest. As Pershing worked his way through the 78th Company, the first sergeant noticed that he was inspecting the officers' pistols but not the sergeants' weapons. Fritz eased up behind Lieutenant Worton, who was in charge of the company that day. The old sergeant unclasped the lieutenant's holster, plucked out Worton's filthy .45 automatic, and dropped his own inside.

After looking over the company, Pershing complimented Captain Messersmith on his "very fit body of men" and proceeded to the 79th Company.[68] Sure enough, when the general centered himself in front of Worton, he immediately demanded, "Let's see your pistol, young man." Worton drew the pistol, locked the slide to the rear, and handed it to the most powerful general the U.S. Army. "Unusual," muttered Pershing, as he handed Worton back his pistol. "It's clean."

When Worton later thanked Fritz for saving him from embarrassment, the first sergeant gently remonstrated the lieutenant. "This isn't Quantico, you know," he advised Worton. "You may have to use it tomorrow night, and if it isn't clean, you'll have a misfire." He could have smugly allowed Pershing to teach Worton the same lesson in a more unforgettably public fashion. But Fritz was a first sergeant of marines and was not about to let an army general find fault in *his* company.[69]

About this time, Brig. Gen. John Harbord, an army officer who had served as Pershing's chief of staff, relieved marine Brig. Gen. Charles Doyen as commander of the 4th Marine Brigade. Lieutenant Sellers neatly summarized the reaction in 2/6: "At first we were insulted at having an army general in charge of a marine brigade." But the 78th Company noted a few changes right away. On Harbord's orders the company was marched to a large barn, where they were issued clean new uniforms (probably army olive drab) from head to toe. "And from that time forward we were served vegetables and fruit at meals. We swore by the new general after that."[70]

Harbord had taken command in time to push the brigade through its final training, which his marines plunged into smartly. On May 10 the 6th Marines's executive officer, Lt. Col. Harry Lee, issued a jumbled special order in the name of the regimental commander providing guidance for this period of instruction. Lee directed exercises in patrols, outposts, advance and rear guards, and attack and defense. The order recalled his fascination with machine-like musketry. In his self-anointed position as the regiment's proponent of small-unit tactics, Lee directed that squads and platoons "be carefully trained in fire direction, control and discipline and in the use of signals concerned. Careful instruction and training of the collective fire units, get fire superiority and spells *success*."[71]

Notwithstanding Lee's gibberish, the following few weeks consisted of rehearsing the French trench-attack doctrine in open terrain with a few poorly considered modifications. In the division's training memorandum, commanders were admonished not to fixate on rigid adherence to the prescribed formations. "The deployments shown herein are suggestions only and departures there from to secure the objective sought are not only authorized but required." The memorandum later stressed the point again: "It must be understood that in attacking from trenches no stereotyped formation can be relied upon. The organization of units is prescribed in orders to meet existing conditions." Yet in sequencing its training, the division emphasized achieving precision in maneuvers before adding complex tactical problems for small-unit leaders. "The troops will be drilled until mechanically perfect in taking up and advancing in the prescribed formations after which all attack formations will be made pursuant to a specific tactical situation and the operations of the troops will be accordingly conducted."[72]

In order to be ready to relieve the U.S. 1st Division, then engaged at Cantigny, the 2nd Division spent several precious days moving from one area to another. Instead of training for a month on open warfare, 2/6 devoted at most fifteen days in May: five days at Changy, and another ten at Serans. With its training time cut in half, the men likely did not proceed beyond attaining mechanical perfection. In a compelling observation, Sergeant Paradis reveals that in practice the battalion had once again pursued razor-sharp perfection in its maneuvers at the expense of flexibility and initiative: "we continued to drill as we had from platoon to company formations. We were maneuvered from section column to section column to skirmish line to wave formation punctuated by one hour a day bayonet drill. Unfortunately few of these dated maneuvers would fit the war we were entering. But I am sure the whole company could have drilled in their sleep."[73]

Ominously, division headquarters also instructed commanders to abandon the principle "that the way to the front must be 'blasted' by the Field Artillery." Incredibly, they believed that alternating rushes coordinated with small-arms fire would mitigate the lack of a rolling barrage.[74] Even more than tactical proficiency at the battalion level, this faith in fire superiority by riflemen would prove a fatal miscalculation.

(All photos are from the National Archives unless otherwise noted.)

1. Thomas Holcomb
2. Harry Lee
3. Robert E. Messersmith
4. Donald F. Duncan

5. Bailey Coffenburg
6. James McBrayer Sellers
7. Graves B. Erskine
8. Clifton B. Cates

9

10

9. Lucian H. Vandoren
10. John J. Kelly
11. Don V. Paradis (MCU Archives)

11

12

13

12. Training at Quantico. "There are dummies for bayonet practice, and at all hours of the day enlisted men can be seen slaughtering these dummy Germans."

13. Bayonet training at Quantico. "Half of it wasn't worth a hoorah."

14

14. With actual grenades in short supply at Quantico in 1917, marines practiced by lobbing stones.
15. Marines of the 3rd Platoon, 96th Company hone their musketry skills to machine-like perfection. (MCU Archives)
16. A few marines of the 3rd Platoon of the 96th Company in May, 1918. (MCU Archives)

15

16

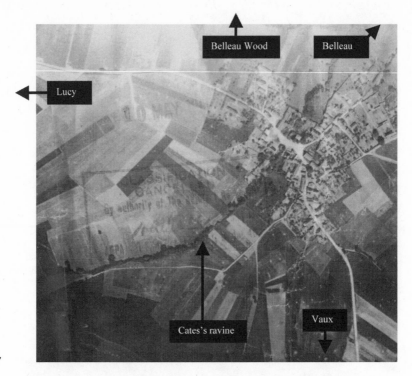

Belleau Wood

Belleau

Lucy

Cates's ravine

Vaux

17

18

17. An aircraft from the French 252nd Squadron took this previously unpublished image of Bouresches on June 6, 1918, the day 2/6 captured the town.

18. Bouresches as it would have appeared to Captain Duncan and the 96th Company. This photograph was taken after the war.

19

20

19. As Lieutenant Cates's platoon cleared Bouresches, Pvt. Herbert Dunlavy shot dead a German machine gunner who was raking the streets from this steeple. Dunlavy was killed a few minutes later. (MCU Archives)

20. Around June 19, a Signal Corps photographer captured this image of the exhausted marines of 2/6 after their three days in Belleau Wood.

21. The officers of 2/6 soon after their first period in the line in Belleau Wood. From left to right: Lts. Gordon Grimland and George White, U.S. Navy; Lt. Graves B. Erskine; Capt. Egbert T. Lloyd; Capt. Randolph T. Zane; unknown (possibly Maj. Franklin B. Garrett); Lt. E. J. Stockwell, U.S. Army; Maj. Thomas Holcomb; Lt. Clifton B. Cates; Lt. Amos R. Shinkle; Lt. John C. Overton; Lt. John G. Schneider. (MCU Archives)

22

23

24

22. Wethered Woodworth
23. Robert L. Denig
24. On July 19, 1918, 2/6 attacked across this open ground toward
the Soissons–Château-Thierry road in the distance.

25. This is purported to be a rare photograph of marines in
combat. The ground suggests it may have been taken at
Soissons.

3 The Triangle Farm and Bouresches

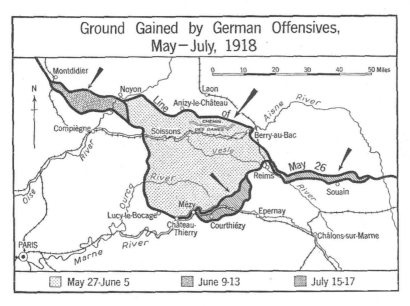

Ground Gained by German Offensives, May – July, 1918

Montdidier · Noyon · Laon · Anizy-le-Château · Compiègne · Soissons · Berry-au-Bac · CHEMIN-DES-DAMES · Line Of · Vesle River · Aisne River · May 26 · Reims · Souain · Mézy · Epernay · Lucy-le-Bocage · Château-Thierry · Courthiézy · Châlons-sur-Marne · Oise River · Ourcq River · Marne River · PARIS

0 10 20 30 40 50 Miles

N

May 27-June 5   June 9-13   July 15-17

STILL SEEKING A DECISIVE BLOW to finish off the British, General Ludendorff launched Plan Blücher on May 27. The purpose of his third great offensive of 1918 was to pull French reserves away from Flanders in preparation for another bid there to finish off the British Expeditionary Force. Crown Prince Wilhelm's army group blasted south over the Chemin-des-Dames heights and across the Aisne and Vesle rivers, reaching the Marne by May 30. The German offensive devoured French reserves "like drops of rain on a white hot iron." German columns closed to within thirty-seven miles of Paris, the closest they had come since 1914. Ludendorff sensed Plan Blücher might offer the knockout blow he was seeking, and he reinforced Crown Prince Wilhelm's attack in the hope of exploiting the unexpected success.[1]

While some Allied leaders panicked, Marshal Ferdinand Foch viewed the deep German salient between Soissons and Rheims as a potential opportunity for a grand counterattack. Perhaps Ludendorff had overextended himself and the tide of war could be reversed. It would take time to assemble the divisions and organize the blow, however. Therefore, Foch needed to establish a defensive line along the Marne River to contain the offensive.

Flowing east to west, the Marne is dominated by steep hills on both banks that make an opposed crossing extremely difficult. Along the south bank of the river, the French Army managed to repel German efforts to push across. Ludendorff planned to exploit Plan Blücher's success through offensives near Noyon and Montdider at the northwest shoulder of the salient. While marshalling reserves for this attack, he needed to gain an advantage of position and so ordered Crown Prince Wilhelm to continue his attack westward along the north bank of the Marne. When General Pershing offered his 2nd Division to assist Foch in the crisis, the French swiftly organized transportation to carry the doughboys and marines to the point of decisive action. The Americans would anchor the southwest corner of the salient, blocking the Paris-Metz road west of Chateau-Thierry. The coming clash would be a grapple for the initiative, a tipping point to decide whether Foch or Ludendorff would be first on the trigger to unleash the next great offensive of 1918.[2]

War Becomes Real

Shortly after reveille on May 30, Colonel Catlin summoned Major Holcomb to the 6th Marines regimental headquarters, a fact noted and discussed by many in 2/6. The battalion had concluded its training in open warfare and was preparing to depart from its billet at Serans, a few miles west of Paris, to relieve the 1st U.S. Division near Cantigny. The air was charged with anticipation, and discussions ran thick with rumor. The young leathernecks had access to newspapers and speculated widely upon their coming role in the unfolding calamity. All hands sensed something big was afoot.

When Holcomb returned in the early afternoon, he ordered Lt. Pere Wilmer to sound adjutant's call and muster all company runners on the double quick. Sure enough, the runners returned to their companies carrying the anticipated orders for movement. The battalion would board trucks at 10:00 P.M. for the front. Action at last! There followed a brief ecstasy of falling in and falling out, of orders barked and orders countermanded. Packs were tightly rolled and seabags stuffed with articles to be left behind. A few final, hasty letters were dashed off, and the men fell in to muster once more in the street.

There they stood, and there they waited. Ten o'clock came and went, but no trucks appeared. An hour passed. After a second hour, the first sergeants sent the men back to their billets. Few could shake off their excitement and sleep. Reveille sounded at 4:00 A.M. with no trucks in sight. At last, around six o'clock, a column of fifty trucks chugged into sight. The drivers were something to behold: weary Asian soldiers from French Indochina who had not slept in days. Despite the marines' eagerness to dash off straight away to rescue France, another two hours passed without explanation before the hurry-up-and-wait ordeal concluded.[3]

Veterans recalled the ensuing twenty-hour ride as a bouncing and jarring carnival of fatigue and emotion. The route first took the marines past excited townspeople, curious to see these American soldiers upon whom so much depended. There were many flowers and a few pretty girls and often cheers of "Vive les Americains!" Pleased as the town folk seemed to be to see the fit young men trundling to the front, these were not riotously jubilant crowds. Their melancholy unease clashed with the Americans' enthusiasm. In a poignant reflection, the 80th Company's Private Hemrick perceived "an apparent mixture of sadness, fear and pleasure." After surviving the war, Hemrick would ascribe this sadness and fear to the terrible losses the French people had come to associate with the coming of battle and to their dread that so many of these young Americans would meet a fate similar to that of so many young Frenchmen.[4]

After passing Meaux, the crowds dissipated and the leathernecks now began to rattle past forlorn columns of refugees. Cpl. Glenn Hill, an NCO in the 79th Company, could not forget the "tragic sight as we watched miles and miles of French families with the few possessions they could assemble as they trudged along the road in their carts." His platoon commander, Lt. Jack West, noted that there was "no cheering from them now, no singing from the troops. War suddenly became real to us."[5]

While it is apparent now that Ludendorff's third offensive was losing momentum well before this convoy of Americans reached the front, and that it is equally apparent that Paris was in no imminent jeopardy, such facts were not at all evident on the last day of May 1918. From the cargo bed of a French lorry, all signs pointed to the approach of an epic battle. This point of view fostered an important, albeit exaggerated, psychological advantage for these marines. In their first major action, Holcomb's men believed that both the fate of the war and America's reputation rested upon their shoulders.[6]

Having survived their bouncing odyssey, the marines clambered off the trucks in the small village of Montreuil-aux-Lions along the Paris-Metz road about 4:00 A.M. on June 1. Montreuil lay about four miles from the front, and its inhabitants had joined the exodus witnessed along the way. Holcomb ordered his company commanders to get their men under cover in the buildings and to sleep while they could.

There followed a brief orgy of slaughter as the famished leathernecks chased down and butchered every chicken and rabbit in sight. Corporal Hill and his brother cleaned and fried some rabbits and vegetables, sharing their feast with the regiment's new dentist, Lt. Weeden C. Osborne.[7] With full bellies, and often as not a sample of wine, the men at last fell asleep among the stone houses.

Around 2:30 P.M. on June 1, General Harbord arrived and ended the marines' siesta. Harbord had scrounged together a column of Packard trucks from the division supply train to whisk 2/6 up the Paris-Metz road. The French defense was crumbling in the face of Crown Prince Wilhelm's persistent assaults, and the 2nd Division was being thrust in to stiffen the line. In short order Holcomb had his companies loaded up and moving forward. Just under ten months

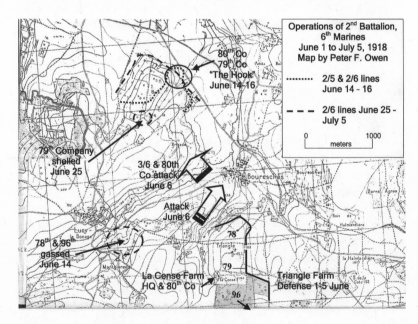

had passed since Holcomb had organized his battalion at Quantico. The Marine Corps's doctrine, training, organization, equipment, leadership, discipline, and most of all spirit were about to be tested in a punishing thirty-day ordeal.

Old Man Fear Joins

Following immediately behind Holcomb in the second truck, Sergeant Paradis discerned the crack and rhythmic thump of rifle and machine-gun fire ahead. French stragglers shuffled past the advancing marines on the shoulders of the road. A battery of French 75-mm howitzers, still in the fight, blasted at unseen targets to the east.

German artillery was trying to range the battery. Abruptly, one of the shells probing for the French 75s detonated in front of Holcomb's truck. The major decided that that one was close enough, and he halted the column. His marines scrambled out, formed into attack formation with commendably little fuss, and smartly marched into the battle.[8]

For the next four days, 2/6 would defend a low ridge between the Paris-Metz road and Belleau Wood to the north, a key position in the 2nd Division's line. Harbord had assigned Holcomb the right-hand sector of the 4th Brigade. Colonel Catlin accompanied the major to the front and outlined 2/6's sector on the regiment's only map. Holcomb's right would tie in with the 3rd Brigade's 9th Infantry on the Paris-Metz road at a collection of houses known as Le Thiolet. His line would run from Le Thiolet north for about twenty-two hundred yards to a steep ravine, then turn sharply west. The next unit to Holcomb's left would be 1/6, more than sixteen hundred yards to the west of the ravine at the town of Lucy-le-Bocage.[9]

While this was excellent defensive terrain, it was too much area for a single battalion to cover. Holcomb's marines would occupy high ground with an excellent view toward Belleau Wood to the north and Bouresches Wood to the northeast. About half of his line ran through forested areas, affording his men some concealment. A steep, nearly impassable ravine cut through the angle at the center of the sector. This ravine offered shelter and concealment to individual soldiers moving along it, but its steep sides constituted a substantial obstacle to any large formation attempting to cross it.

Holcomb weighted the right half of his sector. He ordered Captain Duncan's 96th Company forward to defend Le Thiolet adjacent to the Paris-Metz road north to the Triangle Farm. Captain Zane's 79th Company centered on the Triangle Farm. Captain Messersmith's

78th Company defended north of the Triangle Farm to the steep ravine, where his line curved around in a buttonhook. Each of these
companies was responsible for about six to seven hundred yards
of front. Between the 78th Company's left flank and 1/6's right lay
nearly sixteen hundred yards of open ground. French infantry occupied Belleau Wood to the 78th's left, but their strength, dispositions, and intentions were unclear to the Americans. Holcomb kept
his remaining company, Captain Coffenburg's 80th, in reserve in the
center of his position among the buildings of La Cense Farm. From
there Coffenburg could reinforce or counterattack anywhere along
the battalion front. The three frontline companies dug double rows
of fighting holes and peered toward the east for signs that the Germans had arrived.[10]

The first indications appeared overhead. The Germans had
achieved local air superiority and floated observation balloons
along the front. Because much of his front and most of his rear
lay exposed to enemy observation, Holcomb's command was ap-
pallingly vulnerable to artillery fire. The battalion had experienced
harassing artillery at Verdun but had not yet experienced the ham-
mering of a full-scale bombardment. Having scraped fighting holes
out of the earth, many men in the platoons unwisely returned their
entrenching tools to their field packs, which they staged several
yards behind their positions. Content with their shallow holes,
the marines did not immediately begin improving their entrench-
ments. Battalion headquarters and the 80th Company in reserve did
not dig in at all, relying instead upon the walls of La Cense Farm for
protection.[11]

Late in the day, two companies of the 6th Machine Gun Battalion reinforced 2/6 with their thirty-two Hotchkiss guns. Holcomb's
disposition, oriented to the east and northeast, provided a strong
position against the expected direction of attack, but it still left a gap
between the 78th Company and 1/6 at Lucy to the west. Holcomb
walked the line before darkness set in, approving each company's
dispositions. The weary marines enjoyed a quiet night, their last un-
interrupted night's rest for days to come.[12]

At first light on June 2, Holcomb's marines began reporting German troops filtering into Bouresches Wood. Wilhelm was continuing
his westward attack, and Gen. Max von Conta's corps was unaware
the American 2nd Division had dug in across its path.[13]

At 8:30 A.M. grenadiers emerged from the woods to Holcomb's
front, and the fight was on. The marine riflemen watched French

artillery and thirty-two marine Hotchkiss guns rip apart the thick waves of advancing infantry seventeen hundred yards away. The long-range fire forced the Germans to slow down and creep ahead by short rushes of smaller groups. The Hotchkiss guns cut down more enemy soldiers as they attempted to dash through the wheat. Holcomb's riflemen picked off a few diehards when they popped up close to the marine positions. In the center of the battalion line, Corporal Hill felt that "at three hundred yards it was like being on the rifle range."[14]

At one point the brief action precipitated a false report from a French officer who mistook a working party for a general withdrawal by 2/6. When this report reached Harbord, the general impetuously dispatched a flurry of orders by runner before signalmen repaired the telephone line to Holcomb. The major was hot at the implication his men had wavered. He assured the general that when his battalion moved, "it would be in the other direction."[15]

Holcomb's marines had witnessed artillery and machine-gun fire cut down the German 10th Division's 398th Infantry Regiment. The enemy riflemen had advanced without the benefit of concentrated artillery fire as the rapid pace of earlier advances had outrun the artillery ammunition trains. German artillery had not been able to stockpile sufficient ammunition to keep pace and was unprepared to support the repeated attacks against prepared positions. A few high-explosive shells did detonate on top of a few unlucky marines' holes, killing three and wounding another six. Unknown to Holcomb's men, they had beaten off the only attack they would face in this sector. The IV Reserve Corps's divisions aborted further assaults after the probes on June 2 had revealed the strength of the American positions.[16]

French infantry in Belleau Wood and Bouresches had repulsed the center and right of the 10th Division's attack. Their stand had protected the gap between the 78th Company and 1/6 at Lucy. On the evening of June 2, Colonel Catlin plugged this gap with 3/6's 97th Company. With his left flank now secure, Holcomb could rest more easily.[17]

Around dusk that same evening, an ammunition detail from the 80th Company tottered up the cobblestone road toward the battalion command post at La Cense Farm. The marines were staggering under heavy and painful loads of rifle-ammunition bandoliers slung from wooden poles. Private Hemrick idly watched from the farm buildings. The slow-moving detail also caught the eye of artillery spotters above the German lines. Holcomb's marines were about to learn the lethal power lurking behind the observation balloons.

The first shells exploded among the farm buildings of La Cense. One crashed through the roof of a barn occupied by a platoon of the 80th Company, collapsing one of its stone walls. Sgt. Leo Liptac's foot was crushed by the falling debris. The rest of Liptac's platoon bolted out the barn's double doors toward the woods one hundred yards distant. They had just cleared the barn when another shell erupted among the fleeing men, knocking more than a dozen to the ground.

Moments later, shells began to drop among the ammunition bearers. The dust and smoke at first obscured the detail from view. Hemrick watched in horror as his buddies emerged from the clouds, still carrying their ammunition as they tried to sprint to cover between salvos. More shells blasted the road, and several marines fell. The wounded lay exposed on the cobblestones. Hemrick dashed from the cover of the farm buildings to pull those still alive to safety. After several close scrapes from near impacts, Hemrick made it to the wounded men.[18]

Lieutenant Wilmer had Sergeant Paradis move the battalion runners to the safety of the wood line. As he dashed for the trees, Paradis was horrified to see the carnage outside the barn. First Sgt. Frank Glick, fatally wounded with both legs sheared off, smiled at Paradis as the runners trotted past. When Paradis reached Holcomb's location in the woods, the young sergeant reported on the wounded he had seen and asked for volunteers to head back to help. Lt. John Schneider, Sergeant Major Ingram, and Cpl. Archie Smith headed back into the shellfire with Paradis. He and Schneider placed Pvt. Fred Lomax on a shelter half and managed to pull him to cover, though shells continued to force them to the ground every few feet. Lomax succumbed to his wounds, as did First Sergeant Glick, Gy. Sgt. Max Krause, and four other marines. Ambulances carted away eight wounded, including Lt. Tom Whiting and Sergeant Liptac, who would have his crushed foot amputated. "Old Man Fear joined us that day," observed Paradis.[19]

Having learned a harsh lesson, the headquarters and 80th Company marines dug protective holes among the trees before trying to sleep that night. As the evening shadows lengthened over the quiet farm, a sickened Hemrick caught sight of hungry hogs sniffing among the cobblestones and licking up tiny pieces of flesh with their bloody snouts.[20]

Notwithstanding the horrific end to the day for 2/6, on June 2 Ludendorff's Plan Blücher had reached its apex. Over the next two days, Holcomb's men received only harassing shelling and no more frontal attacks. The IV Reserve Corps cleared the French from Belleau Wood and Bouresches on June 3 but then shifted to the defense. Meanwhile its commander, General Conta, contemplated another attack to consolidate his position west of Château-Thierry. He determined that his corps could be ready no earlier than June 7.[21]

"The Spectacle was Inspiring" — Bouresches, June 6–10, 1918

Gen. Joseph Degoutte, commanding the French XXI Corps, hoped to wrest the initiative away from Conta by striking first. Degoutte issued orders at 3:00 P.M. on June 5 for the French 167th and U.S. 2nd Divisions to attack the next morning. In what would prove the largest operation up to that time for the American Expeditionary Forces and the U.S. Marine Corps, Harbord planned two attacks on June 6 for his 4th Brigade. The 5th Marines would move in the morning to the north to seize Hill 142, just over a mile west of Belleau Wood. In the afternoon the 6th Marines and 3/5 would strike in a northeasterly direction to clear Belleau Wood and Bouresches.[22]

In preparation for the 6th Marines attack, the 23rd Infantry relieved the 79th and 96th Companies at 3:00 A.M. on June 6. Messersmith's 78th Company remained in its position east of the steep ravine. Zane's 79th Company relieved 3/6's 97th Company across the ravine and to the left of Messersmith. Duncan's 96th Company joined Holcomb's headquarters in the woods south of La Cense Farm. Coffenburg's 80th Company had relieved the 75th Company of 1/6 on the night of June 4–5. The 80th was the farthest from Holcomb's command post, for they occupied a line of trenches sixteen hundred yards from La Cense, just northeast of the town of Lucy.[23]

Holcomb joined Catlin at his command post at Lucy, anticipating orders. His battalion dug in and awaited developments, unaware of the purpose behind these maneuvers and somewhat oblivious to the impending operation. Harbord's staff did not issue the brigade attack order for the 6th Marines until 2:05 P.M., having been consumed all morning with the 5th Marines's attack on Hill 142. Harbord's aide jumped on a motorcycle and roared off to the 6th Marines command post at Lucy, where he finally handed Catlin a copy of the order at 3:45. This left the colonel just an hour and fifteen minutes to prepare for the 5:00 attack. Catlin was dumbfounded to discover the order placed him in charge of not only his own battalions but of 3/5 as well. Realizing that he did not have sufficient time to locate the commander of 3/5, Maj. Benjamin S. Berry, Catlin rushed over to the 2/6 command post near La Cense Farm and issued orders orally to

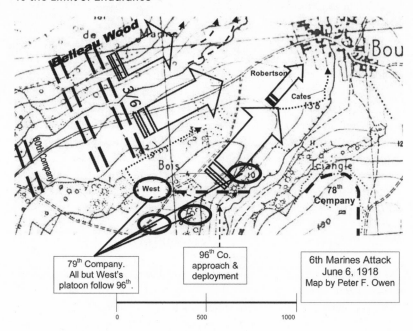

79th Company.
All but West's
platoon follow 96th.

96th Co.
approach &
deployment

6th Marines Attack
June 6, 1918
Map by Peter F. Owen

0   500   1000

Holcomb and Maj. Berton Sibley, the commander of 3/6. Unable to communicate with Berry, Catlin believed 3/5's attack was doomed. He likewise had no opportunity to coordinate with the machine-gun and artillery commanders supporting that unit. With only a little over an hour to go before the scheduled assault, Catlin reviewed the brigade order as written with Holcomb and Sibley, making one last-minute change—he ordered Holcomb to attack alongside 3/6 with one company to support Sibley's advance.[24]

Between the 79th Company's position and Belleau Wood, a wide, open valley, flush with green wheat, ran northeast from Lucy to Boure-sches. Within Belleau Wood the thick forest hid defending Germans from aerial observation. High ground in the southeast corner of the wood offered commanding fields of fire over the valley. Huge boulders provided superb protection for the machine gunners from shellfire. The stone buildings in Bouresches afforded similar cover and con-cealment. For the attacker, only a few clumps of trees dotted the flat meadow sloping down from Zane's position to Bouresches. The steep ravine between Zane and Messersmith to his right along with an east-west ravine running along the south edge of Belleau Wood offered the only cover. Twilight lasted until nearly 10:00 P.M. this time of year, allowing the marines nearly five hours of daylight for the attack.[25]

Harbord's order gave only perfunctory mention of the enemy situation, and Catlin had only a general idea of German dispositions in front of him: Holcomb's men had spied Germans infiltrating into Belleau Wood and Bouresches on the heels of the French. And although Catlin's intelligence officer had attempted to scout enemy positions in the woods, he could not penetrate their screen of outposts. The colonel knew that "there might have been any number of men in there, but we had to attack just the same."[26]

The IV Reserve Corps had nearly as many men and machine guns facing the marines in this sector as Harbord committed to the attack. The 461st Regiment of the 237th Division defended Belleau Wood with approximately two thousand men and between thirty and forty machine guns. Its main line of resistance ran from the northwest corner of the forest to the southeast corner. The 461st Regiment placed machine-gun strongpoints in small outposts in front of its main line and on the small hill in the southeast corner of the wood. The 398th Regiment of the 10th Division defended along the railroad line north and east of Bouresches. But the Germans along the rail line could not bring effective fire upon the marines attacking toward Belleau Wood and Bouresches from the west and southwest.[27]

Bouresches was a large triangular town five hundred yards in breadth, with between sixty and seventy stone buildings. Two companies of the 398th Regiment established an outpost of about one hundred soldiers and six to eight machine guns in the town. Machine guns from these outposts and in others upon the high ground in the southeast corner of Belleau Wood dominated the valley between Bouresches and Lucy.[28]

According to Harbord's order, in the first phase of the attack, 3/5 would attack on the left and Major Sibley's 3/6 would attack on the right in a northeasterly direction from the vicinity of Lucy-le-Bocage to seize Belleau Wood. Only after these battalions cleared the forest would 3/6 continue the attack in the second phase to seize Bouresches and the railroad station there. Harbord merely tasked Catlin to have 2/6 "advance its left to conform to the progress made by the battalion on its left [3/6]." Catlin directed Holcomb to attack with one company and seize the enemy line south of Bouresches, conforming his advance to that of 3/6.[29]

In an optimistic attempt at surprise, the 2nd Field Artillery Brigade planned only brief preparatory bombardments. Nearly two hundred U.S. and French artillery pieces would focus on counterbattery and interdiction fire. This was a generous allocation of firepower for a regimental attack, providing a ratio of nearly one artillery piece to every fifteen attacking riflemen. Yet in a major shortcoming, the plan omitted the "rolling barrage," an indispensable part of French doctrine. Two machine-gun companies and the 6th Marines's 37-mm gun platoon would support the attack with overhead fire. The battalion commanders had no control over these supporting arms and would have to request fire support by sending couriers to the regimental command post. The 6th Marines were about to test the 2nd Division's assertion that infantry could achieve fire superiority without artillery "blasting the way forward."[30]

Holcomb assembled his company commanders at his command post and issued a hasty order around 4:30 P.M. He had precious little time. Holcomb told Captain Duncan to take his 96th Company and pass through Zane's 79th Company, then wheel to the right and attack to seize the enemy line south of Bouresches, guiding on 3/6 to the left. He ordered Captain Zane to follow in support of Duncan with his 79th Company. Coffenburg would follow in support of 3/6 after Sibley's battalion passed through his lines. Holcomb's intentions for the 78th Company is uncertain. Captain Messersmith left the meeting believing that Duncan was going to pass through his unit and that he, not Zane, would follow the 96th Company over the top. From the available evidence, it appears Messersmith misunderstood the order and that Holcomb wanted the 78th Company to stand fast to maintain contact with the 23rd Infantry on the battalion's right.[31]

Duncan's company was located near the battalion command post, and the captain assembled his officers as soon as Holcomb had finished. Duncan's orders were hasty, as they had to be—he had only fifteen minutes to move about a mile to his jump-off position and deploy into attack formation. The series of rushed orders from brigade to regiment, regiment to battalion, battalion to company, and now company to platoons culminated in misunderstanding and confusion. Lieutenant Cates recalled his instructions as "very ambiguous." Duncan gave brief direction on the deployment of the company. He ordered Cates, who would have the leftmost position in line, to take his 4th Platoon across a wheat field to the edge of Belleau Wood and attack on line with the lead companies of 3/6. The purpose of this tactic was to maintain contact between the two battalions. As Cates digested this, Duncan assembled his platoons in column and led his 250 men in a brisk jog up the steep ravine. "We didn't know where we were going," recalled Cates.[32]

Zane's 79th Company was already at its starting point for the attack, though spread out in fighting holes on the wooded ridge overlooking the ground they would soon attack across. Zane assembled his officers and gave a quick order that mirrored Duncan's instructions. Lieutenant West would attack on line with the support companies of 3/6, following Cates. The other three platoons would follow in support of the 96th Company. Lt. Graves Erskine, who had just returned from the Gondrecourt School the day before, was acting as company second in command. He went forward to check on his old 2nd Platoon, temporarily under the command of Lt. Wallace Leonard. Corporal Hill remembered Leonard as "a slim, small man with a whisper of a mustache." He was evidently unpopular with some of the marines, an unfortunate situation aggravated by the fact that Leonard was an army reserve officer. While marine lieutenants attended schools, army lieutenants of mixed quality were often assigned to 2/6 as temporary replacements. Erskine was eager to take back his platoon and pleased to find his men in high spirits. While he was with them, artillery fire began to crash into Bouresches, and the excited marines hooted and cheered.[33]

Duncan reached Zane's position right before 5:00, just in time to watch the final rounds of the barrage hit. The artillery preparation by all accounts did little to suppress the German defenders. Pvt. Charles Vanek remembered no artillery barrage at all. Erskine called it "ten minutes of very light artillery." The barrage did alert the expectant German defenders to the forming assault. Shrapnel began to pepper the 79th Company, aided by the direction of a huge Zeppelin.[34]

It was now 5:00 P.M. Duncan deployed three platoons in line to the left of the ravine, and Cates maneuvered to the left in anticipation of locating 3/6 advancing from Lucy. As Cates jockeyed to get his platoon in position, his men became intermingled with the 79th Company, and Captain Zane directed him to clear out. Cates shifted to his right, caught sight of the rest of his own 96th Company deploying, and decided to fall in on the left of the company line. The 96th Company front now measured more than 250 yards long, from the 1st Platoon's right on the ravine to Cates's 4th Platoon on the extreme left. Each platoon formed into the four skirmish lines they had practiced to perfection. Duncan positioned himself near his 1st Platoon, on the right, and had his second in command, Lieutenant Robertson, on the left near Cates.

The battlefield was serenely quiet as Duncan's marines emerged from the wooded crest and waded into the knee-high green wheat.

They could see the southern border of Belleau Wood five hundred yards to their front and Bouresches eight hundred yards to the northeast. The company pivoted smartly to the right, toward Bouresches. Maj. Edward Cole, commander of the 6th Machine Gun Battalion, watched the 96th Company's dressed lines advance across the wheat and thought it was "the most beautiful sight he had ever seen."[35] Witnesses and participants all agreed on one point: the marine formations looked as perfect as a parade. A German marksman snagged Colonel Catlin with a rifle shot as he admired the advance of his two battalions from an exposed position near Lucy. "I say they went in as if on parade, and that is literally true," wrote Catlin. The commander of the 23rd Infantry, on Holcomb's right, reported: "The marines were seen advancing in splendid order. The spectacle was inspiring." Corporal Hill remembered proudly: "Our spacing was just as in drill. And we kept our platoon front even." A German officer who wrote a history of the battle claimed the machine gunners "could not have desired better targets."[36]

The 96th Company's formation was designed to follow a rolling barrage a short distance in advance to the enemy's front lines. It favored mobility and centralized control to penetrate a defensive position rapidly but sacrificed firepower to the front. In theory artillery "accompanying the attack" would have compensated for the masking of the fire of the three rear ranks. Adjacent units advancing alongside would have drawn fire from the defenders, preventing the enemy from concentrating against a single company. Of the 96th Company's adjacent units, 3/6 was just jumping off from its start line near Lucy, more than a mile to the west, and the 78th Company on its right stood fast, waiting for Duncan to pass through, according to Messersmith. With no rolling barrage and no troops on either flank, the 96th Company walked naked and alone into its baptism of fire.

The company advanced at the regulation pace of one hundred yards a minute. For the first two to three minutes, only occasional shells thumped into the soft earth, hurting no one. The battlefield remained calm enough for marines to banter back and forth.

On the right Lockhart's 1st Platoon had eased ahead of the rest of the company during the right-hand pivot. As bullets began to zing through the air, Duncan strolled over to Lockhart and coolly ordered him to pause and allow the other platoons to catch up on his left. Sergeant Sheridan jokingly asked the captain if he thought they would see much fighting. Duncan replied in good humor, "Oh yes, we will give and take, but be sure you take more than you give!"[37]

As the lead waves of the 96th Company reached a point approximately six hundred yards from Bouresches, the Germans unleashed a hailstorm of machine-gun and artillery fire that ripped apart the marine formation. A burst tore through Captain Duncan's abdomen. Dozens of other marines crumpled into the wheat. The 96th Company hit the deck.[38]

First Sgt. Joseph Sissler, Sergeant Sheridan, Lt. Weeden Osborne (the navy dentist with whom the Hill brothers had shared their rabbit), and a hospital apprentice rushed to drag their captain to safety. The four men pulled Duncan up to a grove of trees, where the regiment had located an aid station with the regiment's one-pound guns. The poorly sited station was in clear view of German artillery to the northeast of Bouresches. As the four men treated Duncan's wound, a direct hit by a shell killed all but Sheridan.[39]

Holcomb's command group, which had followed behind the 96th Company, took shelter in some abandoned German fighting holes in a small patch of woods in the ravine. When word reached him of Duncan's death, Holcomb wept.[40]

After the 96th Company had passed through the 79th, Lieutenant Leonard fired his .45 automatic in the air and yelled, "Come on men, for God's sake don't fail me now!" Because the company was in support of the 96th Company, each platoon initially advanced in a "line of half platoons." This meant each advanced in two parallel columns for ease of control. As Sergeant Benjamin of Leonard's 2nd Platoon recalled: "I led the first half platoon in column of twos out of the woods, then did column right and headed for town. Sergeant B[aldwin] led the second half platoon thirty yards away and on my left. Lieutenant L[eonard] walked between, smoking. I remember that I laughed at him."[41]

Zane's company followed in trace of Duncan's fourth wave, covering only one hundred yards before machine-gun fire began to chop up the formation. Sergeant Benjamin wrote, "We were unable to advance more than a few hundred yards before we were forced to form a skirmish line." The casualties quickly mounted. "I don't ever think I shall ever be able to write or relate the happenings of the next two hours for they were too terrible," wrote home Trumpeter Hugo Meyer. Corporal Hill and his brother both fell from bullet wounds to their left knees. Private Vanek took a bullet and lay where he fell for three hours. A round glanced off Sergeant Benjamin's left jaw and severed his helmet strap. Lt. Arthur Worton was struck twice, in the neck and through the left lung. He would survive but was finished for this war.[42]

Cpl. Thomas Gragard rose to look for a less-exposed position for his squad and crumpled to the ground, killed. Gragard had been Cpl. Oscar Rankin's best friend, and the former minister was consumed with rage. Erskine watched as Rankin "sprang to his feet and swore as no parson had ever sworn," driving his squad across the field toward Bouresches.[43]

After forty minutes Lieutenant Erskine could muster only five of Leonard's fifty-seven-man platoon. Erskine told a marine wounded in the nose to tell Zane that they were pinned down. "About an hour later this poor kid crawled back to report the captain's words: 'Goddammit, continue the advance.' We continued the advance."[44]

By the time West had returned to his platoon in the 79th Company, 3/6 had begun its attack. Major Sibley had deployed his battalion with two companies in the lead and two companies following in support. West maneuvered his 3rd Platoon into position by crossing the wheat field in squad rushes. The platoon formed a thin skirmish line and advanced alongside the 97th Company, the right rear company of 3/6.[45]

West's platoon soon stumbled upon casualties from the 3/6's lead waves. The lieutenant paused to tighten the puttee strings of a marine shot through both calves. He was galled by the number of wounded left unattended. "The pitiful allotment of stretcher bearers to a battalion or company made no impression to an attack of this kind," West later lamented. After he moved on, a shell landed on top of the man he had aided, blasting him apart.[46]

West's men now began to die. A single shell killed Pvts. Horace Ward and John Kaiser. Pvt. Roy Trow, "with his stomach and testicles shot away, a mass of blood," was carried on an unrolled pack by four men several hundred yards to the dressing station where Duncan had been killed; Trow succumbed to his wounds. The platoon slowly advanced until it reached the stalled lines of 3/6, "where we lay in that wheat . . . and took it."

Captain Coffenberg had deployed the 80th Company with two platoons following the left-hand companies of 3/6 into Belleau Wood and the other two platoons following the right-hand companies across the wheat field to the south of the wood. According to *Instructions for the Offensive Combat of Small Units,* Coffenberg should have followed about a thousand yards behind 3/6. But as that battalion came under increasingly effective machine-gun fire from the 461st Infantry, its attack stalled, and the marines of the 80th Company quickly closed the gap. Coffenberg's platoons became intermingled with the support companies of 3/6, and many of his marines joined in the fighting in Belleau Wood.[47]

In front of Bouresches, the rifles of 2/6 were insufficient to gain fire superiority over the German water-cooled machine guns hidden in the buildings to their front and the forest to their left. With no supporting arms under his control, Holcomb could only scribble field messages and hope his messengers reached someone who could direct suppressive fire on the enemy positions to his front and left. The counterbattery fire of the combined French and American artillery brigades began to silence many German batteries, though not the German machine gunners pummeling the wheat field. "They had no definite [German] locations and were obliged to shell at random in a sort of hit-or-miss fire. It must have been largely miss," Catlin wrote. Cole's machine guns shooting over the heads of the 96th Company provided the only effective fire at the Maxims in Belleau Wood and Bouresches.[48]

Holcomb could see the 79th and 96th Companies pinned down in the wheat from his location in an abandoned foxhole. A 78th Company messenger arrived with an inquiry from Messersmith. The 96th Company had never passed through his unit, so Messersmith had not moved. What did the major want him to do? Perhaps perplexed at the misunderstanding, Holcomb told Messersmith to hold fast.[49]

It was no cake walk for the 78th Company. High-explosive rounds erupted so often that marines mistook the toxic smoke for gas. The unit lost a number of men to enemy fire. When Lieutenant Sellers attempted to crawl to Messersmith to report the situation, a German rifleman inflicted a serious wound to Sellers's groin.[50]

Holcomb had lost contact with the 80th Company. He sent Sergeant Paradis off to comb the battlefield for Coffenburg in order to get a report. Paradis grabbed Private Slack and zigzagged across the fields recently crossed by the attacking companies. Countless times the two hugged the earth as shells and machine-gun bullets rained around them. The smoke was so thick that Paradis had trouble finding the unit. He was astounded by the number of dead and steeled himself to disregard the calls of his wounded buddies. Reaching the ravine along the south edge of Belleau Wood, Paradis stumbled into Major Sibley at the 3/6 command post. Sibley gave him Coffenburg's location farther down the steep ravine and directed the sergeant to urge Holcomb not to move the 80th Company—3/6 had been badly mauled and might need their support. Paradis grabbed Slack and quickly covered the ground to Coffenburg, who confirmed the 80th

Company's location. Once more Paradis dashed into the fire-swept field. Slack demurred and attempted another route; Paradis never saw him again. When the sergeant had delivered Coffenburg's message, he asked Holcomb to let him return to help the wounded. No, replied Holcomb. There would be more messages.[51]

For nearly an hour the remnants of the 79th and 96th Companies suffered in the wheat field. German fire steadily ate away at the dwindling number of marines. Men prayed for nightfall to end the ordeal. North of Lucy 3/5 had been cut to ribbons. In Belleau Wood 3/6's left-hand companies were in a life-and-death struggle with machine gunners in the German outpost zone. Holcomb's lead company commander was down, and his two attacking companies lay pinned in the open wheat. By 6:00 P.M. the attack was in peril of breaking apart.[52]

The lieutenants in the 96th Company had only a fragmented perspective of the situation. They knew they were in the attack but not the purpose for it. They could see the right-hand companies of 3/6 stopped cold to their left, Bouresches lying directly to their front. The wooded ravine to their right offered a covered avenue to the town. Through either Holcomb's design or omission, his lieutenants determined in the absence of guidance to capture the town on their own.[53]

The 96th Company executive officer, Lieutenant Robertson, walked out in front of the company, waved his .45 automatic, and yelled, "Come on, let's go!" The 2nd, 3rd, and 4th Platoons formed a skirmish line and followed him toward the town, six hundred yards distant. The 1st Platoon, at the far end of the company line, was under cover in the ravine and likely did not see or hear Robertson.

Marines dropped at every step. Three hundred yards from the town, the 2nd Platoon flopped to the ground and attempted to cover the advance with rifle fire. Their Springfields and Chauchats were no match for the Maxims. The 2nd and 3rd Platoons continued to rush forward for another hundred yards until the survivors gave it up and sought cover in the ravine to their right. Something smashed into Lieutenant Cates's helmet, knocking him out cold. Unbelievably, Robertson pushed on with the remnants of the 4th Platoon through the barrage and criss-crossing machine-gun fire.[54]

In Belleau Wood a small band of 3/6 marines under Lt. Louis Timmerman stumbled into a squad of Germans emplacing two machine guns. The guns would have perfectly enfiladed Robertson and his men. Timmerman and his marines massacred the machine gunners with boots and bayonets in a bloody close-quarter scuffle.[55]

A four-man Chauchat team under the 79th Company's Sgt. James McClelland had joined the charge toward town. As Robertson's men rushed through the barrage, McClelland worked his way around their left flank. Emplacing the Chauchat at a good vantage point, he had his automatic rifleman fire repeated bursts at close range into the stone houses of Bouresches. McClelland's support was desperately needed; the German machine gunners later reported engaging Robertson's men at a range of ten yards. With the aid and intrepidity of Timmerman and McClelland and a great deal of luck, Robertson entered the west side of Bouresches with fewer than two dozen men.[56]

Cates came to after about four minutes and found himself alone on the battlefield. He admitted later that his first instinct was to race for the rear. Then he saw four marines from the 3rd Platoon in the ravine to his right and dashed over to join them. One of the men had gone into the attack with a bottle in his haversack, and he poured wine over the lieutenant's wound. "Goddammit," sputtered Cates. "Don't pour it on my head, give me a drink." He then armed himself with a discarded French Lebel rifle and worked his way up the ravine to the edge of town with the four marines.

About this time the two companies of the 398th Regiment began to pull out of Bouresches, leaving a machine gun posted in the belfry of the church and a stronger force at the north end of town. The 398th had never intended to hold Bouresches but had merely used it as an outpost for its main line along the railroad.[57]

Cates and his four men made it to the center of town without running into any Germans. The lieutenant then spied Robertson and his tiny band withdrawing from the western edge of town. He blew his whistle and Robertson came over. "Come on," Cates said, "Let's go on and take the rest of the town. There's nobody in here now." Robertson had another idea and turned the platoon back over to Cates. "You go in and clean the town out," said Robertson, who said he would go back for reinforcements. "Which I thought was a helluva thing!" recalled Cates.[58]

The center of Bouresches is the junction of three roads: the Lucy road heading west, the Belleau road heading north, and the Vaux road heading southeast. Cates had about twenty-one men in the middle of a town of three times that many stone buildings. The townspeople had long departed, and he was not sure where the Germans lurked.

Cates sent Gy. Sgt. Willard Morrey down the Lucy road with six men. He had Sgt. Earl Belfry take another six men down the Vaux road. Cates took the remaining marines and started inching his way north on the Belleau road.

The Maxim in the church belfry fired a burst into Cates's group. One bullet punctured the officer's helmet while another tore off his gold lieutenant's bar, grazing the shoulder. Cates and his men scurried back to the town center. Undaunted, he divided his band into two teams. They worked their way up either side of the church belfry. Pvt. Herbert Dunlavy single-handedly maneuvered into a position from which he could pick off one of the gunners. The other gunner surrendered himself and his gun, which Dunlavy turned on the retreating Germans. Cates and his marines continued up the street until a second Maxim at the north end of town hammered at his squad. This time the marines did not escape unharmed as several fell wounded. Cates decided he had extended himself far enough and organized his remaining men into four outposts to await reinforcement.[59]

Robertson found Holcomb at his command post in the ravine at about 8:30 P.M. and reported what he had done and seen in Bouresches. The major was glad to get some good news, and appreciated the report, but he was a bit put out that Robertson had left his men to make his report in person. Robertson may have been shaken up, now that he had survived his brush with death. According to Sergeant Paradis, Holcomb had to direct the lieutenant to return to Bouresches.[60]

The 398th Regiment had committed a major blunder. Withdrawing its outpost companies from Bouresches was consistent with the principles of the elastic defense. But in abandoning the town, the Germans had handed an important strongpoint to the marines. Its location afforded the leathernecks observation and fire into the open fields east of Belleau Wood. By holding Bouresches, Holcomb's men could partially isolate the 461st Regiment in the woods as well as deliver supporting fire into its left flank in the southeast corner of the woods. Likewise, by denying the Germans the town, 2/6 could protect troops and supplies moving up to 3/6's position from enfilade fire on their right flank. Holcomb instantly grasped the importance of Bouresches and determined to reinforce Cates with every man at his disposal before the Germans counterattacked and drove out the plucky lieutenant.

The survivors of the 96th Company soon found Cates's route up the ravine, soon followed by Captain Zane with the members of the

79th Company who were still on their feet. As Zane's men filtered up the ravine, they stepped over the bodies of 96th Company men who had sought refuge there. Trumpeter Meyer wrote: "Dead were piled up three and four deep in that ravine. Men with skulls shot off or both legs; oh it was terrible, and the moaning, God, how I prayed."[61]

As the survivors of the 79th Company crept into town, Cates put them into defensive positions. When Captain Zane arrived around 9:00 P.M., Cates gladly turned over command to him. Zane sent a runner to Lieutenant West, who brought his platoon over to the ravine and into town: "Less than half the men who, four and a half hours earlier, had jumped off." West's platoon set up a defensive position on the west side of town, just north of the Lucy road. Stretcher bearers began the heartrending task of manhandling wounded marines to the hospitals.[62]

At 9:27 Holcomb, still unaware that Catlin had been wounded, sent the colonel a report on the situation in Bouresches and his intentions: "Will ask 23rd Infantry to hold Messersmith's line and if they will do so, will send him into town. Our line of resistance from Lucy to Messersmith should be reinforced at once."[63] The 23rd Infantry apparently could not accommodate Holcomb, for Messersmith held his position where he had been since June 1.

At dusk Lieutenant Leonard and the wounded Sergeant Benjamin, who had been pinned down all afternoon, brought back a handful of men to the original jump-off point. Orders from the army arrived at regiment that night directing Leonard to return to the United States to train recruits. Holcomb received notification of this by telephone from Maj. Frank Evans. Within two minutes he had Leonard packed and on his way.[64]

An uneasy night followed in Bouresches. Both the 79th and 96th Companies, each 250-plus strong before the attack, had suffered losses of well over 50 percent.[65] Platoons from different companies, battalions, and regiments were intermingled in the woods, wheat fields, and town. Marines with hair-trigger nerves mistook sporadic enemy firing for local counterattacks. West's men worked the bolts of their Springfields "like machine guns."[66] The officers had only a dim understanding of where their own troops and the Germans were.

At 11:30 P.M. Holcomb had sent a runner off to find either Lee or Harbord with a report that the Germans still held Belleau Wood and the railroad station northeast of Bouresches. Holcomb believed his battalion could not push any farther: "unless Sibley can do something in the way of taking left part of the objective [Belleau Wood], we are in a hole. We also need reinforcement to hold our line of resistance. Send me some word."[67] Lieutenant Erskine reported to Zane at the road junction in the town center. Zane's first priority was to determine what the Germans were up to around his town. He ordered Erskine to lead a reconnaissance patrol northwest of the town. Erskine asked for volunteers from among the survivors of the 2nd Platoon. "Every man in the vicinity volunteered," Erskine proudly reported. He picked Cpl. Oscar Rankin and two privates.

The night was clear and cold for late spring, with dew covering the landscape. A bright moon illuminated the fields and stone buildings as the patrol crept through the wet strands of wheat. The silent marines had slipped to within fifty yards of Belleau Wood when a fusillade of rifle shots sent them hugging the earth. Escaping unscratched, Erskine led his three marines southwest, covering another hundred yards parallel to the wood line. Three more rifles cracked in the pitch-black forest, and again the patrol dove to the ground.

Satisfied he had found the information Zane needed, Erskine retreated back in the direction of town. The marines heard movement as they neared the ravine between Bouresches and the southern edge of Belleau Wood. Erskine froze and lay in wait, listening. He concluded that there were no more than three men in the ravine and brashly decided to spring upon them in the dark in the hope of nabbing a prisoner.

Hearts pounding in their ears, the four marines skulked up to the edge of the ravine. A burst of profanity in an Irish brogue startled them. Erskine hopped into the draw and found Private Mazereeuw, the former sergeant, cussing at the top of his lungs. Mazereeuw had a painful gunshot wound in his knee. He cussed the German who shot him and he cussed the army for not sending an ambulance to deliver him from the field. The four marines hefted their comrade out of the ravine, vainly trying to shut him up before the Germans decided to investigate his shouting. Erskine found an outpost of 3/6 men three hundred yards west of town, where he sent Mazereeuw with two of his men. Erskine and Rankin then snaked up the ravine toward the railroad station. After evading bursts of machine-gun fire and rifle shots from the station, Erskine returned to make his report. He found Zane in his command post in a cellar near the town's center at about 1:30 A.M. on June 7.

From Erskine's report, it was apparent to Zane that 2/6 held Bouresches and 3/6 had a toehold along the southern edge of Belleau Wood. The Germans clung to the southeast corner of the forest and defended the railroad line northeast of town in strength. Anticipating an attack from either direction, he bolstered his defenses to the northeast and northwest. Zane had previously placed West's 3rd Platoon on the northwest side. He had Erskine collect his 2nd Platoon to defend a hedgerow just north of an old farm track facing the railroad. Zane held a third platoon in reserve in the center of town. Robertson's 96th Company marines were intermingled among the 79th Company positions.[68]

In response to Holcomb's earlier plea, Harbord poured reinforcements into the town. The 6th Machine Gun Battalion sent ten Hotchkiss guns to Zane. Sibley pushed marines from his chopped-up 84th and 97th Companies into the town. Division gave Harbord two companies from the 2nd Engineers, and they found their way down to Bouresches as well. Holcomb also requested two Stokes mortars and two 37-mm guns from regimental headquarters. Cates later estimated between six and seven hundred American troops defended Bouresches.[69]

The Germans pounded Bouresches with artillery, and riflemen sniped at marines crossing the streets, but otherwise they did not interfere with Holcomb's consolidation that night nor throughout June 7. That day passed in surreal contrast to the violence of June 6. With more troops than needed in Bouresches now, the 6th Marines pulled out 3/6's 84th and 97th Companies after dark. That evening Allied artillery dropped one shell every fifteen minutes into the town. Vainly Captain Zane fired signal flares, but the shelling continued. A runner finally reached higher headquarters, which terminated the bombardment.[70]

Just after midnight on June 8, Sergeant Paradis returned to Holcomb's command post in the steep ravine south of Bouresches. Paradis had been running messages to Sibley and Coffenburg and was soaked to the skin from his waist down from the dew-covered wheat. Holcomb had moved into a tiny rock cave, squeezed in with Lieutenant Wilmer and Sergeant Major Ingram. Paradis had just finished digging a hole under the opposite side of the rock from the cave when "all hell broke loose." A German barrage erupted around the command post and along the front lines. Thick smoke, explosive gas, and burning grass choked the marines as they hunkered in their holes. The 10th Division was counterattacking at last to recover Bouresches.[71]

Lieutenant Erskine's marines, dug in behind a hedgerow on the east side of Bouresches, were pinned in their holes as a machine-gun barrage from the railroad line raked their parapets. The fire abruptly ceased, followed by a shower of grenades. Attacking infantry had crept up to the far side of the hedgerow under cover of the machine guns and were heaving grenades from ten yards away. The hedgerow saved the 2nd Platoon from annihilation, for the grenades arced over the five-foot hedge and exploded harmlessly to the rear. Despite the surprise and close quarters, the marines held their ground and fought furiously. Springfields and Chauchats flashed in the night. Marines tossed their own grenades until their supply was exhausted. A squad of army engineers had bolstered Erskine's strength, and the soldiers fought every bit as tenaciously as the leathernecks. Two marine Hotchkiss guns added their firepower to the close-range fight. Magnesium flares turned night to day, and Erskine spied a Maxim setting up thirty yards up the farm track from his right flank. He directed the Hotchkiss guns to take it out before the Germans could open up on his men. The attack fell apart against the relentless fire, and the Germans withdrew with heavy losses. Morning broke on June 8 with the village still firmly in American hands. The 79th Company's Cpl. Lloyd Pike counted ten Germans heaped in front of his Chauchat.[72]

Sending Men to Hell: The 80th Company, June 8

Having failed to penetrate the main defensive line in Belleau Wood, Harbord directed 3/6 to resume the attack on the morning of June 8. Harry Lee, now commanding the 6th Marines, attached Captain Coffenburg's 80th Company to Major Sibley for the attack. Sibley ordered Coffenburg, whose unit was still relatively unscathed, to protect his left flank with two platoons and to keep the remaining two platoons in reserve on his right.[73]

The Germans had fortified each position with earth and logs. Their guns covered each other in an inescapable crossfire. The thick woods made it impossible for Sibley to accurately fix the location of these positions. Twenty minutes before H-hour, artillery rained down on Belleau Wood. The barrage could not suppress the forward machine-gun outposts for fear of hitting Sibley's frontline companies in the dense woods, and the shells fell harmlessly to the rear of the posts. The regimental Stokes-mortar platoon supported with indirect fire, but observers could not see through the dense woods, and their rounds likewise caused little damage.

Pvt. Levi Hemrick could see Sibley from his position in the ravine on the south edge of the woods. According to Hemrick, the major was furious about the order to attack. Sibley walked up and down the ravine, with his field shirt rolled up to his elbows, popping his fist in his palm and decrying the hasty, inadequate planning for the coming attack. Hemrick overheard him assert that he was infuriated that he had been "ordered to send men to hell."[74]

Coffenburg's marines fixed bayonets and went over the top with 3/6 at 6:30 A.M. Each platoon formed a simple skirmish line, for the complex French attack formation proved impractical in the dense woods. On Sibley's right, Hemrick's 2nd Platoon and another of the 80th Company crossed a small wheat field between the ravine and the woods and plunged into the forest. Zane's garrison in Bouresches hit the southeast corner of the woods with a machine-gun and rifle barrage.

A blizzard of rounds "like a swarm of wasps" sent Hemrick hugging the earth. One German gun's trajectory passed just inches above his head. As he pressed himself into the dirt, Hemrick could not locate a single German position. He was paralyzed with fear.

Hemrick's platoon sergeant was Paradis's buddy, Sgt. Grover O'Kelley. O'Kelley was leading from the front today. He urged his men to follow him against the German machine guns at the crest of the hill. "Come on men, get them out of there!" he roared. O'Kelley had closed within a few yards of the position when an unseen Maxim, its muzzle just protruding between two massive boulders, cut down the brave sergeant and Pvt. William Huey, another Detroit pal of Paradis. A bullet had creased O'Kelley just above an eye, knocking him out cold.

That burst took the fight out of the 2nd Platoon. Some anonymous voice broke out above the gunfire, "When the machine gun fire holds up, get back to the trench!" The marines scurried to safety. They dragged many wounded to the shelter of the ditch, but O'Kelley and Huey, presumed dead, were left where they lay.

Without artillery or heavy weapons, the marines had no hope of suppressing the concealed, fortified strongpoints. The 2nd Battalion, 461st Regiment, reported, "the repeated tenacious attacks of the Americans break down in our machine gun fire at a range of about 50 meters." Sibley's force retreated to its jump-off line in the ditch on the south edge of the wood. The attack had failed miserably. Marines from 3/6 and the 80th Company had captured just three machine guns, avenging their losses on the gunners with their bayonets. Five hours later the major reported that his battalion was "too much exhausted for further attack."[75]

In front of Sibley's lines, Huey regained consciousness, still under the muzzle of the German machine gun. Thinking the rounds overhead were friendly, he raised to his knees, shouting, "For God's sake don't shoot! We're marines!" The merciless machine gun cut down Huey once more, and he fell lifeless across O'Kelley. The sergeant played dead all day, with Huey's body growing cold across his back. After nightfall, German medics bandaged the American's wound and carted him off to a hospital. O'Kelley survived the war but tortured himself for years with the delusion that he had let down his fellow marines that day.[76]

Harbord withdrew Sibley's men and the 80th Company from the woods that night. The company had lost twenty-four killed, eighty-six wounded, one missing, and one captured. Like the 79th and 96th Companies, the 80th had lost over 50 percent of its strength.[77]

Get Your Head Down, Greeny

As Holcomb's marines had defended the Triangle Farm, the AEF had trucked the Marine Corps's 2nd and 3rd Replacement Battalions to the front in anticipation of the losses the 4th Brigade would suffer. Each replacement battalion was organized in similar fashion to an infantry battalion so that replacements of every rank from private to major were on hand. Each battalion included prewar regular officers and NCOs as well as many lieutenants who had been classmates at the Officer Training School with 2/6 lieutenants. Recruits, some with as little as four months' service, made up the overwhelming majority of the rank and file.[78] The ability of 2/6 to emerge victorious would rely increasingly on the quality of these green recruits.

Pvt. Carl Brannen, who had resigned from Texas A&M in December, had arrived in France aboard the *Henderson* with the 2nd Replacement Battalion in May. Trucks had dumped Brannen and his comrades on the Paris-Metz road the night of June 6 a short distance from Lucy. As dawn broke on June 7, ambulances ominously sped by, rushing to the hospital with the shattered men he and his fellows would soon replace.

After the 80th Company's attack on June 8, Brannen and forty others joined Coffenburg's decimated ranks. In the worst possible fashion, the replacements joined their platoons in their frontline holes. It would have been greatly preferable to withdraw Holcomb's hard-hit command to the rear area and assign replacements there. Men could have become acquainted with their NCOs and rehearsed tactical drills with their new units.

Lieutenant Colonel Lee, now commanding the 6th Marines, was so impressed with the conduct of Brannen and his fellow replacements that he penned a laudatory letter to the commandant of the Marine Corps. Extolling their conduct during the movement up to the front, Lee wrote: "The Regimental Sergeant Major [John Quick] reports that the men obeyed orders without a word, moved in splendid order and across a terrain which was shelled by the enemy with high explosives and lighted up by flares. Their arrival in the lines of the 2nd Battalion relieved a pressing need for men at a vital point. The remarkable steadiness of these men . . . under conditions that would have been trying to veteran troops, is eloquent evidence of the fine material from which the Marine Corps is drawing its men in a critical hour of the nation's history."[79]

In the meantime 2/6 clung to its shallow holes around Bouresches, the gaps in its ranks partially filled with bewildered young replacements like Brannen. Leaving his foxhole one day to fetch water from Bouresches, Brannen paused to speak to a group of old hands on the edge of the woods. "Get your head down, Greeny!" one marine warned. Brannen ducked just in time to escape a volley of rifle fire. In similar fashion Cpl. Melvin Krulewitch joined Messersmith's 78th Company south of Bouresches and found himself in a listening post the first night, alone, afraid, and wondering just why he had joined the Marine Corps.[80]

The 4th Brigade was baptizing these replacements so rudely because it had no fresh units to switch out with 2/6. All its battalions were committed or recuperating from equally high losses. On the evening of June 8, Harbord dispatched the following apologetic message to Major Holcomb: "Much to my regret I am unable to relieve your battalion tonight. The holding of that town is too important for me to risk a change at this time. It will be done just as soon as conditions permit. You and your battalion have done fine work and it is much appreciated by myself and the division commander."[81]

It would be June 11 before Harbord replaced 2/6's weary marines with those of 3/5.

Losses and Lessons, June 1–11, 1918

After ten days of fighting, Holcomb's exhausted troops marched to the rear for a brief rest. The official Muster Roll reports that the battalion suffered 60 killed, 186 wounded and gassed, and 4 missing, almost exactly 25 percent.[82] The roots of 2/6's heavy losses in June can be directly attributed to its unsuitable and poorly executed tactics, a cumbersome command-and-control system, and the inexperience of the 2nd Division in general and senior echelons of command in particular.

Division leadership had proclaimed in May that rifle fire could gain and maintain fire superiority without artillery. Accordingly, General Harbord had ordered the 6th Marines to attack without an accompanying rolling barrage, with disastrous results. The 79th and 96th Companies had charged across nearly nine hundred yards of open wheat fields without appropriate artillery support in a formation designed for short rushes behind a rolling barrage. In Belleau Wood the inability of artillery to provide close support had exposed the 80th Company and 3/6 to devastating fire. In a terrible irony, Holcomb's marines had found the open-warfare battle Pershing sought yet had fought it with unsuitable French position-warfare tactics and without the fire support on which such tactics were predicated. When denied the close, continuous artillery support that comprised an integral part of the French doctrine, such tactics invited disaster.

Sluggish battlefield communications had prevented Holcomb from requesting the fire support he needed once engaged. Once he moved away from the telephones in his command post, his ability to request fire support slowed to the pace of his fastest messenger. Machine guns, Stokes mortars, and 37-mm guns remained beyond Holcomb's immediate command. The 4th Brigade's imprecise plan for control of its machine guns, the "machine gunners only work for machine gunners" order, exacerbated the major's inability to direct supporting fires to suppress enemy positions.

While all hands were novices to this style of warfare, the inexperience at higher echelons led to mistakes for which the battalion paid dearly. The inexperience of General Harbord and his staff underlay all the battalion's difficulties throughout June. The 4th Marine Brigade headquarters conducted all planning and dictated precisely the methods of action. Time and again Holcomb could only react to brigade orders. With little time to prepare, he had no choice but to execute orders as written.

Harbord's brigade order arrived a scant three hours before the scheduled attack. By the time Holcomb could issue his battalion order to his company commanders, he had little time to do more than regurgitate the general's instructions. A mere hour or two to consider the problem would almost certainly have led to a less costly maneuver in executing the assault. In hindsight it seems obvious that the battalion's main effort against Bouresches could have advanced under cover through the ravine exploited by Cates. More than any other factor, the lack of time prevented 2/6 from adequately preparing for the attack. In marked contrast to the 4th Brigade's first battle, the 1st Division had meticulously planned and rehearsed their first attack at Cantigny on May 28, supporting it with overwhelming artillery fire, including a rolling barrage. The initial attack was a dramatic success, though the doughboys suffered terrible losses during German counterattacks.[83]

Despite poor tactics, inadequate communications, and inexperienced leadership, the aggressiveness and spirit of individual marines provided the means for success. Holcomb's men demonstrated breathtaking discipline and courage throughout the fighting. His officers and NCOs led from the front, overcoming savage losses with raw fortitude and unhesitating example.

A superb illustration of this resilience of spirit is reflected in the number of men who carried on the fight even after receiving wounds. No less than sixteen 2/6 marines received citations for such action. In another reflection of the quality of the ranks, six gunnery sergeants and sergeants received citations for taking command when their platoon leader fell wounded or killed.[84] These repeated incidents of junior leaders taking charge and of bleeding marines refusing evacuation gave 2/6 the edge to prevail against fearful odds under the most galling conditions. The question remained, would such esprit endure long enough for tactics and leadership to catch up?

4 Belleau Wood

Major Holcomb assembled his weary companies on the morning of June 12 in a wooded area five miles west of Lucy, where the marines enjoyed regular hot chow and bathed in a local stream. Some helped themselves to fresh clothing and boots that the newly arrived replacements had abandoned. YMCA vendors set up shop to sell sundries such as razor blades, soap, and tobacco. Resenting the YMCA enterprise, the men brazenly helped themselves to the goods in the vendor's truck, with their officers looking on with quiet approval. Here also another 162 marine replacements joined the battalion.[1]

First Sergeant Fritz returned to the 79th Company, having recuperated from a noncombat injury he had suffered in May. This created an awkward dilemma, for the 79th Company now had two first sergeants, Fritz and Simon Barber. Astonishingly young and inexperienced for a company first sergeant, twenty-five-year-old Barber had enlisted in Houston barely two years before. He had evidently impressed Captain Zane during the capture and defense of Bouresches. Fritz's absence from this vicious fight probably weighed heavily in the captain's decision to retain Barber as his right-hand man. Perhaps Zane's cup had runneth over with Fritz's generous counsel. In Erskine's words, "If [Fritz] thought something was wrong he'd tell the captain in no uncertain terms, and he knew his business." Erskine asked for Fritz as his platoon sergeant, a request Zane quickly granted.[2]

While Holcomb's marines recuperated, the 4th Brigade had begun to chew its way through Belleau Wood. When 3/6 and the 80th Company had withdrawn from the forest the night of June 8–9, the 2nd Division had temporarily conceded the area to Gen. Max von Conta's IV Reserve Corps. On June 10 the 2nd Field Artillery Brigade blasted the wood for hours before 1/6 attacked due north through 3/6's old positions along the southern edge. With the benefit of a rolling barrage, 1/6 made modest gains, wrestling the outpost zone from Conta's defenders in the southern third of the wood. Harbord followed up this success with a poorly coordinated attack from the west by 2/5 on June 12. This costly attack fortuitously struck the boundary between the 28th and 237th Divisions, and the aggressive leathernecks succeeded in ejecting the 28th Division from the southern half of the forest.[3]

While 2/5 and 1/6 slugged it out with the 237th Division in the northern half of Belleau Wood, 2/6 continued to enjoy its respite. Newspapers found their way into the marines' holes, their headlines exaggerating the American success at Belleau Wood. In the words of Private Hemrick, "The marines hit the publicity jackpot at just the right time."[4] The unexpected fame of their brigade's exploits restored the swagger of many exhausted leathernecks.

Although the marines of 2/6 were well to the rear of the fighting, German long-range artillery occasionally dropped shells among the battalion's holes. When a high-explosive round made a direct hit on the 79th Company, Lieutenant West helped dig out a man buried up to his waist. "We dug hard at first with shovels, then, as we got closer to his legs, we dug with our hands. Finally we came to blood and shredded flesh. He had no legs. A stretcher took him away to die."[5]

The 78th and 96th Companies Destroyed, June 13–14, 1918

The respite, punctuated by such occasional tragedy, was pitifully short for Holcomb's men. At 12:40 A.M. on June 13, the major received an order to move at once to the woods northwest of Lucy as the brigade reserve. Holcomb promptly had his companies on the road and arrived before 4:00 A.M.[6]

Just before dawn General Harbord received a false report that a German counterattack had wrested Bouresches from 3/5. He ordered Holcomb to move two companies to the woods southeast of Lucy to be in position to retake the town.[7] As daylight broke across the wheat fields, Holcomb led his 78th and 96th Companies across the two miles of open ground at the double, directly under the watching eyes of three German balloons. Midway through this dash, a runner from regimental headquarters caught up with Holcomb and informed him that the earlier report was false. No doubt frustrated, the major immediately veered for the cover of a small wood to his right.

With their location now compromised, the 78th and 96th Companies prudently began scooping out foxholes under the trees. Holcomb set up his command post at the Montgivrault Farm nearby. After the shocking bombardment of the 80th Company at La Cense

Farm on June 2, all hands clearly understood the danger facing the two companies. There was little to do during daylight but dig, pray, and wait for nightfall for an opportunity to evade the watching eyes of enemy spotters. German artillery lobbed shells into the wood intermittently throughout the day, removing any doubt that observers had fixed their location.[8]

Well before dusk, a runner handed Holcomb a 4th Brigade order directing 2/6 to relieve 2/5 in Belleau Wood after midnight. Holcomb ordered his companies to sit tight, draw ammunition, feed the lads one last hot meal, and move out smartly at 1:00 A.M. Holcomb no doubt felt guardedly secure after weathering the day without mishap, yet his marines were in greater peril than he realized. German artillery ammunition stockpiles had burgeoned significantly. As the 78th and 96th Companies dozed in their holes, the 237th Division issued ominous instructions that "every concentration of hostile troops will be subjected to a heavy neutralization fire."[9]

Just before midnight, the mess kitchens of the 78th and 96th Companies rolled up, and the aroma of hot slum gullion wafted through the trees. Marines donned their equipment and scrambled out of their holes in the dark. The hungry leathernecks began to shake out their mess kits, anticipating more days of short rations ahead. A shower of high explosive, mustard, and phosgene crashed into the column with the rude abruptness of a tropic downpour. In an instant those men not hit scrambled back to their holes and shimmied into their gas masks. They could not talk through the mouthpieces of these masks and could barely see through the thick lenses. Amid the crashing shells, screaming wounded, and the clouded night, the men could not see, could not hear, and could not communicate.

This was an unprecedented barrage, a "drenching bombardment," in German terminology, of six thousand to seven thousand rounds. Mustard gas had presented little more than a nuisance to the battalion in the past, provided the men could evacuate the contaminated area. This night, the intensity of the high explosives pinned them to their position, and the mustard agent began to seep into their clothing.[10]

Lieutenant Cates fumbled through his tangle of webbing for his mask. Horrified, he could not find it. The smoky darkness disoriented Cates, and he realized that he could not hope to find his hole where he left his mask. Surrounded by the thickening gas, Cates fought back panic. In a flash he recalled that Pvt. Virgil Hall had been showing off a captured German mask. "Hall!" he screamed. Despairing, he screamed louder. "Hall!" Cates barely detected Hall's muffled response. Before the bewildered private knew what the lieutenant wanted, Cates leaped into his hole, found the metal canister dangling from Hall's neck, and ripped out the German mask. It was too small, but it functioned perfectly. Cates had narrowly cheated death again.[11]

Amid the chaos, Cates's platoon sergeant, Gy. Sgt. Fred Stockham, peered through the smoke and gas for his men. He found Pvt. Barrett Mattingly bleeding from shrapnel wounds. As Cates watched in awe, the former firefighter hoisted Mattingly across his shoulders and stepped off toward the aid station. He had marched only a few paces when a deafening crash directly above the pair flung them to the deck. Dazed from the concussion of the airburst, Stockham rose to his feet and fumbled for the wounded marine. He came across Mattingly and quickly looked him over for additional wounds. He found none but discovered a far greater peril: shrapnel had punctured Mattingly's mask, rendering it useless.

Without hesitating, Stockham removed his own mask and, ignoring the shouted protests of his platoon, placed it over Mattingly's face. Stockham then once again heaved the wounded man upon his back, sucking mustard and phosgene into his lungs. He staggered to the regimental aid station at Lucy. Incredibly, the sergeant returned to the wood once more to aid additional wounded marines. Searching among the smoky trees, still inhaling the poisoned air, he finally collapsed. Only after four days of agony in a hospital bed would Fred Stockham mercifully perish.[12]

At some point before dawn, the barrage lifted sufficiently for the survivors to move out. Holcomb collected the two companies and led them past Lucy toward Belleau Wood. High explosives burst around them. Gas shells flashed in a quiet thump, oozing clouds of mustard. Holcomb zigzagged back and forth across the fields, avoiding the heaviest concentrations. He reached the edge of Belleau Wood with a good fraction of the two companies intact.[13]

But mustard had impregnated the uniforms of most of the marines. As the column twisted through the forest, men fell out every few yards. A handful had the time and presence of mind to strip down and lather their skin with soap, a tedious but effective measure that could mitigate the effects of the blister agent. Most of the men had no opportunity to stop and tumbled out of the column as the gas blistered their skin.[14]

The 79th and 80th Companies continued with the relief, crawling through the wheat on all fours toward Belleau Wood. The night was extremely dark, and the southern half of the wood was inundated with gas. Unable to see or speak clearly in their masks, the marines formed a long single file, each man grabbing the pack straps of the one in front. As the 79th Company snaked through the forest, German artillery fired a mix of high explosive and mustard into the area. Sergeant Benjamin, back with the 2nd Platoon now, recalled the shelling: "Men were struck, but we could not stop. We had to leave them where they fell and trust some kind God to care for them. The order came down the line, 'To the rear.' Wondering, we turned and retraced our steps for about half a mile. 'All clear.' Off with the masks, and to my horror only a platoon and a half was present. Some idiot had misunderstood the order 'All clear' for 'To the rear.'" Lieutenant West quickly became frustrated trying to keep his men together. As Benjamin's men fell behind him and the line was cut, the head of the column continued on in ignorance. Splintered trees blocked the way. "It was impossible to keep a line with gas masks on. Off came the masks, gas or no gas."[15]

This attack far outclassed any bombardment that had previously hit the 2nd Division, effectively destroying the 78th and 96th Companies. The 78th Company suffered 16 killed and 190 gassed or wounded. The 96th Company lost 15 dead and 161 gassed or wounded. Of the company commanders, Captain Messersmith was blinded and Lieutenant Robertson was overcome by gas. Of officers and senior NCOs in both companies, only Lieutenants Cates and Shinkle remained on their feet. These two stalwarts took charge of their survivors and charged on into the woods to help 2/5. Among those sticking it out with Shinkle in the 78th Company was tough little Pvt. Johnnie Kelly.[16]

Holcomb reached the 2/5 command post around 3:00 A.M. with the 79th and 80th Companies and the few diehards from the 78th and 96th Companies. Only hours before 2/6 had been the 4th Brigade's most fresh, most fighting-ready unit. When Holcomb counted heads the morning of June 14, he was stunned to discover that his decimated battalion was incapable of relieving the tired marines of 2/5.[17]

Three Days in Belleau Wood, June 14–16, 1918

After tabulating his losses, Holcomb informed Wise that 2/6 had merely 325 effectives. In Belleau Wood 2/5 had been whittled down to less than five hundred men and had lost three of its four company commanders. Opposing the two American battalions was the

237th Division's 461st Regiment, reinforced by the 2nd Battalion of the 462nd Regiment. The commander of the 461st, Major Bischoff, could muster between four hundred and five hundred grenadiers. Wise and Holcomb may not have known that they enjoyed a meager two-to-one advantage over Bischoff, but in their estimate their two torn-up battalions were too exhausted and too disorganized to realize a successful attack. Holcomb attached Lieutenant Cates and his 96th Company survivors to the 80th Company and had Captain Coffenburg fortify a salient in the northeast corner of Wise's line known as "The Hook." Holcomb used Zane's 79th Company and Shinkle's handful of men from the 78th Company to support Coffenburg.[18]

Holcomb's marines found that the contest for Belleau Wood had disintegrated into a punch-drunk struggle of endurance. Men had fought with too little sleep, water, and food for too long, compounding the cumulative effects of stress. Both sides struggled under the strain. One of Bischoff's commanders begged for his company's relief because "the men are completely apathetic." The influenza epidemic of 1918 hit the 237th Division at this time, felling up to one in five soldiers in one regiment and leaving many other soldiers weak and listless. Another of Bischoff's company commanders wrote, "How feeble and sick we were, with fever, and diarrhea, all of us without exception, and yet we held out!"[19]

Similarly, after leading a counterattack on June 15, Sergeant Benjamin of the 79th Company wrote in his diary: "Wounded, hungry, thirsty, and tired, we stumbled along. In some places the woods were afire. The heat was terrific. At one time we were met by machine gun fire. A few boys dropped but we didn't much mind. Nothing seems to make any difference anymore. I am terribly tired." While the two marine battalions in the northern part of Belleau Wood were incapable of offensive action, the 461st Regiment did not mount any serious attacks either during this period. In a curious illustration of the fog of war, both sides reported repelling night attacks, yet no deliberate assaults were launched by either side. These perceived sorties were likely local counterattacks or even random exchanges of gunfire, for both sides were too exhausted to mount any coordinated action. With riflemen on both sides clinging to their shallow holes for dear life, the battle would be won by the side whose infantry could best endure the other's artillery.[20]

The front was nowhere continuous. German outposts, bypassed in the thick brush, were often intermingled with marine positions. Intermittent artillery blasts made sleep impossible. The fumes of bursting shells choked men almost as badly as did gas. Rations of "monkey meat" arrived only at night. Hot, dirty, and dehydrated, the men were lucky if they refilled their canteen once a day. Disorientation, fatigue, and relentless fear gnawed at their nerves, and shell shock began to whittle away at 2/6's foxhole strength.[21]

Levi Hemrick graphically described the trials he suffered: "We were covered with body lice, hungry and thirsty. We were bruised in body and soul, tired and weary, dirty and weakened by dysentery, that lousy messy kind that requires lots of paper and sanitation, but we had none. There was human blood on our hands that had to go for many days before they could be washed." The strain took its toll of all ranks. On June 16 an artillery round detonated over the 80th Company command post, slightly wounding Captain Coffenburg in his arm. Fragments from the same shell eviscerated a lieutenant named James S. Timothy. A sharp Regular Army officer who had led his platoon throughout the June fighting, Timothy died in Coffenburg's arms. Shaken, his face, hands, and torso covered in Timothy's blood, Coffenburg left Lt. John Schneider in charge of the company and headed to the battalion command post to report to Holcomb. The major determined that the captain was in no shape to continue the fight and assigned him as the battalion quartermaster effective June 18.[22]

Lieutenant Cates's optimism helped Schneider keep the 80th Company together. Private Brannen observed: "With his winning personality, he was able to cheer us when everything looked as dark as it possibly could. His lion courage in the face of any danger was enough to bolster one's morale." Notwithstanding Cates's external visage of enthusiasm, even he longed for an escape from the ordeal. In a letter he began June 14 and finished June 16, Cates wrote: "It has been a living hell since I started this. We were shelled all night with shrapnel and gas shells. At times I wished that one would knock me off, but still life is very sweet at its worst."[23]

Cates withstood the strain, but other leaders could not endure. The diary entry of Sergeant Benjamin reveals how he lost the struggle with shell shock: "A high explosive burst near me and my nerves went snap. I shook and couldn't stop. I was ordered to leave the wood this morning. The trip back through the wood to Lucy was a nightmare. The dead, mainly German, lay in heaps. A shell struck a pile of bodies and one hurtling through the air struck me and threw me down. I crossed a great open field always under fire and arrived in Lucy at the Red Cross station almost crazy. The doctors tagged me 'gas and shell shock.'" Incredibly, two hours later the resilient sergeant once again left the hospital and returned to the 79th Company.[24]

Benjamin reached his company as the men were preparing for relief by a battalion of the U.S. 3rd Division's 7th Infantry Regiment. After two weeks of attrition, Harbord's marines were done in, and he had run out of combat-ready battalions. On the night of June 15, the 3rd Division's doughboys relieved the leathernecks in Belleau Wood. As soon as the green soldiers reached 2/6's positions, Holcomb's exhausted men wasted no time filing out of their positions. In the 79th Company the 3rd Platoon had reached a point beyond caring. As the army officer argued with West, his men unabashedly climbed out of their holes and left the bewildered soldiers on their own to find their vacated positions in the dark.[25]

Rest for the Weary, June 17–23, 1918

The exhaustion and apathy exhibited by the marines did not escape the notice of the division's leadership, who decided to assess the battalion's fitness for battle. On June 19 Maj. J. C. Montgomery, the 2nd Division inspector, spent a day with the unit. He reported that 2/6 had departed Serans on May 31 with thirty-one officers and 941 men. In three weeks the battalion had lost twenty-one officers and 836 men and had received only four officers and 361 replacements, leaving just fourteen officers and 466 men fit for duty. This represents a casualty rate of 64 percent of the battalion's original members plus replacements received through June 19. As many as 165 of these replacements may have joined 2/6 after it withdrew from Belleau Wood. If so, the actual casualty rate during the time the marines were engaged may have been nearly 75 percent of the original unit.

Montgomery further reported that Holcomb's men had eaten hot food on only two occasions, subsisting mainly on hardtack and French canned beef, of which Montgomery noted a "general complaint of [the] poor quality." Nonetheless, he found the marines' weapons and uniforms in good condition and reported that "the morale of officers and men is excellent." Major Montgomery's report suggests that Harbord had pulled 2/6 out of the line before the battalion's cohesion had suffered lasting damage.[26]

Acting on this report, the 2nd Division pushed another load of replacements down to the battalion on June 21. Capt. Wethered Woodworth and 135 marines of Company B, 4th Replacement Battalion, reported to 2/6. Woodworth had studied economics and law at Berkeley, spoke French, and had previously served with the marine detachment aboard USS *Rhode Island*. His replacement company absorbed Lieutenant Cates's twenty-five marines and became the 96th Company de facto. Cates took an instant liking to his new commander. Another 130 replacements joined Lieutenant Shinkle and the thirty-two marines of the 78th Company. Capt. Egbert T. Lloyd, a short, conscientious officer with five years' experience, replaced Coffenburg as commander of the 80th Company. Lt. John Overton, the Yale track star who had befriended many of the 2/6 officers at Winthrop, also reported to the 80th Company. These replacements restored the ranks of 2/6 to 75 percent of its authorized strength.[27]

With the superb caliber of enlisted marines the Corps had recruited, leadership vacancies could be easily filled from the ranks. Gy. Sgt. Joseph C. Grayson in the 79th Company, Sgt. George Erhart in the 80th Company, and Cpls. Raymond Hanson and Harold Powell in the 96th Company received commissions as second lieutenants.[28] Forty-seven other marines were promoted to fill vacant NCO positions.[29] The depth of leadership potential among these junior marines would prove key to restoring the battalion's fighting potential and was a crucial element of its future performance.

Captain Zane made the most aggressive leadership changes in his 79th Company. Three sergeants were promoted to gunnery sergeant, including James McClelland, who had delivered crucial Chauchat support to Lieutenant Robertson during the attack on Bouresches. No doubt in reaction to the devastating bombardment of June 14, Zane assigned one experienced gunnery sergeant, Sethie Henson, to special duty as company gas NCO. In an eye-raising move, First Sergeant Fritz was reduced in rank to gunnery sergeant on June 24, also by authority of the regimental commander. This was probably not a vindictive or punitive move on Zane's part. The company rated only one first sergeant, and as previously noted, Zane preferred First Sergeant Barber. Nonetheless, it strikingly underscores the strained relationship between Zane, by all accounts a superb officer, and Fritz, an equally exemplary NCO who had been the captain's right-hand man for nearly a year.[30]

Zane also took the opportunity to punitively reduce two marines who had failed to perform to his expectations. For reasons unstated, Gy. Sgt. Hormidas Laundry was reduced to private and transferred to the regimental supply company on June 18 by the regimental commander's authority. A summary court-martial convicted one of Zane's privates for contracting venereal disease (prior to the battle, presumably).

One indication that the captain might have felt compelled to tighten things up a bit was the sizeable number of his marines absent without leave during this period. The 79th Company reported eleven men missing between June 14 and 30. Ten of these were replacements who had joined the unit on June 11.[31] Certainly these marines could have all gone missing in action. Yet one cannot escape the fact that nearly all were replacements who had recently arrived together. This striking anomaly suggests that the preponderant number of the company's missing simply went over the hill when the 79th Company headed back into Belleau Wood. The egregious number of absentee replacements contrasts sharply with Harry Lee's rosy letter to the commandant about the conduct of these men. Moreover, these possible desertions underscore the challenge 2/6 faced assimilating new men under combat conditions.

"God What a Night," June 26–July 5, 1918
On June 22, 2/6 moved back to a reserve position northwest of Lucy. During the battalion's six-day respite, the soldiers of the 3rd Division had not made appreciable gains, and Harbord's marines were sent back in to finish the job they had started. On June 25, 3/5 swept through the remainder of the forest behind a rolling barrage. After nineteen days Belleau Wood had finally fallen to the marines.[32] The following night Holcomb's battalion set out to relieve 3/5 and defend the wood's northern end. Rather than move the battalion forward en masse, this time Holcomb had each company move up independently. Guides from 3/5 ushered each company directly up to the unit it would relieve.

The 79th Company's route took it to its new position via an old farm lane that cut straight as an arrow across the forest. As Captain Zane entered the thick woods, the head of the column inevitably slowed. The rest of the 79th Company, moving more quickly in the open, began to bunch up at the edge of the treeline, an understandable but dangerous development. Somehow alerted to the ongoing relief, German artillery spotters pounced on this lucrative target. A sudden barrage of shells sliced through the column.

Sergeant Benjamin recalled what happened next: "[T]hose in the lead appeared going to the rear—some of them wounded. And then with a roar a huge shell landed with a smashing explosion right alongside of us. There was a general stampede for cover; men crouched beside trees or under the protection of rocks. Then another shell."[33] Lieutenant West revisited the place twelve years later and recorded his memories:

Cries, screams, cusses. Every man hugging the earth, praying without a prayer, hoping without hope. Captain Zane, severely wounded, was sent to the rear, refusing a stretcher, later dying of his wounds. First Sergeant Barber, one of the finest soldiers, with both legs in actual shreds. Nothing could be done to stop the flow of blood from those legs. He knew this. We lit a cigarette for him and talked to him until a stretcher took him away—far away. Humphrey, company runner, with the same unmerciful wound, followed Sergeant Barber, dying too. Other men killed and wounded. More shells cracking down on us—they could not miss. Cries of "First Aid," "Stretcher Bearer," pitiful, pleading cries, cursing positive demands. "Christ, Christ, Oh, God." Wounded men pleaded with me to kill them to put them out of their misery. God what a night.[34]

The company lay trapped under the bombardment, its company commander and first sergeant down. Hugging the earth in unfamiliar ground, in a nearly identical dilemma faced by the 78th and 96th Companies twelve nights earlier, the 79th Company tipped on the verge of annihilation.

Gunnery Sergeant Fritz took in the situation at a glance. Once again the senior NCO in the company, the former priest strode amid the bursting shells to Lieutenant Erskine. Saluting smartly, Fritz barked, "Sir, you are in command! What are your orders?"[35]

If Erskine had seemed uncertain what to do, Fritz's prompting swiftly snapped him into action. His first concern was that the sergeant would get hit by the shrapnel slicing through the air. After ordering him to get down three times, Erskine finally got the gunnery sergeant to take cover. Mercifully, the shelling paused after about four minutes. Erskine and Fritz jumped to their feet and began collecting the marines scattered among the trees.

Lieutenant West realized 3/5's guides had all been killed or wounded by the shells that also devastated company headquarters. As Erskine assembled the men, West unholstered his Colt automatic, grabbed a big replacement private named Peter Bonner, and dashed down the lane in search of the front line. He soon stumbled across a 3/5 rifleman in a foxhole. The marine took him to his company command post, where the company commander confirmed that his was the unit the marines had been sent to relieve. He gave the lieutenant two more guides, whom West and Bonner led back down the lane.

Along the way they ran into Lieutenant Erskine, leading the preponderance of the company. West gave Erskine one guide, who led
the marines on to continue the relief. West, Bonner, and the other
guide rounded up stragglers and then followed. Before sunup the 79th
Company had taken over the defense along the edge of the woods,
and 3/5 had departed. When Fritz took muster in the morning, he
found that the 79th Company had escaped remarkably unscathed.
Besides Captain Zane and First Sergeant Barber, the 79th Company
lost just three other marines killed and twelve wounded. Through
their quick thinking and steadiness under fire, Erskine, Fritz, and
West had averted a potential disaster.[36]

Aside from this nightmare, the relief proceeded unremarkably,
the remaining companies moving in without mishap. The marines
unexpectedly passed a quiet nine days defending their sector. Having been ejected from Belleau Wood, the Germans proved content
to dig in among the hills and towns facing the forest. Each night the
frontline companies of 2/6 sent out wiring parties, and the battalion
and regimental intelligence sections conducted contact patrols in no
man's land.[37]

Interspersed among the battalion's holes were German and
American corpses, growing putrid in the summer heat. Huge bottle
flies swarmed over the rotting bodies, also descending upon living
marines trying to eat, drink, or sleep. One night Sergeant Paradis
resolved to bury those nearest the battalion command post. The runners collected blankets from the packs of the dead and carried five
bodies, one at a time, to a clearing fifty yards from their position.
As the men stumbled through the ruined forest, putrid fluid oozed
through the blankets, soiling their boots and uniforms. Harassing
artillery frequently interrupted the detail, and the marines hugged
the earth alongside the bloated remains. Paradis collected a dog tag
from each dead American before entombing his comrade under a
rude cross. Frustrated and nauseated by the odious work, the sergeant returned to his hole dejected. To his distress, Holcomb was
encouraged by Paradis's meager success and ordered him to give it
another go the next night.[38]

Over in the 79th Company, twenty-year-old Graves Erskine was
enjoying his temporary command. The irrepressible lieutenant
amused himself by pinpointing the location of a German machine
gun in a ravine three hundred yards in front of his lines. He notified
Holcomb of the gun's suspected location. To Erskine's delight, an
artillery barrage smothered the ravine with shells.[39]

The night of July 2, Lieutenant Cates led thirty-two men from the 96th Company into the open fields north of Belleau Wood with the ambitious mission of emplacing double apron wire across nearly five hundred yards of the battalion's front. Holcomb told Cates that 2/6 would be relieved once the wire was in place, a dubious but nonetheless stimulating incentive. The night was especially dark, and the marines muffled the blows of their sledge hammers with sandbags. Cates worked the men hard and finished the job in time to eat a quick hot meal and crawl into his hole at the company command post just before daybreak.

The marines had completed their work just in time, for a heavy German barrage plastered the wood before dawn. Cates dashed down to his platoon's position. He was confident the wire would foil an attack if one followed on the heels of the shelling but was concerned how the sudden bombardment would affect his new replacements. He later wrote home: "They are a fine bunch, but still a little green and excitable. Gee! I wish I had the old men back."[40] Cates fired a few flares and peered into the new wire, but he saw no movement. Surmising this was merely a harassing barrage, he scurried back to report his findings to Captain Woodworth. A succession of high-explosive airbursts knocked him to the deck. Amazingly, the lucky lieutenant picked himself up and discovered that he had once again survived a close call without a scratch.

Anticipating relief, Cates passed an anxious day waiting for the night. About 5:00 P.M. the lieutenant learned that not only would he be leaving the front immediately but that Holcomb had selected him to lead eighty marines from the battalion, twenty from each company, in an Independence Day parade through Paris the next morning. Cates selected Gy. Sgt. Ben Taylor and other old hands where possible. The lucky men eagerly rolled their packs and followed Cates and Taylor back to a rendezvous point, undaunted by the risk of moving during daylight. Cates survived yet another close call when his keen hearing detected an inbound shell. The men hit the dirt as one, and the round detonated harmlessly just twenty feet away.

In Paris that night the happy marines joined the other lucky leathernecks and doughboys from the division. They were able to clean their bodies, uniforms, and gear and to sleep on cots, incredible luxuries after over a month in combat. Cates discovered that his men were penniless, so he divided his roll of cash among them. The parade the next morning was overwhelming, with bouquet after bouquet of fresh flowers handed to the Americans as they marched along. The next event was even grander: a champagne luncheon at a munitions factory where ten thousand women were employed. Less than twenty-four hours before, these young men had been under fire, surrounded by filth and death. They had survived, and now they celebrated their reprieve from death with gusto to match the occasion. Cates wrote that French women fought over the marines, who ended up "screwing whenever and wherever and whatever they could."[41]

While Cates and his detail raised the roof in Paris, Holcomb received word to turn over his sector to a battalion of the 26th Division's 103rd Infantry on the night of July 5. The battalion's last tour in the line had been comparatively docile—only nine marines were killed and twenty-three wounded. Nonetheless, the men were worn out physically and psychologically. As the 79th Company scrambled through the woods in half-platoons, Lieutenant West's fourteen-man section took cover from a light barrage on the way out. "We scurried out of there like rabbits—scared rabbits. A month before, this would not have affected us this way. Now our nerves could not stand it, shell-shocked in a degree. I was ashamed of myself."[42]

The Business of War

Once again, the aggressiveness of the individual marines and the ability of 2/6 to maintain its cohesion in the face of destruction were inspiring. Armed with the tough lessons of its initial combat, such a spirited combat organization was well poised to couple its aggressiveness with more appropriate tactics. Accordingly, the battalion's effectiveness might have been expected to improve considerably in its next few actions. But the cumulative effects of exhaustion and attrition would continue to affect Holcomb's splendid marines, jeopardizing the assimilation of their experience.

The aggregate cost to the battalion in human terms is staggering. In thirty days of fighting, 2/6 had suffered 104 killed and 662 wounded, gassed, or missing. This catastrophic toll compels one to wonder if the unit had retained enough old hands to benefit from its trial by fire, or if the bloody tide had washed away any vestige of experience the battalion had so dearly bought.

Beyond the numbers evacuated, anecdotal evidence suggests that most of those supposedly fit for battle had suffered from varying degrees of shell shock, or post-traumatic stress as it is now described. The Marine Corps had fielded a magnificently disciplined and spirited battalion in 2/6, the best the United States could offer. Yet the obvious, widespread erosion of the mental health of the men raises the question of how many more such battles these superb marines could endure.

The battalion's trials in the latter half of June revealed two worrisome trends. First, the assimilation and training of replacements was still questionable. The 79th Company had lost a disturbing number of replacements missing, and Cates had seemed unsure whether his new men would measure up to his "old gang." Second, higher echelons of command continued to fumble as they learned their business, as illustrated by the 4th Brigade's mishandling of 2/6 on June 13.

Harbord had not anticipated employing his reserve in a counterattack against Bouresches. When the threat arose, the 79th and 96th Companies exposed themselves to observation balloons while moving to a supporting position, a blunder that led to the devastating gas barrage. With more frontline experience, the general and his staff might have recognized the crucial importance of Bouresches and positioned the brigade reserve in a more central location under cover of darkness.

Yet there were definitive signs that the division and brigade leadership had learned important lessons from the attack of June 6. Of critical importance, Harbord ensured that the successful attacks by 1/6, 2/5, and finally 3/5 had been fully supported by artillery with well-coordinated rolling barrages.

In another encouraging development, many leadership vacancies within 2/6 had been seamlessly filled through rapid promotion of junior sergeants, corporals, and privates. These tough young marines had stood the test of battle, retaining the battalion's high standards of discipline. They were proficient in the doctrine impressed through a year of training, yet more impressed with the tricks and techniques that had brought them through a month in Belleau Wood alive. Many of their comrades evacuated for slight wounds and gas burns would return as well. Of those evacuated in June, 285 would see combat again with 2/6, the preponderant number returning within two months.[43]

Something less tangible had been lost, something no amount of replacements could restore regardless of their proficiency or aptitude. Before Belleau Wood, Holcomb's battalion had trained together for a year, a year in which the men formed lifelong friendships. Looking back twelve years after the war, Jack West reflected: "After Belleau Wood, war for us became largely a business. Men, just numbers, changing constantly. Here, men were living things, personalities, friends. Here, many of those friends gave all they had."[44]

5 Soissons

THE MARINES OF 2/6 HAD DEPARTED BELLEAU WOOD on July 5 mentally, physically, and emotionally exhausted. For the next eleven days, the battalion enjoyed a true respite, first in a reserve position well behind the lines, then from July 13 to 16 in the riverside town of Nanteuil-sur-Marne. There the men washed away a month of grime and dirt in the Marne River, wrote letters home, and slept. Some drew new clothing and equipment, while others less fortunate picked lice from their raggedy uniforms.

After the ordeal of Belleau Wood, the reprieve in the pastoral Champagne country afforded Don Paradis and his mates a new outlook on life: "The trees seemed greener, the wheat fields a more beautiful brown, interspersed with green hay fields and orchards along the beautiful Marne River winding down the valley toward Paris. We drank it all in with a new and deeper appreciation of the world the good Lord had given us." The men sorely needed time to recuperate. As an organization, the battalion just as sorely needed to synthesize the lessons it had learned into improved tactical doctrine. Yet the brief respite afforded little opportunity for something so ambitious, and the tired veterans would have had difficulty benefiting from a vigorous training schedule. The battalion would fight its next engagement with the same organization, doctrine, tactics, and equipment as in June. On the one hand, the experience Holcomb's marines had gained in Belleau Wood accorded all the individual skills and psychological advantages of veterans. On the other hand, his companies had suffered such heavy casualties that this experience was diluted by a flood of replacements.[1]

The new men fortunately constituted but a tiny minority of the battalion's leadership. The roster of officers reflects abundant changes, but nearly every new officer had previously proven his ability to lead men in combat. Maj. Robert Denig replaced Major Garrett as Holcomb's second in command. Denig had been a marine for twelve years and had already commanded an army battalion in the 3rd Division. Jovial and slightly rotund, he did not fluster easily and was not afraid to exercise common sense when it ran against the grain of direct orders. Holcomb retained Captain Wilmer as adjutant, Lieutenant Vandoren as scout officer, Captain Coffenburg as quartermaster, and U.S. Navy lieutenants Grimland and White as battalion surgeons.[2]

Of the original company commanders, only Messersmith, commanding the 78th Company, remained. The captain had returned in time to deal with his chronic ne'er do well, Pvt. Johnny Kelly. Now that the company was out of the line, Sgt. Henry Bogan decided to rein in Kelly, ordering the hotheaded private to police the company area to peacetime perfection. Kelly later explained how he then picked up his fourth court-martial. "I told him to go----himself!" Messersmith docked two-thirds of Kelly's pay for the next three months. The private rejoined his squad, seething at the authority of the Marine Corps. "Listen to me, God!" he loudly declared. "I'm going to kill Sergeant Bogan!" Bogan ran off to report this obstinacy to the captain, and Kelly ran off to Paris.[3]

Messersmith would have to fight the coming engagement without Kelly, but he enjoyed proven leaders as lieutenants. Amos Shinkle resumed his post as second in command. Three platoons were led by new second lieutenants commissioned from other companies in 2/6, including the former battalion sergeant major, Charles Ingram. Messersmith lost his first sergeant in the trade as John Dean stepped up to take Ingram's place as sergeant major.[4]

The 79th Company's officers completely turned over. Stalwarts Graves Erskine and Jack West were hospitalized with unidentified illnesses on the eve of battle. First Sergeant Fritz, demoted to gunnery sergeant in June, was commissioned along with Lt. James McClelland in July. Both officers transferred to command platoons in the 96th Company. Fortuitously, Carl Wallace had recovered from his Verdun wounds and returned wearing captain's bars to take command from Erskine. Only two platoons would be led by lieutenants: one by George Ehrhart and another by Delos McKenzie, both commissioned from the ranks. Gy. Sgt. James Crandall stepped into Fritz's shoes as first sergeant.[5]

Captain Lloyd retained the 80th Company. Short in stature, Lloyd was proving somewhat punctilious and did not enjoy a bond of mutual respect and affection with his men. This strain was offset by the reputation enjoyed by his rock-hard second in command, John Schneider, one of the few remaining "old" officers in the battalion. In addition to John Overton, the popular Yale track star, Lloyd had three recently commissioned NCOs, Lts. Charles Roy, Harold Powell, and Hugh Kidder. The company's gunnery sergeants included acting 1st Sgt. Frank Yohner, German-speaking William Ulrich, and one old hand who had recovered from gas, John Schrank.

In contrast to Lloyd, Captain Woodworth seemed most capable and was respected by the officers and men of the 96th Company. Woodworth would have a superb team helping him lead his unit in the next battle. James Robertson, now a captain, returned as second in command. Clifton Cates continued to lead his 4th Platoon. Cates was chagrined to stand in formation on July 10 to watch Robertson decorated with the Distinguished Service Cross for the capture of Bouresches, though he did not permit the event to affect his irrepressible optimism. With former NCOs Fritz and McClelland and recent replacement Robert Duane commanding the other platoons, the 96th Company would be well led in the approaching battle.[6]

The Allied Counteroffensive against the Aisne-Marne Salient
The marines' stand at Belleau Wood had helped contain Ludendorff's Plan Blücher offensive inside a vulnerable salient between the Aisne and the Marne rivers. This pocket, measuring thirty miles across and thirty-seven miles deep, was a liability that the Germans now had to defend. Ludendorff still held out hope for one final offensive in Flanders to knock Great Britain out of the war. Not yet ready to launch this attack, he instead planned a succession of local offensives to keep the Allies off balance and thus retain the initiative, exacting what he hoped would be exorbitant attrition from his opponents. The first of these, Plan Rheims, would begin on July 15 east of Château-Thierry.[7]

French intelligence detected indications of Plan Rheims in early July. Foch sensed the opportunity to regain the initiative and issued orders July 12 for a counteroffensive by four armies against the Aisne-Marne salient. This counterattack would begin July 18, three days after the German attack, in order to strike when the Germans would already be committed to Plan Rheims and most vulnerable. Foch's main effort, an attack by Gen. Charles Mangin's Tenth Army, would cut eastward into the base of the salient near Soissons. If Mangin's army cut the main supply route from Soissons to Château -Thierry, he could force the German Eighth Army to withdraw north of the Aisne. To weight Mangin's attack, Foch gave him the massive U.S. 1st and 2nd Divisions, arguably Pershing's most capable organizations.[8]

Moving Up: A Balancing Act of Time and Friction, July 16–18, 1918

Foch's efforts to conceal his preparations would thwart the 2nd Division's efforts to conduct detailed planning and thorough preparations, with a corresponding price in operational efficiency. Until July 16 Holcomb had no inkling of the impending attack, one in which 2/6 would play a vital role only three days hence. Harbord, promoted to major general, had taken command of the 2nd Division. Brig. Gen. Wendell Neville, the 4th Brigade commander, was down sick, leaving Lieutenant Colonel Lee as acting brigade commander. Because that left Holcomb in command of the 6th Marines, Denig had the responsibility of getting 2/6 to its destination, though neither he nor Holcomb had an idea of where that was.[9]

Denig had the men draw extra ammunition and grenades and had the battalion staged by company along the highway near Nanteuil at 5:00 P.M. on July 16. All hands were accustomed now to the punctuality of the French transportation corps, and no one was surprised when the trucks did not appear until midnight. Denig and Wilmer climbed into a touring car and led the column off to the front at 1:00 A.M. on July 17, in front of the column if not actually directing its movement. Almost as soon as the caravan started, a German long-range gun scored a lucky hit alongside the tenth truck, killing the drivers and two marines and wounding five more. At the front of the column, Denig and the first nine trucks hurtled on, oblivious to the carnage behind. The major discovered the break before long but had a painful time rounding up the remaining fifty trucks.[10]

In the 79th Company, Pvt. Neal Van Haften remembered a terrifying and wretched ride:

> The night was black as ink, and starless, and the trucks carried no lights save a single miserable oil lamp on each machine. Mile after mile reeled off over a seemingly endless road. Accidents were frequent; occasionally a truck would be passed, thrown to the side of the road, with its nose in a ditch or up a tree. In addition, the road was clogged with ammunition carts, commissary trucks, or artillery on its way to the front. At times detours had to be made through fields where the road was blocked by such obstacles. The French chauffeurs were well supplied with wine which they kept stowed away under the front seat between drinks, and as a consequence they drove recklessly, hopping all over the road when there was no apparent reason for it. This did not suit some of

the marines who were becoming seasick at traveling such a pace, and forthwith, to remove the cause they stole the wine. It was good but unfortunately there was not quite enough to go around among the twenty-four huskies with a single thirst. When next the chauffer felt a thirst and discovered his loss there was excitement aplenty, mussed up French expletives, and cussing by a wild eyed "Frog" chauffeur who denounced all marines as robbers, pigs, and thieves. He was answered by jeers or a wealth of good old American slang. Then the humor of the whole affair got under each man's skin and everybody had a good laugh; cigarettes were lighted on the sly; jokes and stories floated around, and the motor cars sped on and on.[11]

The weather began to try the marines' good humor, though. After midnight a thunderstorm unleashed torrents of rain onto the men riding exposed in the backs of the trucks. Lightning struck trees alongside the narrow road, snapping limbs and trunks into their path. The marines bounced and jarred through the night and into the next morning, soaked to the skin, unable to grab a moment's sleep.[12]

The drivers dumped Denig and his marines around noon that day a few miles west of the huge Viller-Cotterets Forest. Unknown to Denig, under cover of these woods Mangin was assembling his Tenth Army. In the absence of further information, Denig saw no point in wearing out a thousand marines in a blind search for the rest of the 2nd Division. He tucked the battalion into a ravine, where the men could grab some rest and drink water from a brook, while he waited to see what developed.[13]

Denig found out their destination later that afternoon when Major Sibley marched by with 3/6. Sibley told him that they were to head to Montgobert in the north end of the forest, and there was no time to lose. Denig weighed the inevitable wear on his men against the need for haste and decided to take a chance and wait awhile longer, allowing the humid air to cool slightly. The July day was dreadfully hot, and there was likely to be a battle in the morning. Shortly after 4:00 he assembled the battalion and led his hungry leathernecks into the forest.

Artillery, tanks, infantry, and cavalry clogged the roads, forcing the stumbling marines onto the shoulder to bypass traffic jams. Van Haften called it "the darkest night I have ever seen, so dark that a man could not distinguish his leader five paces ahead." The leathernecks resorted to grabbing onto the equipment of the man in front as they lurched along. Paradis recognized the rumble of not-too-distant artillery, and "Old Man Fear crept back into our bones." Despite the miserable conditions, the medley of activity convinced the marines that "an important development was imminent," breeding an infectious sense of purpose in all hands. Just before they reached the Montgobert Farm around 10:00 P.M., a second thunderstorm cascaded onto the weary men. Soaked for the second successive night, the marines had no alternative but to roll up under raincoats and shelter halves and sleep as best as they could.[14]

About 2:00 A.M. an officer woke Denig and informed him that the 6th Marines were assembling as the corps reserve at Le Verte Feuille Farm on the east edge of the forest. Le Verte Feuille was about four miles away. Reckoning that he could gain little and lose much rousing the battalion in the middle of the storm, Denig let the men sleep awhile longer. At 4:35 General Mangin held reveille for him in the form of a colossal barrage. Foch's great counteroffensive had begun.

As the first sergeants assembled the companies along the forest lane, Denig delightfully gulped down a steaming mug of coffee poured for him by the hospitable gunners of an adjacent French battery. Before daylight 2/6 was once again on the move, pushing ahead through the congested woods. As sunlight revealed distinguishable shapes around the column, Denig spied an enormous supply dump along their path. His famished marines had not eaten a proper meal since falling in at Nanteuil thirty-six hours previously. Over the protests of the supply officer, Denig had his men stuff their packs and pockets with hardtack, monkey meat, canned hash, condensed milk, and sugar. Glum prisoners and fiery-eyed wounded, the residue of victory, flowed past. German planes strafed the woods, sending leathernecks, doughboys, and *poilus* scrambling and leaving corpses and dead horses in their wake. A few French fighters chased the Germans away, and the battalion reassembled on the road.[15]

When the column passed 2nd Division headquarters, General Harbord pulled Denig aside to ensure that the major understood the situation and where he was to take 2/6. The 2nd Division had attacked to the east that morning as part of the French XX Corps. The XX Corps included the 20th Moroccan Division north of the 2nd Division and the U.S. 1st Division beyond the Moroccans. The 6th Marines were the corps reserve, still assembling at Le Verte Feuille. The 2nd Division's other three regiments had barely made it into their positions that morning, but the attack had progressed well thus far. Denig accepted a few pancakes from the general before the chief of staff, Col. Preston Brown, shooed him away. The major easily caught up with his column and reported to Holcomb at Le Verte Feuille around noon. Lee having returned to command the 6th Marines, Holcomb now resumed command of 2/6.

Denig had creditably delivered 2/6 to the correct destination in one piece, as fresh and ready for action as possible under the trying circumstances. He had done exactly what is expected of a second in command: he had assumed command, made decisions, and taken action. Denig could easily have worn out his men, eschewing rest, water, and food, or lost marines to straggling and misdirection by marching through the night. He could just as easily have been the heel as the hero had XX Corps needed to commit 2/6 to the battle on the morning of July 18. As it turned out, 2/6 had not been needed. Once again in command, Holcomb led the battalion forward into a ravine five hundred yards southeast of Le Beaurepiere Farm, where the marines dug in and awaited orders.[16]

The Tactical Situation, July 18–19, 1918

Mangin's attack had caught Army Group Crown Prince Wilhelm off balance. Although the 5th Marines had barely reached the line of departure on time and the division's three machine-gun battalions had not closed up, the 2nd Division had advanced almost three miles on July 18. The 5th Marines and 3rd Infantry Brigade had seized the important Vierzy Ravine, breaching the German artillery protective line along the way. But the attack had cost the infantry heavily, and the 5th Marines and the 9th and 23rd Infantry were intermingled throughout the division's zone. By nightfall on July 18, the disorganized battalions of these three regiments had established a line roughly fifteen hundred yards east of Vierzy.

At 2:00 A.M. on July 19, Harbord received an order from the XX Corps to continue the attack two hours hence to breach the Château-Thierry road. With Harbord's other three regiments too shot up to participate, XX Corps released the 6th Marines to the 2nd Division to conduct the operation. Harbord immediately recognized that he had no hope of meeting the scheduled time of attack. The 2nd Division would delay, but there was a sense of urgency. If Harbord postponed the attack for too long, the Moroccan division on his left would be left unsupported, and German reserves would bolster the defense along the Soissons–Château-Thierry road. Seeking an

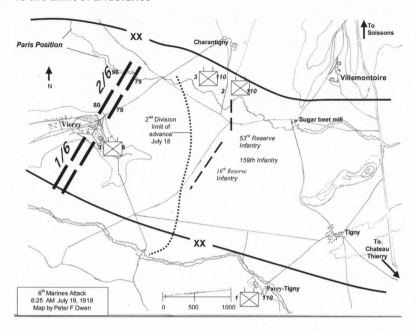

Paris Position

XX

Charantigny

To Soissons

N

2/6 96
79
80
78
3
6

Vierzy

2ⁿᵈ Division limit of advance July 18

3 ↑10
2 ↑10

Villemontoire

Sugar beet mill

53ʳᵈ Reserve Infantry

159th Infantry

16ᵗʰ Reserve Infantry

1/6

XX

Tigny

To Chateau Thierry

6ᵗʰ Marines Attack
8:25 AM July 19, 1918
Map by Peter F Owen

0   500   1000

Parcy-Tigny
1 ↑10

achievable start time, Harbord approved a 7:00 advance for the 6th Marines.[17]

Harbord scrambled in vain to position the 6th Marines in time. The headquarters of the 2nd Division, the 6th Marine Regiment, and all three battalions were located in close proximity to each other at the Beaurepaire Farm, which should have simplified coordination. Shortly after division received the XX Corps order, Lee was summoned to the division command post to review it. Apparently caught off guard, the 6th Marines dawdled. While Lee poured over the order and maps with the division staff, his battalion commanders were not immediately alerted. It was 3:30 before the regimental adjutant, Capt. Walter Sitz, woke Holcomb to inform him that the regiment would attack in just three and a half hours. Another hour passed before Lee and Sitz huddled with the battalion commanders to coordinate the one-mile march from Beaurepaire to Vierzy. Another two hours passed before the regiment filed down the road, Holcomb's battalion leading, followed by Hughes's 1st Battalion and then Sibley's 3rd Battalion. The marines donned gas masks as they passed through persistent clouds in the Vierzy Ravine.[18]

At the railroad station, Lee once again assembled his three battalion commanders and their staffs and issued a verbal order. It was now 7:00, the time specified by XX Corps as the time of attack, but the 6th Marines were still sorting out their plan. Lee's regiment would emerge from the Vierzy Ravine and pass through the 5th Marines fifteen hundred yards to their southeast. For nearly two and a half miles the attack would cross flat, open ground of waist-high wheat and plowed fields. Lee placed Holcomb's battalion on the left and Hughes's 1st Battalion on the right, with Sibley's 3rd Battalion in reserve. Holcomb's left flank would brush along an old trench line called the "Paris Position," which zigzagged in a southeasterly direction just inside the division's boundary with the Moroccans to the north. The Paris Position had served as a support trench to a similar line that ran along the 1st Battalion's right flank to the south.[19]

The three thousand riflemen of the 6th Marines would face about two thousand infantrymen of the 14th Reserve Division. The German defenders were bolstered by at least fifty-six machine guns. The 2nd and 3rd Battalions of the 110th Grenadier Regiment occupied the Paris Position trenches in front of Villemontoire. To the south, the 1/110th Grenadier Battalion had fortified Parcy-Tigny. Between the Paris Position and Parcy-Tigny, remnants of the 16th and 53rd Reserve Infantry and the 159th Infantry had dug hasty positions in a line running south from Charantigny to Parcy-Tigny. These last three regiments had suffered 50 percent losses in the previous days' fighting and had lost hundreds more to influenza and exhaustion. The 2nd Division had captured a trove of German artillery on July 18, but elements of three more artillery battalions occupied firing positions northeast of Tigny. From the higher ground there, they could inflict direct fire on the 6th Marines crossing the open ground.[20] Unless supporting fire could protect Lee's marines, the Germans would have more than sufficient artillery and machine guns to cut his regiment to shreds.

To suppress these defenses, the division's artillery brigade, reinforced by a French artillery regiment, had begun a one-hour preparatory bombardment at 6:00 A.M. The division did not plan a rolling barrage for the 6th Marines. Had it attacked on schedule, the regiment's start position fifteen hundred yards to the rear of the division's frontline units would have complicated the advance behind the creeping shellfire. The artillery brigade had insufficient time to coordinate such a complex mission, made doubly difficult by the necessity to precisely coincide the barrage with the 6th Marines passage through the division's forward limit. Instead, the 2nd Field Artillery Brigade planned and directed all fires. Four artillery regiments would be supporting the attack of a single infantry regiment. Their forward observers would enjoy excellent visibility from the lip of the Vierzy Ravine, where they could telephone fire-direction instructions to engage targets of opportunity. Yet the artillery support appears to have been planned without coordination with the marines. Although Lee and his battalion commanders were not far from the artillery brigade command post and would pass a stone's throw from its forward-observation posts near Vierzy, neither the marines nor the artillerymen appear to have attempted to plan in collaboration. Unquestionably, once the marines went over the top, communication and liaison between them and the batteries would be nonexistent.[21]

Partially compensating for the uncoordinated artillery support were five machine-gun companies allocated for the attack: four from the 6th Machine Gun Battalion and the 73rd Machine Gun Company, 6th Marines. Their Hotchkiss guns could have provided long-range fire from the vicinity of Vierzy or could follow in support of the advancing battalions, suppressing German strongpoints at the direction of the rifle-battalion commanders. Yet the 6th Marines failed to fully exploit the advantage these guns offered. It is a generally accepted tactical principle that supporting fires are wasted if stashed in reserve and are best exploited when utilized throughout every phase of an engagement. It is apparent from the available records that Lee kept at least half of his eighty Hotchkiss guns in reserve at the Vierzy Ravine throughout the attack on July 19. These forty guns remained silent until at least 4:00 P.M., and their crews added nothing to the battle aside from aiding nearby casualties. Further diluting the regiment's firepower, its Stokes mortars and 37-mm guns never arrived; the trucks carrying these heavy weapons were lost somewhere in the Viller-Cotterets. Lee used their gunners and other marines from his headquarters company as additional riflemen for the regimental reserve. The 6th Marines would attack without a rolling barrage, without Stokes mortars or one-pounder field guns, and with half its machine guns tucked away in the Vierzy Ravine.[22]

A comparison between the plan for July 19 and the experience of June 6 presents ominous parallels. In both attacks three battalions of marines attacked a force of roughly two thousand German defenders. Preparations for both assaults were characterized by hasty planning and insufficient time for reconnaissance and refinement at the battalion level and below. In both the infantry advanced without the indispensable support of a rolling barrage, while German artillery could fire directly into the advancing infantry from dominating high ground. On June 6, 3/5 and 3/6 had battered through a mixture of wheat and woods, while 2/6 had advanced across eight hundred yards of exposed ground; at Soissons the entire regiment would attempt to advance five times that distance across a field described by Holcomb as "the most open country I have seen passed over in an attack."[23] To any officer who had survived the attack on June 6, the situation must have appeared dismal.

Nonetheless, there were differences that justified a glimmer of faith in the plan. The 6th Marines would be exploiting the previous days' successes, possibly delivering the *coup de grâce* to the shattered regiments of a beaten foe. The large number of prisoners taken on July 18 certainly indicated that the morale of German defenders was unquestionably lower here than at Belleau Wood. And in an even more promising development, the marines would have tanks joining them for the attack.

The offensive at Soissons marked the largest use of tanks to that time. XX Corps reinforced the 2nd Division with twenty-eight tanks for July 19. Slow and lightly armed with either machine guns or light one-pounder cannons, these Renaults nonetheless could withstand machine-gun fire, and the German infantry had no antitank weapons. But German artillery on the commanding heights east of the Soissons–Château-Thierry road could fire directly into the lumbering vehicles. What is more, Lee's marines had never worked with tanks, would have little opportunity to coordinate their actions before the attack, and would find it almost impossible to communicate with their French crews amid the fighting.[24]

Holcomb had 2/6 drop packs and fill canteens before he led his leathernecks out of the shelter of the Vierzy Ravine just after 7:00. Most marines would attack this hot day toting merely rifle, gas mask, and cartridge belt, about twenty pounds. Chauchat gunners and loaders would have to lug their heavy automatic rifles and heavier fifty-pound clip bags.

As his companies filed out of the ravine, Holcomb deployed them along the Vierzy-Charantigny road. After organizing themselves into attack formation, the men lay prone. The ground here was in slight defilade, but German artillery and indirect machine-gun fire impacted within the battalion's formation, inflicting the first casualties. Lieutenant Cates described another close call as the 96th Company deployed: "Just as I was getting my men into position, a machine gun bullet cut thru my rain coat that I had rolled on my back and went through my coat and stuck in my shoulder. I thought that someone had hit me with a rock at first, so I had a man look at it and he pulled a bullet out. It had just broken the skin and had caught in my coat." A high-explosive shell hurled shrapnel into the 80th Company. Gy. Sgt. John Shrank dropped just ten feet from Sergeant Paradis. Hospital corpsmen rushed over to bandage Shrank, a Belleau Wood veteran who had rejoined the company just six days before. Lieutenant Cates was nearby and stooped to take his pulse. "Don't bother, he's dead," Cates told the corpsmen.[25]

The Attack at Soissons, July 19, 1918

The 6th Marines were not ready to attack when the preparatory barrage lifted at 7:00 A.M. Cpl. Victor Sparks, in the 78th Company, wrote in his diary, "Our barrage commenced but we never received the order to follow it." Major Denig wrote in his diary that 2/6 was ready to go but had to wait for the French tanks. Lieutenant Cates's official report of the attack also ascribes the delay to the late arrival of the French armor, as does Gy. Sgt. Gerald C. Thomas's account. The eight Renaults finally came up and took position in front of 2/6; Denig noted that their commander hobbled about on a peg leg. The Germans noticed the tanks too and fired a few rounds to confirm the range. They then ceased fire, content to wait for the marines to enter the killing ground.[26]

Ascribing the blame to the French tanks is only partly justifiable. It appears that the attack was further delayed as Lee waited until Sibley's 3/6 closed up. Sergeant Paradis stated: "We were held up because of the 3rd Battalion failing to reach its zero hour position. In fact the 3rd Battalion was lost." The official history of 3/6 acknowledges that the unit had to wait for the other battalions to pass, then vaguely remarks, "It was understood that the hour set for the attack was 8:00 A.M." As noted above, General Harbord had set the time for the attack at 7:00, and Lee was still issuing his orders to Sibley, Holcomb, and Hughes in the Vierzy Ravine at that time. In fact, Paradis vividly remembered that the French tanks began to move out before 3/6 was up and that marines had to chase down the vehicles and inform their crews that the attack had been delayed. Although 3/6 would initially hold back near Vierzy in reserve, Lee waited until they arrived, which they finally did at 8:15.[27]

After nearly an hour and a half of lying along the Charantigny road, an order swept through the ranks of 2/6: "Pass the word quietly to fix bayonets. We are going over." At 8:25 the two thousand marines of the 1st and 2nd Battalions arose from the wheat and began the advance.[28]

As on June 6, the formation was something to behold. Arrayed on perfectly flat ground, the two thousand leathernecks advanced in perfect alignment. Denig admired the sight: "For two kilometers the four lines of marines were as straight as a die. Their advance over the open flat plain with their bayonets shining in the bright sunlight was a picture I shall never forget." Cates agreed: "It was the most beautiful attack I have ever seen. As far as you could see up to the right, there were just waves and waves of men."[29]

Holcomb followed the leading tanks with two companies up and two behind. On the left Wallace's 79th Company led, with Woodworth's 96th Company in support. On the right Messersmith's 78th Company led, with Lloyd's 80th Company in back. The command group, thirty strong, followed in trace of the 80th Company. The companies attacked with four platoons abreast, each platoon in four waves—the "platoon as assault echelon" from the French *Offensive Combat for Small Units*. This formation gave the battalion a frontage of one thousand yards.[30]

The German artillery had been waiting for the marines to move into the open and now wreaked havoc on the neat formations. High explosives ripped apart clumps of men as they paced slowly behind the lumbering tanks. After the battle, every report would decry the slow rate of advance of the sluggish machines, probably no faster than fifty yards per minute, just half the regulation pace.[31] This excruciating shuffle doubled the time the battalion was exposed to enemy artillery.

The 78th and 79th Companies passed through the 5th Marines at about 9:00, and machine guns began to scythe through their ranks. About this time, Lee committed two companies of 3/6 to fill the widening gap between 1/6 and 2/6. As 2/6 closed with the German infantry, German artillery dropped a protective barrage directly across the battalion's path. Sergeant Paradis described the terrifying scene: "The concentration was so great that it seemed like a black curtain, and it seemed to me that Holcomb was headed for the thickest and blackest part of that German line. Men went down all around us from rifle fire and machine guns and cannon. I was in the first wave [of the battalion headquarters]. A man was hit in the wave back of me about twelve yards back and he yelled, 'Paradis, help me!' I looked around, he grabbed his stomach and fell. I started back but Holcomb yelled, 'Let the medics take care of him!'" Exposed to enfilading fire from the Paris Position to the left, the 79th Company quickly suffered debilitating casualties. Wallace was hit in the legs, putting him out of the war for good. In the 78th Company Corporal Sparks "had already said good-bye to mother as I could not believe anyone could live under such shelling. I had no fears but I was sure this was my last day." As the shelling knocked gaps through the waves, platoons quickly merged into a single skirmish line.[32]

In the 96th Company Cates turned to his sergeant and cautioned: "'Look at Captains Woodworth and Robertson getting right together there. That's bad business.' And I hadn't any more than said it when a shell hit close to them and they both were down." Woodworth hobbled to the rear past Holcomb's command group, eyes sparkling despite obvious lacerations on his head, arm, and leg.[33]

With Woodworth and Robertson wounded, Cates took command of the 96th Company. He proudly noted that his marines continued unwavering through the shelling. "As fast as they would cut our men down, the waves would close up and take up a perfect formation again." Before long he had lost two more lieutenants, leaving just Lieutenant Fritz. Then shrapnel pierced Fritz's hand, cutting a nasty wound that would cost him his arm. A shell landed next to Cates in another close call, slitting his trousers just above the knee. He pressed on with his company.[34]

The 80th Company also suffered terribly as it followed the 78th Company. Lloyd advanced in the first wave, swinging his cane and urging the men onward. Pvt. Carl Brannen advanced alongside his buddy Pvt. Forest "Red" Williams. A high-explosive shell detonated between them, hurling Brannen to the deck. His hands were scorched by the blast, but he arose, amazed to find himself otherwise unhurt. Red Williams lay writhing and groaning on the ground. Following standing orders, Brannen pushed on.[35]

It dawned on many that litter bearers might never find a wounded man in the waist-high wheat. Someone seized upon the idea of jabbing the felled marine's Springfield into the dirt by its bayonet. Without such markers, wounded such as Williams were otherwise abandoned to the forlorn chance that the overwhelmed litter bearers and hospital corpsmen would stumble across them. Williams's luck ran out; he succumbed to his wounds.[36]

Pushing on while holding his position in formation, Brannen could not hear his platoon commander but could see him out in front. Lieutenant Overton walked backward, shouting encouragement to his men and waving his .45 automatic and cane. More artillery plastered the platoon, ripping out Overton's heart as he walked. Another shell killed the platoon sergeant. Brannen continued forward.[37]

The 80th Company's numbers were dwindling quickly, and Captain Lloyd felt too many of his riflemen were leaving the ranks to assist the wounded. He ordered his first sergeant, Frank Yohner, to move to the rear of the company and stop able-bodied men from leaving the advance. Evidently, Yohner did not carry out the instructions; in a report Lloyd signed after the battle, he accused the first sergeant of ignoring his orders and himself leaving his post to assist a wounded marine to the rear.[38]

The Germans were pummeling Holcomb's men with relative impunity because the 20th Moroccan Division to the left had not cleared its zone of attack. The French had started their advance four hours earlier than the 2nd Division and had captured a thousand prisoners, but by 9:20 they had made it only as far as Chazelle, which lay to the left rear of the 2nd Division's limit of advance of July 18.

In the battalion command group, Holcomb watched the terrifying spectacle as the shrapnel and bullets ripped apart his battalion. The headquarters marines followed the 80th Company into the dense smoke and flame of the German defensive barrage. "From that time on I am not very proud of my actions," admitted Sergeant Paradis. "I probably became very near a shell-shocked condition."[39]

Major Denig fought to retain his aplomb as a man nearby was torn in two. He began talking inanely to Captain Wilmer just to keep his mind occupied. The major pointed out that the rounds start on the right and work to the left. A rabbit broke and ran, and Denig watched its flight. "Good rabbit," thought Denig, "he took my mind off the carnage." It occurred to him that he was carrying the hefty sum of one hundred dollars and told Wilmer to be sure and get it. With the same graveyard humor, Wilmer retorted that his chances of living that long could be bought for a nickel. "You think of all kinds of things," Denig reflected.[40]

As the battalion came upon the 16th and 53rd Reserve Infantry positions, the German infantry panicked and fled back across the Paris Position to the northeast. The few remaining French tanks routed a pocket of riflemen who had rallied at the sugar-beet mill southwest of Villemontoire. As each company's left flank neared the trench line, the marines instinctively angled toward the fire, pivoting the direction of attack from southeast to almost due north. The battalion formation dissolved as it broke into pursuit. Cates watched his marines dash ahead: "Soon we were up into the boche trenches and they jumped out and ran like wild deer. Up to that time the men had kept perfect formation, but when the boche commenced running the men swarmed after the boche shooting as they ran. The men yelled like a bunch of cowboys as they chased them."[41]

Cates realized that his men were heading into the Moroccan sector and reined in those marines he could. He organized a very thin north-south skirmish line of around twenty men at about 10:00 three hundred yards west of the mill. A straggler told him that Captain Lloyd was off to his left front with a similar group. Cates sent two runners to locate Lloyd, but after they set off, he never heard from or saw them again. Determined to locate Lloyd, Cates dropped most of his equipment, stuck his .45 in his blouse pocket, and wormed his way eastward toward the mill. One hundred fifty yards from the mill, he spotted three Germans among the buildings there kneeling to take a bead on him. Just in time he dove for cover into a tiny eight-inch depression. As rifle bullets punched through the air above his supine body, the lieutenant looked for better cover. He spied a mound of earth to his right and skipped across it as the errant rifle shots peppered the ground behind him. Cates dove over the mound, landing square atop Captain Lloyd and his tiny knot of eight men.[42]

Brannen's platoon now came across the trenches of the Paris Position. Brannen watched a few marines started down the trench in a small group. His instincts told him to stay clear of the bunched-up men, and he veered to the right, hurdling a few strands of barbed wire. Sure enough, a high-explosive round crashed into the trench, making a "clean sweep" of the marines there. Rifle and machine-gun fire began to clip at the 80th Company men around him, piercing one through the shoulder and amputating another's finger. Brannen patched up both men, who then took off for the rear. He figured it was time to go to ground and sprinted for the shelter of a sunken road. Brannen beat a burst from a machine gun by inches.[43]

Holcomb and his headquarters group dove into a group of foxholes abandoned by the Germans. Paradis and the others piled atop each other, cowering from the incessant barrage. "I laid there with every muscle in my body twitching, hardly knowing what I was doing." Holcomb could see the last three tanks burning in front of their line, struck by artillery firing across the Château-Thierry road. Watching tank after tank erupt in flames "was a mighty hard blow to our morale," thought Paradis. The attack had died out.[44]

Despite his wounds, Woodworth was still forward of the Vierzy Ravine and had watched the battalion's advance. From his perspective, it appeared that the left-hand companies had broken through to the Soissons–Château-Thierry road. He summoned a runner and scribbled down the following message at 9:30, sending copies to both Lee and Holcomb: "96 and 79 gained objective, but can't hold for wounded are coming thick. I am hit. Lieutenant Robertson hurt badly. We must have reserves as we cannot hold." But had Woodworth's marines reached the Château-Thierry road? Such a thing would be possible in this fluid fighting. Major Denig also claimed that marines of the battalion crossed that road. Yet regardless of whether they reached it or not, the two pockets of troops led by Lloyd and Cates and a sprinkling of other riflemen at that point constituted the nearest thing to a cohesive line.[45]

Lee proudly reported the following from his command post near Vierzy at 9:50: "Advancing nicely. Think Tigny ours. Tanks are doing fine work. The enemy are retiring. Things going well. Casualties normal." Lee's assessment was highly optimistic. Casualties were devastating, and the tanks were burning. Marines caught in an open beet field near Holcomb's command post dug in where they were, using the bodies of dead leathernecks as breastworks. These small groups of men still had fight left in them, though they would not constitute a major threat to a determined counterattack.[46]

The same could not be said of the German defenders' morale. In an uncommonly candid admission, the 14th Reserve Division stated that "our own infantry was retreating in droves." The 16th Reserve Infantry reported short rounds from German artillery landing among its troops at Villemontoire and stragglers looting liquor from the division commissary. "A considerable number of the artillerymen, above all the drivers, were very drunk." The 14th Reserve Division was coming apart at the seams. Yet the strongpoints at the sugar-beet mill and Parcy-Tigny remained in the hands of the 110th Grenadiers, and the 20th Division was en route with orders to counterattack and recover the ground as far west as Charantigny.[47]

With his front line thin, Holcomb feared such a move could sweep his battalion away. At 10:23 he sent this note to Lee: "Woodworth wounded. Reports 1 company nearly all casualties. They have merged with 79th—left line company. He believes they reached the Chateau-Thierry road and had to fall back." At 10:45 Cates penned his own report: "I have only 2 men left out of my company and 20 of other companies. We need support, but it is almost suicidal to try to get it here as we are swept by machine gun fire and a constant artillery barrage is on us. I have no one on my left and very few on my right. I will hold." Holcomb forwarded Cates's report to Lee along with the following amplifying note: "I am in trench 179.0–285.9. Cates is on my left in the same trench. Lt. Garnett of Sibley's bn is here with 30 men. No report from my right."[48]

The battalion command group lay scattered among shallow German foxholes near the mill. Wilmer and Vandoren hunkered down not far from Holcomb and Denig, but they could neither communicate with their commander nor move closer. As a headquarters the group could hardly function. Denig busied himself deepening his hole with his entrenching tool. Holcomb, who had not carried one, asked to borrow the shovel. Denig demurred; Holcomb could wait until he was done with it. As his second in command flung dirt out of his hole, Holcomb was generous with encouragement and advice, "with the result he soon had the spade," recalled Denig. "I then watched him burrow down and passed his advice back with embellishments."[49]

Lee sent the following update at 11:45: "Reports indicate growing casualties, amounting heavy, say 30 percent. 78th Company by runners say have only one platoon left. All are requesting reinforcements and M.G. and Chauchat ammunition. First Battalion reports no French troops on right, and are held up 300 yards in front of Tigny. Have in line from right, First, Third, and Second Battalions; Reserves, Battalion Engineers, Headquarters Company and two companies 6th Machine Gun Battalion. Have ordered line to dig in."[50]

Corporal Sparks fired about forty rounds in the general direction of the enemy, then burrowed into a foxhole for the day. A gunnery sergeant took charge of the marines around him, but no officer was in command. The 78th Company officers were all casualties, and the tiny group had no communication with Holcomb or any other officers. Sparks wrote angrily in his diary: "Light machine guns were useless. They were Chauchats and jammed after a few rounds, so that those who had them threw the ammunition away."[51]

With only a few hundred riflemen holding the 2nd Division's front, the 2nd Artillery Brigade provided the firepower to secure the division's hard-won gains. From posts around Vierzy, the brigade's forward observers directed devastating barrages onto every concentration of German troops that threatened the 6th Marines. The 12th Artillery passed along fire requests from the 4th Brigade to bombard Tigny, Parcy-Tigny, and to hit the German batteries that were shelling the 6th Marines. At 12:30 the 12th Artillery's 1st Battalion reported its activity to the 2nd Brigade commander: "Chateau-Thierry

Road being shelled with all calibers, both time fuse and percussion being employed. The road south of Charey-Tigny continues to be shelled. Many small groups of men had been observed on hill northwest of Villemontoire headed in this direction."[52] This reveals that the division's artillery spotters were having a field day, encircling the 6th Marines with protective fire and disrupting any German attempts to assemble a counterattack.

At 3:45 Lee officially ordered what had already become fact: "The Division Commander directs us to dig in and hold our present lines at all costs. No further advance will be made for the present. He congratulates the command on its gallant conduct in the face of severe casualties." The feared German counterattack did not materialize, though it certainly would have faced little opposition. In 2/6 alone, 87 marines had died, 280 were wounded, and 36 were missing, a total of 403 casualties—a rate of at least 40 percent. Many of the missing no doubt died undetected somewhere in the wheat.[53]

The day passed with occasional humor, though more commonly with terror and tragedy. "Throughout the day you could hear men calling for help in the wheat and beet fields. Their cries would get weaker and die out," Denig recorded. Nearby, Cates observed: "Every time a man would start in with a wounded man, the damn boche would cut at him with a machine gun or a one pounder. Some day those damn rascals have got to pay for such things."[54]

Cates himself continued to lead a charmed life. Scurrying between the positions of his marines, he heard the whiff of an incoming shell and hit the dirt. The blast occurred close enough to blow a shovel he carried out of his hand, leaving him holding a piece of the handle.[55]

The many able-bodied marines who carried casualties to the rear had depleted the battalion's fighting strength even more. Worse, some may have shirked their duties. Private Brannan disdainfully recalled "fifteen or twenty men who claimed they got lost off during the night and were not in the terrible slaughter in the sugar beet field."[56]

Suffering Was Extreme

The attack had petered out, but the ordeal of the wounded continued. One unintended consequence of the lack of detailed planning was the total failure of casualty treatment. Those wounded lucky enough to reach the Vierzy Ravine swamped the capacity of the 5th and 6th Marines's aid stations. Captured German medical troops worked alongside the Americans to treat casualties from both sides but still could not keep up.

Lee summarized his regiment's plight at 6:40 P.M.: "It is impossible to move from one position to another without drawing all sorts of fire. Losses are placed by Battalion Commanders at between 40 and 50 percent. Their appeals for doctors, ambulances, and stretcher bearers are pathetic. Cannot the ammunition trucks and any other transportation that may appear tonight, be used to evacuate the 200 or more cases now in the Regimental D. S. [Dressing Station] under Dr. Boone? Some may be saved by prompt removal."[57]

Over two thousand American, German, and French wounded had clogged the gas-choked ravine. The critical shortage of ambulances and stretcher bearers prevented medical corpsmen from evacuating stabilized patients to field hospitals farther to the rear. Despite Lee's pleas for ambulances, no casualties were removed from the Vierzy Ravine until after dark on July 19, when medical officers commandeered empty ammunition trucks from the 2nd Field Artillery Brigade. According to a surgeon in the 5th Marines: "Passing through poisonous gas and over shell-torn roads undergoing terrific bombardment, these trucks, with their groaning and screaming cargoes bouncing around, rushed to clear the area and reach possible safety many kilometers away. Suffering was extreme and many died en route." The artillerymen sped to the rear but had no idea where to take the injured men. If Mangin's Tenth Army had issued a medical plan, it was a mystery to the 2nd Division. Many wounded were dropped at the division supply dump, where they froze under a torrential rain that night, then were plagued by the blazing sun and insects the following day. Death by shock and infection were too common.[58]

Near twilight, Major Denig chanced a reconnaissance of the battalion's positions in the growing darkness. Along a trench not far from his hole, he found three men blown to bits, another with no legs, a fifth with no head, and a shell-shocked marine pointing at them all, shrieking, "Dead men! Dead men!" Denig found Vandoren, who joined him on his tour of the lines. They found eight wounded men sharing a large shell hole, one of them blind. "There was nothing to do but leave them."[59]

After nightfall on July 19, the French 5th Algerian Division relieved the 6th Marines. Not until July 23 would this division take the Château-Thierry road. By then, however, Ludendorff had decided to evacuate the Aisne-Marne salient. Holcomb's survivors collected as many wounded as they could and started the long hike back to the

Viller-Cotterets Forest. Carl Brannen and two other 80th Company men found a buddy, Pvt. Horace Cooper, who had bullet wounds to his leg, arm, and head. They lay Cooper on a blanket and staggered to the rear. The blanket proved a poor litter and slipped out of their grasp, dropping Cooper painfully to the ground. Unlike too many others, Cooper survived his ordeal.[60]

At daylight the battalion assembled in the Viller-Cotterets Forest. Paradis shuffled along to the assembly area, weary after helping carry a wounded man to the Vierzy Ravine. He spied Holcomb sitting on a stump alongside the road. The sergeant had been at the major's side during the attack on Bouresches and throughout the fighting at Belleau Wood. Heretofore Holcomb had always projected an aura of calmness through every calamity. After witnessing the slaughter of his marines on July 19, though, even Holcomb showed signs of battle fatigue. "I thought perhaps he was sick so I went over and asked if he needed any help. He said, 'No thanks. Just get your men out of here as soon as possible.' He was a very weary and dejected man, if ever I saw one."[61]

The Worst Kind of Warfare

On July 19, 2/6 lost nearly half its strength and failed to seize its objective, the Château-Thierry road. While Holcomb's undaunted marines had routed elements of four German regiments, his command no longer constituted a cohesive fighting unit by the time the attack went to ground south of the sugar-beet mill. It was well for his battalion that the Germans here were on the ropes. The thin line of foxholes south of the mill could hardly have withstood a determined counterattack. Nonetheless, the attack by the 6th Marines did maintain the momentum of the Tenth Army's offensive, and it contributed materially to achieving the intent of the operation: forcing Army Group Crown Prince Wilhelm to evacuate the Aisne-Marne salient. The expectation at XX Corps that the 6th Marines alone would break through to the Château-Thierry road had been overly ambitious. In comparison, after relieving the regiment on July 20, it took the French 51st Division two more days to reach the road, and even then the French fell back against German counterattacks.[62] In light of this, 2/6's performance at Soissons can be considered a tactical success, though one achieved once more at an exorbitant cost.

Reflecting on this day and the battalion's earlier fights, Lieutenant Cates wrote home: "This warfare is the worst kind of warfare. It is not open warfare nor is it trench warfare. It is a mixture."[63] A comparison of factors contributing to the battalion's severe losses reveals an ominous trend: 2/6 was suffering for the same reasons it had lost so many men at Belleau Wood. Not surprisingly, the French trench-warfare tactics proved just as inappropriate at Soissons as they had been at Bouresches. Moreover, inexperience at higher echelons had again denied 2/6 a rolling barrage. In this instance XX Corps and General Harbord had again ordered an attack without allocating sufficient time for the 6th Marines to prepare adequately.

One is tempted to sharply criticize the regiment's colonels and majors for lacking the gumption to object to this ill-conceived and hastily assembled plan. Certainly the flaws in the division's plan of attack of July 19 leap out of the historical records. But one must recall that when time is short, a commander must trust that his superiors have considered the costs and the potential gains and made the best calculated risk. The potential gains were as real as the casualty lists: the success of the Tenth Army's attack at Soissons has been called the turning point of 1918. When roused in the dead of night and informed of the impending attack, Lee and his battalion commanders concerned themselves with executing the division order as effectively and efficiently as they could, not with questioning the wisdom of the plan.

It does seem obvious that the regiment moved with inexcusable lethargy in the hours leading up to the attack. Recall that on June 13, when alerted in the dead of night to reposition as brigade reserve, Holcomb had 2/6 up to Lucy within four hours. The regiment must have expected an attack order for July 19, yet its officers appeared taken by surprise when it arrived. After the battle there may have been some recrimination within the 6th Marines. Assessing Holcomb's despondency on July 20, Paradis opined, "I think there had been some difficulty between him and one of the other majors in one of the other battalions had got lost and probably he was a little bit worried that something was going to reach back to headquarters."[64] The sergeant is referring to Sibley's late arrival, which is pointedly avoided in the official histories. Notwithstanding Paradis's account, the delay truly may have been due to the late arrival of the French tanks. Never having enjoyed the support of either tanks or a rolling barrage, waiting for the armor was an understandable error, one that the officers who conducted the attack would not forget. The question remained whether any experienced leaders down at the battalion level could survive until higher echelons became proficient.

Once it was obvious that the timeline could not be met, Lee and his battalion commanders chased the battle rather than seized control of it. Having delayed the attack by nearly an hour and a half, the 6th Marines appears to have taken it as a given that the 2nd Field Artillery Brigade could not conform its fire plan to the new timeline. Passing such detailed changes by telephone to twelve U.S. and nine French batteries while the scheduled barrage was well underway may well have been beyond the command-and-control ability of the 2nd Division. Reacting to the battle as they found it, the marines fixed bayonets and hoped for the best.

Other recurring factors hurting the battalion's efficiency at Soissons include the unresponsive command-and-control system and the lack of organic heavy arms. Both of these factors hampered Holcomb's ability to support the maneuvers of his rifle companies. A Lewis-gun platoon in every rifle company could have saved the lives of a significant number of Holcomb's dead and wounded. Tanks portended to fill this gap, but the battalion's lack of training in cooperation with them diminished their effectiveness, and their slow rate of advance left most marines skeptical of their worth. After the battle Cates wrote: "I do not like to advance with them [tanks] as they go too slow. They are very good when it comes to breaking down barb wire or destroying a machine gun nest, but otherwise I had rather advance with the infantry alone."[65]

The pathetically inadequate medical support available exacerbated attrition. The division medical troops had had insufficient time to deploy prior to the battle. Likewise, the failure of the regimental heavy weapons to arrive reduced the amount of supporting fire 2/6 received. The 2nd Division just did not have the mobility and flexibility to rapidly deploy from the march into the assault. Organized as a ponderous giant capable of sustaining heavy losses without requiring relief, the division could not nimbly jump into the attack as it had been required to do at Soissons without outpacing its heavier support. For all its rhetoric on maneuver and open warfare, the AEF had constructed the 2nd Division to fight a war of attrition.

Of even more severe consequence to future combat effectiveness, the losses hit the officer ranks disproportionately. In the four rifle companies, of the nineteen officers who started the attack, only Shinkle, Lloyd, and Cates walked away.[66] The battalion needed more than replacements and a few days rest to regain its former efficiency. It needed to rebuild its core of small-unit leaders, and the new team would then need to train together. Moreover, the appalling losses at

Belleau Wood and Soissons underscored the need to change tactics. But with no new doctrine yet rolling out of AEF headquarters, the burden of innovation would fall on the shoulders of the battalion's veterans.

Corporal Brannen's description of the appearance of 2/6 as it straggled off the line on July 20 attests to the fatigue gnawing at their endurance: "The surviving marines who left the battle line were a terrible looking bunch of people. They looked more like animals. They had almost a week's growth of beard and were dirty and ragged. Their eyes were sunk back in their heads."[67]

After Soissons the marines of 2/6 would have an opportunity to pause, rest, refit, and retrain. For the AEF it was a time for self-examination. Surviving officers in the 1st Division, who had undergone a very similar experience to the 2nd Division at Soissons, learned similar lessons about liaison between infantry and artillery, rolling barrages, the use of cover against frontal attacks, and integration of heavy weapons.[68] Few American units had an opportunity to retrain after a period of heavy combat. The 2nd Division was among the fortunate few. Having suffered aggregate casualties totaling 100 percent of its original strength, it remained to be seen how well 2/6 would adapt to its experience.

26. Ernest C. Williams (MCU Archives)

27. Before dawn on September 15, 1918, Major
Williams led 2/6 down this road into the Bois
de la Montagne. The Mon Plaisir Farm lies on
the high ground in the distance.

28

29

28. Taken from the same position alongside the road to the Bois de la Montagne, looking east. Hill 231.5 is center left. Le Rupt Rau runs along the bottom of the ravine.

29. Taken from the Essen Hook, looking north. Blanc Mont is in the distance to the left. German machine gunners in this position cut into the left flank of 2/6 as the marines advanced toward Blanc Mont.

30. John H. Pruitt

31. The summit of Blanc Mont, showing
numerous bunkers.

32

33

34

Facing page

32. Looking north from the summit of Blanc Mont. The marines of 2/6 attacked across this ground on October 5. Saint-Étienne is in the distance to the left.

33. Looking east across the Meuse-Argonne battlefield. The town of Remeauville is in the distance. Here 2/6 followed in support of 3/6 as the 2nd Division attacked north on November 1, 1918.

34. Near Mouzon, 2/6 attempted to cross the fast-moving waters of the Meuse River on the last night of the war.

35

35. During the occupation of Germany, these 32 original members of the 79th Company assembled for a group portrait. They had numbered 250 a year before.

6 Saint-Mihiel

THE TWO-MONTH PERIOD AFTER SOISSONS constituted the single major reshaping period for 2/6. The battalion would not see major fighting again until the Saint-Mihiel offensive in mid-September 1918.

This long break was notable for the changes in leadership at both the division and battalion level. Shortly after Soissons, Maj. Gen. John A. Lejeune, the senior marine in France, took command of the 2nd Division. Lejeune, whose name has become synonymous in the Marine Corps for the fatherly style of leadership he practiced, recognized the urgency of tough, realistic training. But the general never wavered from his first priority, which he described as "the kindling and fostering of a division spirit, or esprit, which would animate the hearts of all its officers and men."[1]

Under Lejeune's leadership, the division would scrutinize the lessons learned in its previous battles to rethink both how it trained and how it fought. Combat efficiency in 2/6 would benefit dramatically from these changes, but the battalion's overall competence would be diluted by the large number of replacements in its ranks and hobbled by the mule-headed leadership of its new commander.

Enter the Bull

Few officers were more antithetical to Thomas Holcomb than Maj. Ernest C. Williams. Holcomb, promoted to lieutenant colonel, had moved up to second in command of the 6th Marines, where he would personally hold the reins for both operations and intelligence. Lt. James Sellers remembered Williams as "a simple kind of soul who liked to leave everything up to his adjutant while he would try to get up to the front-line with an automatic rifle." Lt. Clifton Cates concurred: "He had all the courage in the world, but I wouldn't say he was the brainiest or friendliest man in the world." Lt. Graves Erskine said that "Major Williams was not the best map reader in the world, and he didn't listen to his junior officers very much." Sgt. Don Paradis, with characteristic bluntness, stated: "He was an alcoholic, drinking from one half to two quarts of whiskey a day. . . . I learned to detest the man."[2]

A high school graduate and the only son of a newspaper editor in Sidell, Illinois, Williams had served two years as an enlisted marine before earning his commission in 1909. By 1916 he had accumulated three disciplinary infractions on his official record, one for threatening an NCO while attending officer training at Parris Island, another for returning late aboard USS *Helena* from leave, and the third from the commander of the 4th Marines for unspecified "conduct of prejudice to good order and discipline." Williams's repeated misconduct was rare among marine officers of the period. Nonetheless, he had advanced to first lieutenant and reported to Santo Domingo, where his career took a decided turn for the better. In command of the 47th Company at San Francisco de Macoris, Williams captured a small rebel fort in a *coup de main*. Pistol drawn, he personally shouldered open the fort's gate and charged into a bloody ten-minute gunfight in which eight of his twelve marines fell wounded. This audacious assault dazed the unsuspecting garrison, buying time for his support element to exploit his foothold and overwhelm the defenders. One hundred guerrillas surrendered, while another two hundred fled. Six months later Williams received the Medal of Honor for his intrepid action, along with his sobriquet, "The Bull."[3]

Williams's audacity under fire overshadowed his past misconduct and excessive drinking. As the Marine Corps wrestled with wartime expansion in the twenty-two months following his attack on the fort, he had catapulted to major, shipped to France, graduated from the AEF Infantry School of the Line, and as an observer with the army's 38th Infantry, participated in the 3rd Division's famous defense of the Marne during July. On August 10, 1918, Williams took command of 2/6 at Point-a-Mousson. He was thirty-one.[4]

The Western Front demanded hard men with tremendous physical courage, which Williams had in abundance. But nothing in his prewar service had prepared him for the technical aspects of commanding a battalion of one thousand men, and nothing in his personality suggested that he would be a quick study.

A Tactical Renaissance

When Williams took command, 2/6 occupied a quiet position at Pont-a-Mousson on the west bank of the Moselle River. In the two weeks following Soissons, the battalion's survivors had moved through various rest billets before settling into this sector for a ten-day stretch on August 7. The marines noted that their new commander led each foot march on horseback, setting a blistering pace for his panting riflemen to maintain. Once ensconced in the fortified position at Pont-a-Mousson, the men took advantage of the respite to bathe in the Moselle, blast fish to the surface of the river with grenades, and scour the countryside for cognac.[5]

While the marines and doughboys enjoyed their deserved break, the 2nd Division's senior officers determined to remedy the glaring shortcomings in tactics and training revealed at Belleau Wood and Soissons. On August 19, 2/6 moved into billets at the Bois de l'Eveque for twelve days of intense training. General Lejeune's guidance stressed realism and flexibility. He demanded that his instructors "require their subordinates to dispose their troops in accordance with the situation, and discuss the exercise with officers and non-commissioned officers with the view to developing the best method. . . . The adoption of 'normal methods' of attack or defense, which limit the use of troops to fixed formations, is prohibited." These exercises, based on the division's previous engagements, trained the troops in enveloping machine-gun nests and strongpoints, consolidating their own defenses to repel counterattacks, and the integration of machine guns, mortars, and 37-mm guns.[6]

The 2nd Division was not the only American unit learning from its first engagements. The AEF published a revealing document on August 29, "Combat Instructions for the Troops of First Army." Recognizing the imperative of the rolling barrage, headquarters now proclaimed that "the rate of progression of the [rolling] barrage must be slow and should include long pauses. . . . [T]he infantry must hug the barrage closely in order to reach the enemy's successive trenches before he has time to man them." A few days later the AEF released another document in which General Pershing himself attempted to clarify the differences between open warfare and trench warfare: "The essential difference between open and trench warfare . . . is characterized by the presence or absence of the rolling barrage ahead of the infantry." The AEF had, however grudgingly, embraced the rolling barrage as an essential component of deliberate attacks. Such thinking was entirely in accordance with Lejeune's ideas, and the 2nd Division would employ these techniques in the coming battles to great effect.[7]

In a major departure from the French doctrine heretofore employed, the marines learned to precede the attacking echelon with a thin line of scouts, spaced ten to fifty paces apart, who would locate

German machine-gun nests. The scouts' job was to signal the location of the machine guns and possible gaps to the company, which deployed in small groups between one hundred to four hundred yards to the rear. These groups would push through gaps in a series of rushes covered by the fire of other groups. In recognition of the inadequacy of mere rifles and Chauchats for achieving fire superiority, first-line battalions would receive a machine-gun company, mortars, 37-mm guns, and occasionally a single 75-mm gun. The 2nd Artillery Brigade developed a new "plan of liaison" between the infantry and artillery that relied heavily on telephones instead of runners. Such tactics promised to revitalize the battalion's efficiency.[8]

The marines of 2/6 also practiced a new technique called "marching fire," intended to suppress defending infantry in order to enable the Americans to close and finish the job. Bracing their rifles and Chauchats against their right hips, the marines would advance on line, blasting a steady hail of fire ahead of them. Pvt. Carl Brannen vividly described the problem and the intended solution: "Heretofore, we had come out of our trench or hiding place and rushed toward the enemy as fast as we could run, while they poured a deadly fire with machine guns. What were left, if any, would go over the spouting machine guns and bayonet or shoot the gunners. Now we were to come out firing from the hip, which kept down the speed of advance, but we hoped to shoot them away from their guns before so much damage was done."[9] That the marines would practice overwhelming fortified Maxims with unaimed bolt-action-rifle fire only underscores the deadly dilemma of the Western Front: attacks against fortified positions almost always achieved only limited success at exorbitant costs.

Regardless of the merits of the battalion's new tactics, a shortage of replacements diluted the effects of this training. The heavy losses of Belleau Wood and Soissons had used up the marine replacement battalions in France, and the brigade was still short twenty-five hundred men. In order to maintain the quality of the Corps's only fighting organization, Lejeune refused to force army replacements upon the marine brigade. Poorly trained soldiers arriving from America had undermined Pershing's effort to build an army of superior riflemen; privates who had not seen a rifle or pistol before reporting to combat units were not unknown. Determined to preserve the 4th Marine Brigade's elite status, Lejeune had the rear areas scoured for leathernecks assigned to provost duty, schools, and hospitals, making up part of the shortage. Yet too many of these men arrived after the brigade had finished its training period on August 31. Between September 1 and 12, 372 marines reported to 2/6. A final training period from September 5 to 10, which focused on attacking through woods and underbrush, provided an opportunity to introduce some of these replacements to the new tactical doctrine.[10]

Notwithstanding Lejeune's efforts, 209 all-new replacements joined 2/6 from the 5th Separate (replacement) Battalion on September 11, the very eve of the Saint-Mihiel offensive. These men had not only missed the 2nd Division's training period but also had not trained in France at all. Typical of these newcomers was Pvt. Thomas B. McQuain. McQuain had enlisted on April 22, less than five months before joining the 80th Company. After basic training at Parris Island and four weeks of machine-gun school in Utica, New York, he reported to the 5th Separate Battalion with time for a mere two weeks of training before the battalion embarked. The unit debarked in France on August 27, where the impatient arms of General Harbord's Service of Supply whisked them along directly to the 4th Marine Brigade. Although Parris Island had ensured replacements like McQuain did not lack for individual esprit de corps, fitness, or discipline (McQuain himself was a rifle expert), the quality of these latecomers nonetheless suffered in contrast with original members of the battalion and earlier replacements. McQuain and his cohorts had received minimal training at Quantico and none at all since arriving in France. Such green troops had no time to assimilate into the ranks of 2/6. The proficiency of 2/6's most junior riflemen had sunk to its lowest level since Quantico.[11]

A handful of returning veterans and several promising newcomers had restored the company-grade officer ranks from the annihilation at Soissons to something close to its previous quality. Captain Woodworth recovered from his wounds and resumed command of the 78th Company, while Capt. Bailey Coffenburg returned to the 80th Company. The other two company commanders, both replacements, appeared highly competent. Capt. George Martin took over the 79th Company. Capt. John Minnis, a Naval Academy graduate whose leadership of a company of soldiers in the 3rd Division's defense of the Marne had earned him the Distinguished Service Cross, now commanded the 96th Company.[12]

Many of the lieutenants were also new to the battalion, but most had seen combat as NCOs in 2/6 or in other battalions of the 4th Brigade. The commandant had astutely decided in late 1917 to accept no more officer candidates from civilian life and commissioned 164 of the marine brigade's combat-proven NCOs after they attended the AEF's officer-training school. Three lieutenants who had been commissioned in July, James McClelland, Delos McKenzie, and Harold Powell, departed to attend this school in August and would miss the coming fight at Saint-Mihiel.[13]

On the battalion staff, Lieutenant Vandoren assumed duties as the adjutant, where his lawyerly thoroughness and organization would offset The Bull's petulance. The irascible Lieutenant Erskine took over for Vandoren as scout officer. Gy. Sgt. William Ulrich, a fluent German speaker who would receive the Distinguished Service Cross for Soissons, moved up from the 80th Company as battalion sergeant major.[14]

Colonel Lee assembled the officers of the 6th Marines on September 11 for additional instruction on operating with tanks. Tanks would support the 2nd Division at Saint-Mihiel, and Lee, perhaps at Holcomb's suggestion, was not about to wait until the last minute again to figure out how to integrate them into his attack. Captain Minnis, the new commander of the 96th Company, had observed French armor on maneuvers on September 7. He prepared a detailed description of their operations and tactical doctrine for Lee that served as the basis for this instruction. According to Minnis, tanks served two purposes: to destroy barbed wire and to knock out machine guns. A company of fifteen light tanks normally worked directly for an infantry battalion commander. In a descriptive analogy, he described tank-infantry teamwork as resembling "that between a hunter and his dog. The infantry is the dog that finds the machine gun, and holds it, while the tank is the hunter that comes up and destroys the hostile machine gun."[15]

Minnis also emphasized the interdependence of the infantry and tank. The tank drew small-arms fire to allow riflemen to rush forward, while the tank depended on the men to locate and destroy antitank guns. Minnis concluded his letter by admonishing, "above all, the fight is the infantry's fight, and they must always consider any help from the tanks as purely 'velvet.'"[16]

This instruction served as a fitting capstone to the revitalized doctrine of the 2nd Division before Saint-Mihiel. While 2/6 would not gain tank support in this fight, the battalion's tactics had matured considerably since May. In the coming action the battalion would fight with a more viable combat doctrine. But without the opportunity to ingrain that doctrine into 40 percent of its manpower, and under the unsteady leadership of Bull Williams, the battalion's overall efficiency was nevertheless retarded while its cohesion eroded.

A Hedge against Attrition

In an effort to preserve that precious cohesion for future battles, the marines took a drastic step to mitigate the effects of attrition. The brigade's leadership recognized that the terrible losses at Belleau Wood and Soissons had frustrated the accumulation of experience within the infantry ranks. In order to preserve a cadre, each company henceforward left one officer and 20 percent of its marines behind when going into action. This calculated insurance against attrition could hardly have comforted the 80 percent who would go over the top. Carl Brannen, who had fought at both Belleau Wood and Soissons yet would not be left behind with the fortunate 20 percent, recalled his fatalistic outlook before Saint-Mihiel: "I reasoned that the war would continue a year or two longer, but that I would not see the finish."[17]

But this measure further deprived the battalion of experienced marines in the coming fight. For reasons both pragmatic and humanitarian, the most experienced veterans comprised this cadre. At Saint-Mihiel the 96th Company would fight for the first time without Lieutenant Cates. "I was glad in one way and I was sorry in another," he recalled.[18] Without Cates and other experienced leaders, companies like the 96th risked suffering higher losses than they might otherwise. In the impersonal calculus of attrition, the marines' leadership had undeniably evaluated the risks and gains and hedged their manpower against annihilation.

Saint-Mihiel: The Operational Situation

The 2nd Division had heretofore fought exclusively as part of French corps. At Saint-Mihiel the division would fight in the U.S. First Army's first major combat operation. Gen. Ferdinand Foch had curtailed the First Army's objective from a penetration of the Hindenburg Line and the capture of Metz to a limited offensive to reduce the Saint-Mihiel salient. Whether the First Army would continue to command the bulk of American divisions afterward was still a point of contention between Foch and Pershing. Accordingly, it was vital to Pershing that the First Army achieve an incontestable success that would put to rest Allied skepticism of American leadership.[19]

The triangular Saint-Mihiel salient measured twenty-five miles across its southern face and sixteen miles up its western face. Ten

Plan of Attack of First Army, September 12, 1918

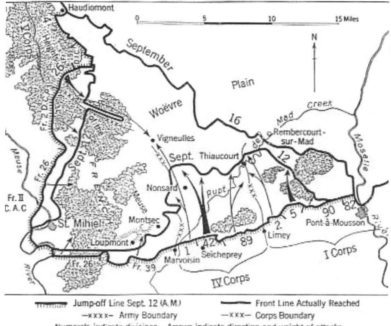

Jump-off Line Sept. 12 (A.M.)   ———— Front Line Actually Reached
—×××— Army Boundary   —×××— Corps Boundary
Numerals indicate divisions   Arrows indicate direction and weight of attacks

German divisions defended five successive defensive lines that had withstood several French offensives. Notwithstanding these well-developed positions, the German leadership recognized the vulnerability of the salient. Gen. Karl von Fuchs, commanding this sector, intended to withdraw his divisions to the more defensible Hindenburg Line, which cut across the base of the salient.[20]

The 2nd Division would attack into the right center of the salient's southern face as the leftmost division of the U.S. I Corps. The division's sector averaged only two miles across, a narrow frontage that would facilitate the concentration of combat power. In rifle strength alone the 2nd Division held something like a 6:1 advantage over the opposing Germans.[21] For the initial attack, the soldiers of the 3rd Brigade would lead with the 9th and 23rd Infantry Regiments abreast. Williams's marines would have a comfortable buffer of four thousand yards and five thousand American infantrymen between themselves and the enemy.[22] Unless things went terribly awry, 2/6 could count on seeing little action on the first day and might even escape heavy combat for the duration of the battle.

Saint-Mihiel, September 12–15

After a four-hour artillery barrage, the 3rd Brigade went over the top amid a torrential thunderstorm. The American shells obliterated the German defenses just as Fuchs commenced his planned withdrawal to the Hindenburg Line. The bombardment shattered German communications, isolating the battalions of the 419th Reserve Infantry Regiment of the 77th Reserve Division from higher headquarters and supporting artillery. Following a rolling barrage that advanced just one hundred yards every four minutes, the assaulting doughboys surged through the understrength 419th. The regiment, whose battalions averaged less than five hundred men, disintegrated before the advancing Americans, who were delayed more by barbed wire than by enemy fire. By 2:00 P.M. the 3rd Brigade had captured Thiaucourt and reached the army objective line, the 2nd Division's assigned mission for the entire offensive.[23]

Bull Williams's battalion followed in support of the doughboys, its operations unremarkable but for the wounding and evacuation of Captain Coffenburg on September 13; Lieutenant Kilduff succeeded him in command of the 80th Company. That evening the 4th Marine Brigade relieved the 3rd Brigade along the army objective line.[24] With the 2nd Division's objective for the campaign secured by the 3rd Brigade, the marines had only to consolidate the sector before turning it over to the 78th Division. Accordingly, the 6th Marines relieved the 23rd Infantry on the night of September 13–14. Consolidation would require the marines to wrest control of the outpost zone from the German 31st Division, which had rushed up to defend the Hindenburg Line.

On the afternoon of the fourteenth, 2/6 occupied a support position just east of the village of Xammes. Lieutenant Erskine slipped into the town and brought back a German helmet full of beer to his delighted battalion commander. Williams's participation in the battle so far had been unremarkable. Notwithstanding the battalion's easy time, Erskine patrolled for more than just booze. For two nights, September 13 and 14, he infiltrated the German outpost zone in the Bois de la Montagne. Erskine knew the Germans had occupied the woods; on at least one occasion he and his patrol exchanged fire with an enemy outpost. Other intelligence reports collected by the division G-2 also indicated the presence of German troops in the woods.[25]

These outposts belonged to Captain von Jagow's 3rd Battalion, 398th Infantry Regiment. The purpose of these positions was to protect the main German defenses in the Hindenburg Line. Jagow had reorganized the remnants of his original seven companies into three 120-man companies, each named for its commanding lieutenant. Kompanie Conrad had established an outpost on Hill 231.5, just east of the Xammes-Charey road, while Kompanie Speer occupied an outpost west of the road. A third company, Kompanie Schatze, manned a support position farther north. Morale, according to a captured German NCO, was "very bad."[26]

The 6th Marines should have had little difficulty chasing the 3/398th out of the Bois de la Montagne. The Americans enjoyed something like a seven-to-one advantage in numbers.[27] But their recent training and revitalized tactics would fizzle due to a series of poor command decisions. Because of the obstinate leadership of Williams and the dim situational awareness of Lee (for which Holcomb, as the staff officer responsible for intelligence and operations, must shoulder some of the blame), the marines of 2/6 would once again suffer avoidable losses indemnifying the poor tactics of their officers. Pvt. Carl Brannen in the 80th Company summarized the situation well: "My military sense didn't approve of what we were doing, but a soldier only obeys orders."[28]

The Bull and the Bois de la Montagne, September 15

The Bois de la Montagne describes the forested slopes of the drainage and valley of Le Rupt Rau, a minor stream snaking southeasterly into the larger Rupt de Mad, which flowed through the 5th Marines'

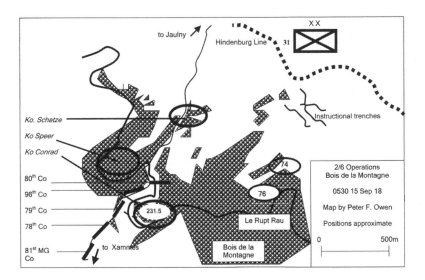

zone. The relatively flat plateaus to the north and south of the forest were cleared farmland, offering superb observation and fields of fire. The Hindenburg Line roughly paralleled the northern edge of the forest at a distance of several hundred yards to exploit these fields of fire. The wooded slopes were uncommonly steep, rising nearly two hundred feet vertically just two hundred yards from the banks of the creek. This afforded both sides concealment and some protection from flat-trajectory artillery, especially the French 75-mm howitzers of the 12th and 15th Field Artillery. The irregular shape of the forest and the twisting draws would complicate control of large infantry formations. Machine gunners burdened with the heavy Hotchkiss guns and ammunition would not be able to keep pace with the lightly loaded riflemen. Likewise, the crews of 37-mm guns and trench mortars would be confined to the roads.

Lee had Sibley's 3/6 occupy the army objective line about fifteen hundred yards south of the Bois de la Montagne. He directed Maj. Frederick Barker, commanding 1/6, to conduct a reconnaissance of the forest with two companies at 6:00 P.M. on the evening of September 14.[29] Lee had not ordered Barker to *clear* the woods, merely to scout it. Clearing a forest that was nearly two miles wide and a mile deep, roughly the size of Belleau Wood, of enemy resistance at night would have vastly exceeded the capabilities of Barker's two companies.

The patrol stepped off by 9:00 P.M. A short time later Barker's column followed a farm track into the Bois de la Montagne. The marines' route kept them a few hundred yards south of Kompanie Conrad's outpost on Hill 231.5. Lieutenant Conrad may have detected the patrol; his machine gunners and riflemen kept silent, but 1/6 reported artillery fire falling nearby as they slipped into position in the northeast corner of the woods just after midnight. Two more under strength companies from Kompanie Schatze moved into the woods, between Kompanie Conrad and Kompanie Speer.[30]

As Barker's companies were establishing liaison with the 5th Marines on their right flank, the 4th Brigade changed Lee's task from a reconnaissance of the woods to the establishment of an outpost line. The division was consolidating their position with a view to turning the fight over to a new division. Lee ordered Barker to bring up the remaining two companies of 1/6 to outpost the north edge of the Bois de la Montagne. At 2:12 he gave Williams the task of supporting Barker: "You will proceed immediately with your battalion and machine gun company north and occupy the line from the

Xammes-Charey Road east across the southern edge of the woods lying between Xammes and Charey along the unimproved road running east-west through the Bois de la Montagne."[31] Nothing Lee said suggested that Williams might encounter the enemy, and nothing the major did suggests that he at all considered the threat of enemy interference with his mission. Lee may have interpreted Barker's lack of contact as an indication the woods were clear of Germans. In doing so he would have been overestimating the marines' ability to have thoroughly patrolled the area in just five hours. Moreover, Barker's remaining two companies would be moving up concurrently with Williams's battalion. In no way could 1/6 have cleared the woods nor secured its northern edge before 2/6 reached the southern edge.

Regardless of whether Lee expected 2/6 to encounter the enemy, Williams's handling of his battalion displayed a cavalier disregard for security. "He gave very sketchy orders," Erskine recalled. No doubt eager to get moving under the dissipating shroud of darkness, Williams formed his battalion in a column of twos on the Xammes-Charey road at 3:30 A.M., with the men dispersed at five-yard intervals. He then marched through 3/6's lines with only Erskine's scouts preceding his headquarters group. The companies followed in the order 80th, 96th, 79th, and 78th Company, with the 81st Machine Gun Company following. The column stretched more than a thousand yards behind him, which would exacerbate the major's ability to communicate with his rearmost company commanders.[32]

So oblivious was Williams to the lurking danger that he led his battalion straight down the road toward the German outposts, riding his horse at the head of the column. As it dawned on Erskine that the major was taking them into the Bois de la Montagne, he urged him not to attempt to cross the bridge across the streambed along the southern edge of woods. Williams ignored his intelligence officer. At 5:00 A.M., by Williams's account, the column descended into the ravine above the bridge.[33]

"There was a very heavy ground fog as we moved out at daylight," recalled Sergeant Paradis, following directly behind Williams's command group in the 80th Company. "Visibility was only about fifty yards ahead of us, which at the time seemed a good thing as it gave us cover from the prying eyes of the enemy. We moved out in a column of twos on a road that proceeded down into a valley into a bridge across a small stream."[34]

Ominously, the column stumbled upon a startled German soldier alongside the road. Erskine continued to plead with Williams, pulling on his leg, begging him to stop. With the vulnerable column winding down behind him from Hill 231.5 into the ravine, across the bridge, and along the road, Bull halted. Years later Brannen wrote that at this point the major ordered Lieutenant Kilduff to take a platoon from the 80th Company to reconnoiter the far side of a clearing.[35]

Angry now, Williams dismounted, pulled out his map, and turned on his flashlight in full view of the German outposts. Erskine recounted Williams's outburst: "'Come here and show me where you think we are! I know where I am.' I said, 'No sir, I'm not coming near that flashlight.' He finally gave me a tongue lashing, got on his horse, and started the march and we hadn't gone fifty yards before it seemed like every machine gun in the world had opened up."[36] Williams's command group and Erskine's scouts, leading the column, escaped the initial fusillade. Through the shadowy murk, the leathernecks caught sight of forty Germans escaping into the forest. Notwithstanding The Bull's ill-considered use of his flashlight, the marines had stolen undetected into the middle of one group of defenders, likely the reinforcements from Kompanie Schatze who had moved up only hours before. Williams ordered Erskine and his scouts to pursue, and Sergeant Major Ulrich commanded (in German) the fleeing soldiers to surrender. Obediently, the Germans hesitated; a few tossed down their rifles. For an odd, awkward moment, the defenders were on the verge of capitulation.

A rifle shot split the silence. Springfields and Mausers erupted, and the fight was on again. Evading Germans snapped off shots as they snaked away through the trees. Erskine's scouts dogged them, brazenly cold-cocking a few of the slower fugitives with helmets and pistols. From Erskine's viewpoint, the fight was turning out marvelously.[37]

Farther back in the column, though, marines were fighting for their lives. The interlocking machine guns of Kompanies Speer and Conrad caught the 80th Company in a hornets' nest of fire. The tail platoon, in column atop the bridge, caught the brunt of the initial fusillade. A barrage crashed to earth behind the 81st Company at the rear of the column.[38]

The battalion's fight unraveled into a collage of confused, disconnected fights by isolated groups of marines. As with most actions, none of the eyewitness accounts tell the same story. What is clear is that Williams's opportunity to influence the fight evaporated with the first burst of German machine-gun fire.

The battalion had conducted drills to respond to such an ambush while in column. According to this exercise, the 80th Company in the lead would form a line to the front, while the 96th, as the second company in column, would come around on its right. The 79th, third in column, would come left, and the 78th would remain in reserve. What the 81st Machine Gun Company was supposed to do is unclear, and those men were likely ignorant of this battle drill anyway. Likewise, many recent replacements had not trained on this procedure with the battalion. This factor of uncertainty, combined with the shock of the machine-gun barrage, broken terrain, poor visibility, and overall confusion on September 15, caused the companies to become intermingled on both sides of the road. "Needless to say we scattered like a bunch of quail," Paradis recalled. "We were only about 50 yards from the edge of a thick underbrush. Most of those left took refuge there."[39]

Private Brannen described what had become of Lieutenant Kilduff's platoon: "When we were a hundred yards or so from the battalion and crossing an acre size clearing, we were fired on by machine guns from the woods. Perhaps half the platoon were shot down, including Kilduff. The rest of us dashed for the woods; those nearest brought the lieutenant, but a bunch of bullets had drilled a large hole in his left side. By this time it was a well established fact that we were surrounded, while the survivors of my platoon had the enemy on two sides and were almost cut off from the battalion." The remnants of Kilduff's platoon intermingled with Paradis's knot of men. As artillery shells detonated around them, Sergeant Paradis took charge. "I gathered about twenty-five men and placed them in a weed-filled ditch at the edge of the woods. There were three Chauchat automatic rifle squads and I placed a machine gun at each end of the line and one in the center with the riflemen spaced at about five yard intervals."[40]

The 80th Company was chopped into isolated pockets, all strung along the road between Kompanie Speer to the west and Kompanie Conrad on Hill 231.5. Williams and his headquarters group were isolated with them at the head of the column.[41]

Trailing the 80th, the 96th Company swung into action against Kompanie Conrad on Hill 231.5. Captain Minnis fell, shot in the chest; he would live but was done for this war. First Sgt. George Humphrey, not as lucky, also fell, dead. The 96th's lieutenants fought on but not as part of a cohesive unit. None of them but Cates had led a company before, and Cates was with the 20 percent left behind.[42]

Following the 96th's platoons up the road, Captain Woodworth tried to salvage the situation. But part of his own 78th Company had followed Captain Martin and the 79th Company to the left side of the road against Kompanie Speer, while others became embroiled in the fight with Kompanie Conrad to the right. Initially the marines on the left of the Xammes-Charey road dug in. Shortly thereafter, a machine-gun bullet tore into Woodworth's leg. He fell, rose again, and second burst to the body knocked him down for good. The Germans had claimed three of 2/6's four company commanders in the first minutes of the fight.[43]

A few marines from the 80th and more from the 96th Company had joined Erskine's scouts in their chase. Fifteen or twenty Germans made a half-hearted stand in a small house, but a few grenades took the fight out of them. They too staggered south under guard. Erskine and the others dashed north again, emerged from the cover of the woods, and walked right into the teeth of the Hindenburg Line.

North of the Bois de la Montagne, the ground opens up for several hundred yards right up to the wire of the Hindenburg Line. The Germans had arrayed machine guns to cover this killing ground, with a heavy strongpoint built into Mon Plaisir Farm. Throughout the morning, groups of marines reached this open ground, stabbed at the enemy position with only their rifles and bayonets, and scurried back into the cover of the woods, dragging along their wounded.

Erskine's story is typical of those who attempted to advance beyond the treeline. Recalling his dash back for cover, he remembered: "before I got to this little patch of woods a column of Germans started coming up. All I had was my pistol, and I got a couple of them. The others sort of dispersed. I was hiding in these bushes, then I ran out into the open to try to get down under some cover, but two machine guns opened up on me and caught me in the leg and busted it up pretty badly, and I lay there till 10 o'clock I guess." Pvt. Archie Vale of the 96th Company found the lieutenant and carried him a half mile to an aid station. Erskine nearly lost his leg. He would not return to the battalion.[44]

When Cpl. Carlos D. Creed, 96th Company, attempted to cross the field, he too was struck down. Under intense machine-gun fire, Hospitalman Apprentice David Hayden rushed to his side. Realizing the severity of Creed's wounds, Hayden continued to apply dressings in the open despite the continuous fire. He then hoisted Creed onto his back and carried him to safety; the young corporal nevertheless perished.[45]

78th and 79th Companies Attack

More than an hour had passed since the ambush. Although cut off from Major Williams, Captain Martin now had sufficient control over his own 79th Company and contact with Lt. James Adams, now commanding the 78th Company, as well as the 81st Machine Gun Company to coordinate an attack. Sometime around 7:00 the two companies attacked on line to the north, each with a four-gun Hotchkiss platoon in support. Martin led his company into the woods to the left while Adams's marines attacked along the Xammes-Charey road and to the right.[46]

From an aid station at the Xammes-Charey road, Captain Woodworth had a unique, clear grasp of the battle. At 7:15 he sent the following message to regimental headquarters: "Major Williams, 80th Company, and one platoon of 96th Company separated from us at dawn. 96th and part of 78th advanced as we were fired upon. Captain Martin, 79th Company, and some 78th Company are now advancing due north against heavy resistance. Some effort should be made to organize as we can only go north and do not know our position." Sgt. Victor Sparks, a 78th Company NCO, vividly described this attack: "It was still dark but we heard the shouts—'The marines are going over.' There was only one way to go and that was forward. We heard that wild rebel yell when the marines made contact and before one could figure out what was happening and a good part of the platoon were on a plain and started to dig in. To the right of us and beyond was an isolated platoon in a field. Germans were peeping out from the distant foliage of their lines." Sparks, having reached the killing ground north of the forest, found himself the senior marine in sight. Maxims emplaced around the Mon Plaisir Farm and among instructional trenches northeast of the Bois de la Montagne prevented the marines from breaking out of the trees. Perhaps in shock by now, certainly under enormous strain, Sparks went berserk. Fearing the Germans would soon overwhelm the isolated platoon on his right, the sergeant stuck his rifle and bayonet in the ground. Drawing his .45 automatic with one hand and his trench knife with the other, he ordered a charge into the German line. Despite intense machine-gun fire, his marines followed him across the open field and into some vacant German dugouts.[47]

Realizing the tenuous shelter of the dugouts, with Maxim rounds snapping overhead and the predictable counterattack looming, Sparks reconsidered his position and began to withdraw his men one at a time. In a testament to the ferocity of the fire, he had to force one marine out of the relative shelter of the dugout at pistol point. As the last man to leave, Sparks now found himself very alone in the dugout. He sprinted for safety, unbelievably reaching American lines unscathed. His mind had had enough, however. By his own admission, Sparks fell apart. A gunnery sergeant held him down while other marines disarmed him and then led him to the aid station.[48]

The attack by Lieutenant Adams and the 78th Company had achieved some success. The marines destroyed a machine-gun position they found tucked *under* the cement bridge, where Kompanie Conrad first sprang the ambush. During this assault, Adams uncovered Major Williams and the battalion command group, who had set up a temporary command post atop Hill 231.5.[49] The Bull was no longer cut off from his battalion, though it would still take him some time to get his arms around the fight.

To the left, the 79th Company did not fare as well. Ignorant of the battalion's mission, Martin reacted aggressively by striking to the west of the road to clear that part of the Bois de la Montagne. But after fighting through Kompanie Speer's position, he continued to push the attack into the Hindenburg Line. There, withering machine-gun and artillery fire forced the 79th Company plunging back into the trees; 3/398 reported repulsing three separate assaults.[50]

Colonel Lee, exasperated by how the operation had unfolded, attempted to get The Bull under control. At 7:10 he had sent a message to Williams by runner: "Halt and reorganize along the south edge of wood at Hill 231 and support Barker who is ordered to occupy north edge of Bois de la Montagne. Sibley [the commanding officer of 3/6] is on the Army Line in your rear as reserve. The idea is to hold these positions as ordered. Report frequently to me on phone. S/Lee."[51]

On the crest of Hill 231.5, Williams now had marines from three rifle companies (78th, 80th, and 96th) and four machine guns, all intermingled. At 7:35, probably before Lee's runner had reached him, Williams sent an erroneous and highly optimistic situation report revealing that he grasped neither the true situation nor his mission. "We have practically cleared the Bois de la Montagne but cannot advance further without artillery preparation. Mon Plaisir Farm appears strongly held." The Bull's last statement about Mon Plaisir suggests that he intended to continue the attack into the Hindenburg Line. German after-action reports describe the marines advancing to within two hundred yards of their trenches before being forced back. Either Williams was sending his marines against the main German defenses or he had not passed on to his subordinates what the battalion's objective for September 15 was, and in the absence of further guidance his men pushed the attack as far as they could.[52]

A message scribbled down by the wounded Captain Woodworth only twenty-five minutes after Williams's communication suggests the latter: "The battalion is totally disorganized as the companies were split before starting. I am in dressing station. . . . 3 bullets. It is near main road—I should advise support of some sort at once owing to the disorganized condition of the battalion and that Captain Martin who has the left does not know our object or directions."[53] Woodworth penned this second message to Holcomb, whereas he had sent his first one to Lee. As the report suggests a crisis in the battalion's leadership, Woodworth may have felt more comfortable communicating with his former battalion commander. Whether or not the captain was aware of Williams's rosier message, he felt compelled to get this unvarnished report into Holcomb's hands.

No doubt in response to Woodworth's plea for support, at 8:00 A.M. the regimental machine-gun company pushed its one uncommitted Hotchkiss platoon up to Hill 231.5, where it reported to Williams. The major wasted no time, ordering the four machine guns over to Captain Martin across the road.[54]

Notwithstanding Woodworth's report, Lee still had two battalions in the Bois de la Montagne and little idea where they were or what his battalion commanders intended to do. If Williams or Barker had field telephones by now, neither spent much time on them. At 8:10 he ordered 3/6, in reserve: "Stay in place on army line until further orders. 2nd Battalion is separated into two bodies, one under Williams and one under Martin. 1st Btn. is in front of Bois de Montagny don't know where. Send patrols to front to locate them and have him [Major Barker] report over phone up at front. Phone in on line with Williams, follow wire up. S/Lee."[55]

The Germans Counterattack

Between 8:00 and 10:00, German artillery continued to pound the marines, especially around Sergeant Paradis's position near the Xammes-Charey road. To the west of Paradis, the 79th Company defended a broken line snaking along the northern lip of the ravine. Eight Hotchkiss guns from the 81st Machine Gun Company strengthened Martin's position. Across the road, the remainder of 2/6 was intermingled for fifteen hundred yards to the east.

Sometime around 10:00, the German's counterattacked Major Williams's disorganized battalion. Their aircraft controlled the skies this day, and they buzzed over the forest, directing artillery fire. West of the Xammes-Charey road, Martin's men fell back in less than perfect order, during which one of the Hotchkiss guns fell into enemy hands. In revealing language, the machine-gun-company commander wrote tersely: "Owing to the speed with which the infantry fell back it was impossible to keep up. The machine guns at one time on that flank were surrounded on three sides by the enemy." Martin reformed at his jump-off line along the southern edge of the Bois de la Montagne. The regimental surgeon reported stragglers from the 78th, 79th, and 81st Companies at his aid station, with no idea as to their units' positions.[56]

While the bulk of the 78th, 80th, and 96th Companies consolidated around Hill 231.5, other knots of marines stubbornly held their ground farther forward. Sgt. Henry Bogan, Pvt. John Kelly (the troublemaker from Chicago who had threatened to kill Bogan before Soissons), and their group of sixteen marines clung to a tight perimeter, fighting off three counterattacks with rifles and a single Chauchat. By the time Lieutenant Adams fought through to relieve their band, bullets had whittled the sixteen defenders down to eight.[57]

Sergeant Paradis and his cluster of marines would not let go of their outpost along the Xammes-Charey road. German spotters knew their location and kept 77-mm and mortar rounds hurling into the ground around them. Expecting a counterattack, Paradis crawled from one marine to another, holding the thin line together by his own will. A shell nearly buried Pvt. Florian Frillman and his automatic-rifle team. "Scatterbrain," as his platoon called him, shook it off and poured fire across the road.[58]

The counterattack died under the well-aimed fire of Scatterbrain's Chauchat and Pvt. Carl Brannen's rifle grenades. Sergeant Paradis observed that "a few Germans came out of the woods towards us but [they] did not gain twenty-five yards." Brannen later wrote, "The boys over the bluff began to retreat under our fire, and we poured it on good and proper until they were out of sight over a ridge."[59]

Williams, finally getting on top of things, called for artillery fire on the Mon Plaisir Farm around 10:20 A.M. He also requested immediate resupply of rifle and Hotchkiss ammunition.[60] But he had already lost control of the Bois de la Montagne.

1/6 Attacks

Distressed at how the fighting progressed, Colonel Lee pushed the rest of 1/6, two platoons from 3/6, and a Hotchkiss platoon from the 6th Machine Gun Battalion into the fight. 1/6's 75th and 95th Companies, reinforced with the 3/6 platoons, would attack on the left of 2/6.[61]

At 11:35 Williams explained the plan as he understood it to his four companies. "Hold until 1/6 passes through, then follow at 1000 yards. Get liaison left and right. Everything is OK."[62] The last sentence suggests that Williams felt that his lieutenants needed some reassurance, or perhaps The Bull needed to reassure himself.

When Capt. George Stowall brought his 75th Company forward and linked up with 2/6, the situation did not look promising: "On arriving at the south edge of these woods, two companies of the 2nd Battalion of the 6th Marines, were found in position. . . . The senior officer of these two organizations stated that they had advanced to the north edge of the woods but had been driven back by heavy machine gun and rifle fire coming from the woods . . . and also from the North East. They also stated that about 100 dead and wounded had been left in the woods, which were very open."[63] Stowall took charge of the intermingled marines. Tasked to clear the woods west of the road, it took him until nearly 2:00 P.M. to sort the men from three battalions into a line of attack. Leading the way was 1/6, two companies strong, with the reorganized 78th and 79th Companies under Captain Martin and Lieutenant Adams following in support. Stowall too reached the northern edge of the trees, killing and capturing Germans along the way, only to meet a hailstorm of artillery and machine-gun fire. The four companies tumbled back, reforming once more on the southern edge of the woods. When the marines pulled back this time, Sergeant Paradis and his weary platoon fell back with them.[64]

Final Counterattacks at Dusk

About the time Stowall led the attack, the 6th Marines passed word that the 310th Infantry of the 78th Division would relieve the regiment at midnight.[65] From that point on, the leathernecks undertook no more offensive action and consolidated their line. On the left flank, 1/6's 75th and 95th Companies anchored 2/6's left flank along the southern edge of the woods. Following the wood's edge to the road, 2/6's line then passed across the front of Hill 231.5. The 74th Company (1/6) still held the ground between 2/6's right flank and the 5th Marines.

About dusk, the 31st Division attempted one more counterattack to drive the marines out of the forest. Fire from the 155-mm howitzers of the 17th Field Artillery plastered the advancing Germans as they emerged from the Hindenburg Line, much to the delight of General Lejeune, who observed the artillery's effect from his command post. Marine Hotchkiss guns further broke apart the attacking formations, and the American line was never seriously threatened.[66]

The doughboys of the 78th Division relieved the 6th Marines on schedule, though the marines left the soldiers with an untidy defense. After dark, German and American patrols hunted for each other even as the units changed over. By dawn, 2/6 had left the woods behind them.[67]

Assessment

Despite Williams's bungling, 2/6 had wrested the Bois de la Montagne from the 3/398th Infantry. Nonetheless, had 2/6 run into a more stubborn opponent on September 15, the operation might have gone completely sour. As it stands, the incompetence of Williams cost an exorbitant number of casualties, a waste of nearly one-quarter of the battalion, in what should have amounted to a minor operation.[68]

It is surprising that the Marine Corps did not cashier or even court-martial The Bull for this fiasco. At the conclusion of a rehearsal for the Saint-Mihiel attack, Lejeune had admonished his officers of the gravity of their responsibilities. "Avoidable ignorance on the part of officers was inexcusable and reprehensible," he recalled saying. Williams's ignorance on September 15 appears entirely avoidable. He deployed his battalion in an inexcusably vulnerable formation, then walked his column into an ambush. He ignored the warnings of his scout officer. Indifferent to security, the major rode a horse at the head of his column into combat and then turned on his flashlight in an unknown, enemy-held environment. Once in contact, elements of his battalion battered themselves pointlessly against the fortified Hindenburg Line because he had not impressed upon them the objective and purpose of the mission. Williams was lost. He may even have been drunk. According to Erskine, the major had been drinking previously.[69] For all these reasons, marines died needlessly.

The reasons his superiors took no action may be inferred. The Bull's Medal of Honor, awarded by a grateful nation only the year before, must have protected him from a certain amount of scrutiny. That aside, any accusation against Williams would also soil Colonel Lee, commanding the 6th Marines, whose mishandling of the whole operation set the stage. Tom Holcomb, as Lee's second in command

and the officer primarily responsible for operations and intelligence, likewise would bear his portion of responsibility for this debacle. Such a public flogging in the Marine Brigade, with Williams and his medal in the center of the impact area, would bring discredit on the tender reputation of the Marine Corps, especially when contrasted with the superb performance of the 3rd Brigade on September 12.

Apart from The Bull's leadership, 2/6's performance reveals instances of both efficiency and imprecision. The battalion's training had provided the means to overcome the shock and confusion of the ambush, with its column-to-line drill salvaging a very precarious situation. The rifle platoons overran the German outposts at close quarters in wooded terrain, a task to which they had specifically trained a fortnight prior. Whether or not any companies utilized scouts or marching fire is a matter of conjecture.

The battalion certainly had not employed supporting arms through the first hours of the fight on September 15. Machine guns were parceled out to the companies but occasionally failed to keep up with the riflemen's see-saw movements. Regiment had attached one 37-mm gun and two Stokes mortars to each battalion, but these weapons saw no action.[70] The steep terrain undoubtedly reduced the mobility of these beastly guns to a crawl. As mentioned, 2/6 received no tank support for this mission. The cumbersome, fragile Renaults would have been constrained to the road had any been available.

The battalion could, and should, have integrated artillery into its operations. Without question, the 2nd Division's artillery was underemployed on the morning of September 15.[71] The first record of Major Williams requesting artillery support came at 10:20, five hours after the fighting began. Had artillery been summoned to isolate the Bois de la Montagne from the Hindenburg Line, as it handily did during the evening counterattack, 2/6 would have had a much easier time clearing its zone. As it was, the marines fought alone, paying a heavy price.

The aggressiveness of small-unit leaders and individual marines put a vital punch in these attacks. Sergeants such as Bogan, Paradis, and Sparks consistently took charge of the action around them and inspired marines to persevere in the face of blistering attacks. Such feats of leadership were not universal, however, nor were they enough to overcome sluggish command at higher echelons. Perhaps the high preponderance of replacements and the grim necessity to leave behind one-fifth of the veterans as cadre retarded the battalion's ability to fight cohesively.

The dilution of the battalion's leadership and the infusion of re-placements had begun to erode the splendid spirit that had protected 2/6 in earlier dark times. Symptoms of poor discipline began to ap-pear in the *Muster Roll*. The battalion reported fourteen marines ab-sent without leave during September. But straggling was far worse in other units fighting in the Meuse-Argonne; the commander of the million-man U.S. First Army would estimate his number of stragglers at 100,000 about this time. Although the rate of absenteeism in 2/6 appears mild in contrast to such widespread straggling, the numbers are nonetheless indicative of sinking morale. Several of those absent were recent replacements in the 79th Company who disappeared to-gether on September 20. Six from the 80th Company, mostly old hands, took off on September 27 on the eve of the next battle.[72]

If the marines of 2/6 had misgivings about their new major before Saint-Mihiel, his actions there did nothing to instill them with confi-dence. Williams had become highly unpopular in the 80th Company since September 15; on September 25 he had handed a field commis-sion to Gy. Sgt. Stephen Skoda, a prewar crony who had a reputation as a martinet, not a fighter. Sergeant Paradis felt that Skoda, who had been Paradis's drill sergeant at Parris Island, owed his commission to his ability to keep The Bull supplied with booze.[73] The six absen-tees from the 80th may well have decided they had had enough of Williams's leadership.

This battalion was not the same bunch who had come over aboard the *Henderson*. Few of the original marines were still around; the spirit of those who remained had been tempered by exhaustion and frustration. To many of the new replacements, 2/6 was a world of strangers with whom the bonds of comradeship had not been formed. To the old timers, the loss of buddies was doubly troubling when coupled with the loss of faith in their commander. At Belleau Wood Holcomb's marines bounced back into the fight time and again as a true band of brothers. Williams's battalion would batter its way forward as a cold, brittle, and impersonal machine.

7 Blanc Mont

WITH ONLY TWO WEEKS AFTER SAINT-MIHIEL before its next battle, 2/6 had time for a mere six days of training. This brief period could not replicate the extensive training the battalion had conducted in August and early September. Nonetheless, it provided an opportunity for the veterans to familiarize the recent replacements with the new tactics developed in August. Both the marines who had joined 2/6 just before Saint-Mihiel and the replacements for the casualties lost there profited from this experience. In another interesting development, a handful of sergeants drew M97 shotguns for fighting in close quarters.[1]

Once again, heavy casualties among the officers required substantial reorganization of the battalion's leadership. According to Lieutenant Sellers, who rejoined the unit after recovering from his wound of June 6, five inexperienced replacement captains joined the battalion after Saint-Mihiel, yet Major Williams did not entrust them with companies. He assigned one of these men, Capt. J. C. Collier, as his battalion second in command. Williams chose to post three lieutenants who had proved themselves in combat, Sellers, Shinkle, and Cates, as company commanders. He gave Sellers the 78th Company, Shinkle the 79th, and put Lieutenant Cates permanently in charge of the 96th. Sellers wrote in his memoir that he suspected Lieutenant Vandoren persuaded Williams to make these assignments.[2] Cates and Shinkle had commanded companies after their captains fell in the heat of battle, and all three were known and respected by their men.

The same could not be said of the solitary captain Williams entrusted with a company. Capt. Walter Powers, who had served in 1/6 before joining the battalion in August as a first lieutenant, took over the 80th Company. A lawyer before the war, Powers had obtained his commission through the Massachusetts Naval Militia along with Arthur Worton. At Soissons, he had served under Maj. Johnnie "The Hard" Hughes. Hughes knew Williams from the Dominican Republic and had endorsed Williams's recommendation for the Medal of

Honor. Hughes likely provided him with a favorable recommendation on the captain, for Powers later claimed that Hughes intended to recommend him for a Distinguished Service Cross for his actions at Soissons. The men in the 80th Company did not know Powers but were prepared to give him a fair shake. "We had heard good reports about his performances on other fronts," recalled Paradis.[3]

Williams's platoon commanders, all seasoned veterans, buttressed these company leaders with at least as much combat time as their superiors. All had either come over as lieutenants with Holcomb or earned their commissions as NCOs in the 4th Brigade. But the number of lieutenants greatly exceeded the battalion's requirements. Recognizing the disruption that heavy officer casualties had caused, the Marine Corps commissioned so many NCOs that 2/6 would enter its next fight with at least eight extra lieutenants. Veterans returning from the AEF's School of the Line included Jack West and former NCOs Maurice Bennett and Edward Fowler. West had gone AWOL from school to rejoin the battalion during the Saint-Mihiel action, while Barnett had stayed the course and graduated. Both had received high marks. They reported to the 79th Company. Fowler, a former South Boston police officer, took command of a platoon in Sellers's 78th Company.[4] West, Barnett, Fowler, and others like them provided 2/6 with lieutenants as well trained and experienced as it ever had. Only the unsteady leadership of Williams and Powers were in question.

Blanc Mont: The Operational Situation
The German performance at Saint-Mihiel testified to the exhaustion of the kaiser's army. Sensing the opportunity to end the war in 1918, General Foch had ordered a final general offensive to commence September 26. The Americans would attack in the Meuse-Argonne, the British would continue their advance near Cambrai, and the French would resume the attack in the Champagne region just west of the Argonne to support the Americans. In order to reinforce the French Army's attack, Pershing passed control of the U.S. 2nd and 36th Divisions to Foch.[5]

Two days into this offensive, the French Fourth Army had shuddered to a halt before an east-west chain of hills north of the Vesle River known as Les Monts. Beyond them to the north, the terrain descends gradually to the Aisne River. If the French could take Les Monts, the Germans would have to withdraw north of the Aisne, thus abandoning Rheims and securing the western flank of the Americans

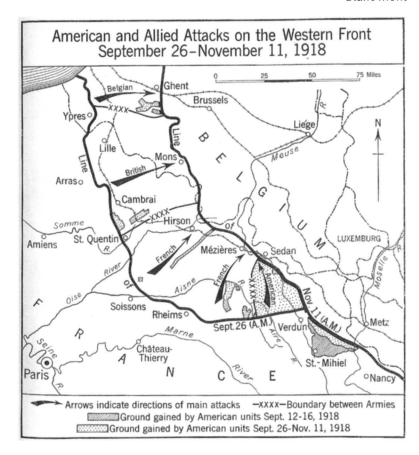

American and Allied Attacks on the Western Front
September 26–November 11, 1918

Arrows indicate directions of main attacks   —xxxx—Boundary between Armies
▨▨▨▨Ground gained by American units Sept. 12-16, 1918
▨▨▨▨Ground gained by American units Sept. 26-Nov. 11, 1918

in the Argonne. The key to breaking through Les Monts was Blanc
Mont, the most formidable and commanding hill in the chain. With
the eager consent of General Lejeune, Foch passed control of the
2nd Division to the Fourth Army for the purpose of assaulting Blanc
Mont.[6]

Blanc Mont is an L-shaped east-west ridge rising gently to a summit more than three hundred feet above and about two miles northwest of the town of Somme-Py. The base of the L points south, toward
Somme-Py (and the French position at the time). The lower slopes
of the ridge, devoid of cover in 1918, afforded unobstructed fields of
fire. Halfway to the top the terrain became broken by light woods
and shallow ravines, which offered shelter to small groups of attackers. From the densely wooded summit, camouflaged observation
posts could direct artillery fire throughout the region. But German

reserve areas to the north were shielded by the ridge from French observation. When Private Brannen first gazed upon the commanding height, he recalled a stanza from the "Marines' Hymn": "'If the Army and the Navy ever look on Heaven's scenes / They will find the streets are guarded by United States Marines.' After looking at that ridge ahead, I decided my next duty might be helping guard the heavenly streets."[7]

German Defenses

The Germans held three lines of resistance: a series of trenches five hundred yards deep just north of Somme-Py, a second line along the crest of Blanc Mont, and a final line through the town of Saint-Étienne. In the 2nd Division's zone, elements of three critically understrength divisions—from west to east, the 200th, the 51st Reserve, and the 203rd Divisions—defended along with a hodgepodge of amalgamated formations. Notwithstanding their small numbers, exhausted condition, and very low morale, the Germans here enjoyed a tremendously strong position replete with deep dugouts and concrete machine-gun emplacements.[8] As 2/6 would learn again, a very small number of defenders generously armed with machine guns could cripple a battalion in minutes.

Directly to the front of 2/6, the 2nd Battalion, 235th Reserve Infantry (2/235) had emplaced its 225 troops in a sprinkling of machine-gun positions in the Essen Trench. To the west, in the Essen Hook, the 2nd Landsturm Kompanie emplaced its machine guns. On a finger running due south from Blanc Mont, the 5th and 7th Companies of the 2nd Battalion, 74th Reserve Infantry (2/74) defended a commanding machine-gun strongpoint. These two companies enjoyed the protection of deep dugouts and had orders to counterattack into the flank of any penetration. The remainder of 2/74 and the 18th Jaeger Battalion manned the German main line of resistance southeast of the summit of Blanc Mont. Several infantry and artillery headquarters of the 200th Division occupied bunkers and trenches on the summit of ridge. The 10th Field Artillery Battalion had deployed two of its three batteries of 77-mm guns on the forward slopes of Blanc Mont, while the combined artillery of at least two divisions could bring fire against the marines' planned advance. In total, 2/6 faced somewhere around twelve hundred Germans in its zone. And in reserve behind Blanc Mont, another two thousand soldiers of the 149th Infantry Regiment stood poised to deliver a counterattack in force.[9]

The 2nd Division would assault Blanc Mont as the main effort of

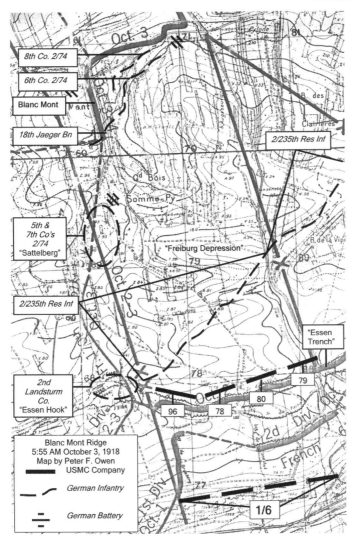

8th Co. 2/74

6th Co. 2/74

Blanc Mont

18th Jaeger Bn

2/235th Res Inf

5th &
7th Co's
2/74
"Sattelberg"

"Freiburg Depression"

2/235th Res Inf

"Essen
Trench"

2nd
Landsturm
Co.
"Essen Hook"

79

80

96   78

Blanc Mont Ridge
5:55 AM October 3, 1918
Map by Peter F. Owen
USMC Company

German Infantry

German Battery

1/6

the French Fourth Army. Lejeune decided to attack with both of his brigades on two converging axes toward the summit of the ridge. The French reinforced the 2nd Division with forty-eight tanks, two regiments of 75-mm howitzers, two battalions of 155-mm howitzers, and two battalions of 120-mm long guns. The French 252nd Aviation Squadron provided aerial reconnaissance and artillery spotting. In addition, French divisions would attack to either side of the Americans to secure the division's flanks. Each of Lejeune's brigades would attack on the narrowest of fronts, with all six battalions in column to penetrate rapidly to the objective on the summit. Williams's 2/6 would lead the six infantry battalions of the 4th Brigade.[10]

The Odor of the Dead

The 2nd Division began moving up on September 30 in a cold rain. After dropping off the 20 percent cadre, 2/6 moved into the line north of Somme-Py. Hiking the seven and a half miles from their assembly area near Sarry, Williams's marines filed through an ammunition point, where each rifleman grabbed two bandoliers of ammunition. In a reflection of the professionalism that now pervaded the seasoned 2nd Division, the ammunition-issue point was set up alongside the infantry's route of march. As the riflemen passed through, supply personnel draped bandoliers over their shoulders, with scarcely a pause in the line of march. This efficiency saved lives as well as time, for it prevented the congestion that could prove an attractive target for German artillery. Riflemen also grabbed two fragmentation and one concussion grenade apiece, while automatic-rifle teams shouldered the heavy Chauchat magazines. Yet the battle-wise leaders in 2/6 were dismayed that signal flares were in short supply and no rifle grenades were handed out.[11]

When Williams's marines relieved the frontline *poilus* on the night of October 1–2, they found that the French had seized a foothold within the first belt of German trenches just north of Somme-Py. French and German corpses littered the trench floors and dugout. "The odor of the dead was very prevalent," observed Sergeant Paradis. He and the other veteran sergeants in the 80th Company wasted no time organizing the position. From right to left, the 79th, 80th, and 78th Companies and the attached 81st Machine Gun Company occupied the southernmost of these four trenches; the Germans still held at least the northernmost trench.[12]

Guiding the 78th Company into position, Johnnie Kelly came across a macabre squad of dead Frenchmen; one corpse sat upright with the top of his brain exposed. Just then Sgt. Carl Schreiber barked into the darkness.

> "Where are my men? Where are my men?" he demanded of Kelly.
>
> "Why, there's a whole gang of them over there," the private responded, pointing to the gruesome assembly in the niche, now indistinct in the growing night.

"Get them for me," said Schreiber.

"Get them yourself," replied Kelly.

The unsuspecting sergeant went over, groped for his men, and as luck would have it, placed his hand upon the dead soldier's uncovered brain. "I laughed like hell," Kelly recalled.[13]

To the left of the 78th Company, the 96th Company slipped into a north-south communication trench, its northern end barricaded where it connected with the enemy-held east-west Essen Trench. The Germans and marines traded hand grenades at points where their lines approached each other. The 96th Company was forced into this peculiar arrangement because the French division west of the 2nd Division had not penetrated the German position. To Cates's left, the enemy line wound up a narrow east-west ridge to the so-called Essen Hook, from which the 2nd Landsturm Company could batter Cates's men with enfilading fire.[14]

Night Attack, October 2

The next day, October 2, Lieutenant Fowler and Kelly asked Sellers for permission to slip up to the Essen Trench and see what the Germans were doing. Sellers assented, and the pair wormed their way up a communication trench. They discovered that the troops to the 78th Company's direct front had withdrawn. Sellers requested permission to seize the vacated trenches lest the Germans return. Capitalizing on Sellers's initiative, Lee ordered 2/6 to seize all of the forward-most trenches at 6:30 P.M.[15]

Williams forwarded Lee's order to his company commanders verbatim: "At 6:30 P.M., you will occupy, by infiltration, the trenches DU PACHE, DE L'ELBE, and D'ESSEN. Two platoons will be up initially, followed by other two as successive trenches are reached. Consolidate and hold with two platoons in front trenches and two in rear." The right-hand companies met little opposition. Paradis found only corpses as he led his platoon over the top, fuming that Lieutenant Skoda, his former drill sergeant, was not leading his platoon from the front. Likewise, Paradis noted that Captain Powers waited until the entire 80th Company had occupied the Essen Trench before following in trace.[16]

Only Cates's 96th Company encountered serious resistance. Cates had proven himself an energetic and courageous officer before, but it would be at Blanc Mont where he would come into his own as a truly exemplary combat leader. Williams had given him some attached machine guns, one-pounder guns, and trench mortars to bolster his assault. Cates directed these and two of his rifle platoons to beat down the machine guns on the Essen Hook, then scrambled over the top with his other two platoons. In contrast to Powers and Skoda, Cates led from the front. The rush to the enemy trench three hundred yards away took only two minutes. Cates wrote later that the Germans "opened up with a few machine guns and I saw about twelve grenades come flying over, but that was all; they ran like sheep."[17]

At 8:00 P.M. Cates sent Williams this happy message: "Attack a success. Few losses. Consolidated. Liaison with 78th on right and French on left. Everything in good shape."[18] No one in 2/6 had conducted a night attack before, but Williams's marines pulled it off rather smartly. The battalion now occupied the same Essen Trench as the Germans to the west, with an empty section between Cates's left and the enemy.

Williams's lieutenants continued to persist in their aggressiveness. Lieutenant West volunteered to lead a small patrol beyond the Essen Trench to scout the nearest German positions. Audaciously, he wormed his way within close proximity to the enemy, collecting detailed information of their locations. Returning to his company's lines, West gave Shinkle a much-valued picture of opposing dispositions in front of the 79th Company.[19]

Just before midnight, a group of artillery forward observers and thirty-six engineers reported to Williams's command post. The large detachment was an initiative by the division artillery brigade to improve liaison with the infantry battalions. Williams learned from them that he would lead the division's assault on Blanc Mont at 5:50 A.M. When the major got through to Colonel Lee by field telephone around 3:30, the colonel confirmed the time of attack and added that the division planned to give Williams a company of twelve French tanks to support his assault. A courier was en route with a copy of the attack order for Williams along with another important missive from Lee on musketry: "Impress all men with the fact that musketry is still KING and they have but to sit tight and shoot straight, insuring superiority of fire and guaranteeing success."[20]

The battalion would be no worse off if Lee's latest sermon went astray, but without the written order, Williams could only grasp a general idea of the plan of attack. The Bull nonetheless had a pretty clear picture of what the division had planned, for he had attended an orders briefing on October 1 for an October 2 attack that XXI Corps had canceled. At 4:30 A.M., no courier having appeared, Williams prudently huddled under a poncho with Vandoren, who scribbled out an attack order on a field message pad by flashlight. Absent detailed instructions, Vandoren scrawled out a plan consistent with the battalion's recent training. The four companies would attack abreast from their present positions at H-Hour, leaning into the rolling barrage. Each would begin the advance with its four platoons on line, arrayed into four waves for the assault.[21]

The company commanders all expected to strike sometime in the morning. But Williams had failed to alert them that 5:50 would be the time of attack when he received that word from the artillery-liaison group. Even after Lee confirmed the attack, Williams continued to wait for written instructions before informing his subordinates. Meanwhile, he and Vandoren continued to draft the battalion plan of attack on a tiny yellow message pad absent the details of a regimental order, a tedious, frustrating process. The minutes ticked away while the companies waited for instructions.

Despite the lack of explicit attack orders, few marines slept that night, and nervous boasting throughout the trenches belied their excitement. Writing years later of these last cold hours before dawn, Lieutenant Sellers could still feel the adrenaline pulsing through him as he listened to the banter of his keyed-up men. Outside the company command post, Kelly boasted that he would be the first to capture a machine gun.[22]

Veterans prepared for the expected attack with an almost business-like sang-froid. Brannen checked his bayonet to ensure it was securely latched in its scabbard and unfastened a few of his ammunition pouches for quick access. He swung his two bandoliers in front of his chest, slid a razor in one pocket, and tucked his Bible in the other. "I was using all the protection I could think of," he admitted.[23]

At 5:40 a breathless runner delivered the anticipated regimental order, too late for Williams to adjust his own instructions. In fact, he and Vandoren had taken too long. None of the company commanders had yet received the major's orders and were still ignorant of such basic information as the time of attack. To make matters worse, the tanks had not yet arrived. After his experience at Soissons, Vandoren no doubt had little inclination to watch another barrage roll away from them, and he likely impressed that opinion on Williams, who likely needed no prodding to attack. It would have been out of character for The Bull of San Francisco de Macoris to sit idly on his haunches, waiting for some French tanks to show up. For all his shortcomings, Williams was aggressive, and he had courage in spades. Runners dashed off to each company with orders to attack at 5:50.

The preparatory barrage erupted on top of the German positions at 5:45. Sellers, Cates, and Powers all reported that the battalion runner did not reach them until 6:00. After the five-minute barrage, the artillery began creeping forward at 5:50, drifting at the ponderous pace of one hundred yards every four minutes. Recognizing the shelling for what it was, company leaders leapt into action. Platoon by platoon, they clambered out of the Essen Trench. The hours of drill now paid off as the platoons assembled into their formations automatically. The barrage was already two hundred yards away, but the tanks were nowhere to be seen. The Bull was not alone in his impatience. The line surged forward. Not a man in 2/6 hesitated.[24]

The Battalion's Finest Hours

The battalion swiftly caught up to the ponderous barrage. Keeping as close to the detonations as possible, Williams's marines caught many of 2/235's defenders still underground. A morning fog helped obscure the Americans until they were nearly on top of the enemy positions. Those Germans who braved the barrage found themselves quickly enveloped by small groups of marines.

For the first six hundred yards, machine guns from the Essen Hook on the left cut swaths through the 78th and 96th Companies. Paradis noticed the incoming artillery fire was quite feeble compared to his previous experience, though the machine-gun and rifle fire was furious. Brannen, running messages for the 80th Company, recalled, "The rows of men moved forward unhesitatingly but fell like ten pins before the deadly machine gun fire."[25]

Twenty minutes into the attack, the 78th Company bumped up against a fortified machine-gun emplacement spitting tracers through the barrage. As a company runner for Sellers, Johnnie Kelly carried only a pistol that day. He eased a grenade out of his pouch with his right hand and pulled the pin. Gripping his .45 automatic in his left hand, Kelly charged through the exploding shells. Emerging impossibly unscathed, he stumbled upon a young retreating German. The teenage soldier threw up his hands and dropped to his knees, begging for his life. Kelly noticed the terrified youngster's eyes shift ever so slightly to the marine's left. He looked too and spied the machine gunner whirling his gun around. In one swift motion Kelly turned, ducked, shot the gunner with his pistol, and lobbed the grenade. The grenade detonated, and Kelly was on top of the hole before the dust settled. Those Germans who could still raise their arms surrendered. Kelly grouped them together, waited for the barrage to pass over, and prodded his prisoners back down the hill through the 78th Company formation. As he passed Sellers, Kelly called out, "I told you I was going to get the first one."[26]

The 96th Company continued to take a beating. Only after Cates's company reached the broken terrain at the stem of L-shaped Blanc Mont could his platoons begin to maneuver under cover. The ridge's intervening finger soon blocked the fire of the Essen Hook gunners, who shifted their attention to the battalions following in trace of 2/6. As Cates's marines moved around this finger, they found an east-west ravine leading around the flanks of a 2/74 machine-gun strongpoint to their left. The German battalion's graphic account of its defeat connotes grudging respect for the 96th Company's effective use of cover and aggressive fire and movement:

Here at about 7:00 A.M. the noise of combat coming from the front lines was audible and orders were issued to occupy the positions. Hardly was the last man at his post when the enemy became visible, urging our men to surrender by waving at them. They had overrun the foremost lines with almost no resistance. Our machine-gun fire, which was launched at once in compliance with orders, brought their advance to a halt. But now the Americans with the machine guns they had speedily brought into position opened a furious fire that combed along the surface of the trench parapets. The company commander of the 5th Company, Lieutenant Soldan, as well as another officer, Lieutenant Louis, personally operated machine guns until jams rendered them useless. The bullets of our machine guns, easily finding their mark in the dense masses of the Americans, inflicted heavy casualties. Meanwhile the enemy, utilizing the gaps in our lines, had surrounded the 5th Company on its left flank, having advanced through the Freiburg depression and the dense shrubbery west of that company. They now launched another assault, advancing and firing their light machine guns [Chauchats] which were operated, while carried by one man under his right arm, by another walking immediately behind. By the artillery bombardment, as well as the machine-gun fire, the company had already suffered bloody losses which amounted to at least 25 percent. Attacked from the front and left flank, partly also from the rear, the remainder of the company, approximately twenty men, had to surrender. Only a few succeeded at the last moment in escaping and even a portion of these men was immediately mowed down by the ensuing pursuit fire. The company commander succeeded in reaching the battalion command post, from which point, standing and firing free hand, he shared in the defense against the overwhelming attack, until here too the envelopment of both flanks brought things to an end.[27]

The companies opposing the 78th Company experienced the same fate. When two guns threatened his platoon, Cpl. John Pruitt, one of the original members of the company, dashed ahead. In a vicious assault he killed or captured the gunners, then pushed on behind the barrage. Reaching a dugout, this one-man hurricane captured forty more enemy soldiers cowering underground from the shelling.[28]

Brannen, separated from his 80th Company, joined a platoon on the right flank of the 78th Company. He vividly described how this group enveloped one of the German machine guns.

Instead of trying a direct assault, we decided to flank it. The lieutenant asked for some men to go around each flank. Three of us went to the left. When we were in close proximity to the nest, we were a little too exposed, and the fellow on my right fell, killed. As I jumped for protection into a ditch nearby, a fusillade of bullets caught me below the heart on the left side, through one lens of the field glasses, and against my bandoleer of ammunition. The best I remember, ten bullets in my own belt exploded, but they had deflected the enemy bullets, saving my life. My own bullets ripped my coat to shreds as they exploded and went out over my left shoulder by the side of my face. My cloth bandoleer and the field glasses caught on fire. I got them off me and then replaced the field glasses around my neck again as they quit burning. I collected myself together and, with the other companion in the ditch, looked for our machine gunner but saw that Americans were now in possession. I suppose we had helped by drawing fire while the others rushed, for on going up there I found three dead Germans stretched [out] by two guns.[29]

Brannen escorted the prisoners to the rear, using them as litter bearers for wounded marines and French artillerymen. At the field hospi-

tal the surgeon checked Brannen's burns and scrapes. The marine felt
that his wounds were superficial and was surprised when the doctor
tagged him for evacuation.[30]

In the 79th Company's first encounter with a German machine
gun, a bullet gave Lt. Amos Shinkle a nasty head wound that took him
out of the war for good. But the ever able Lt. Jack West sprang up and
took command. Shinkle told West that the company's objective was
the Medeah Ferme road, and the company pressed on.

The rolling barrage doubly served as an unmistakable control
measure for the companies of 2/6. The destructive wall of shrapnel
and dust delineated an unambiguous beacon to every marine, guiding their way up the hill. The artillery also dropped a thick cloud of
white smoke in front of the advancing waves that obscured the attacking riflemen from German machine gunners on the crest.[31]

As Williams's marines neared the crest just before 8:30, German
resistance began to disintegrate. The continuous drum fire unhinged
many of the defenders, who fled before it or eagerly surrendered as
it passed. The 2/74 war diary describes the last minutes of the assault:

> But now the Americans appeared also at the front, supporting
> their advance from the direction of Sattelberg with machine-
> gun fire. Again they walked into a warm reception in the
> form of our rifle and machine-gun fire. This, however, was
> greatly weakened by the enemy's previous artillery prepara-
> tion, which, by direct hits and splinters, had rendered useless
> about 50 per cent of the machine guns, there having been no
> opportunity to shelter them by bomb-proof dugouts. The
> light and heavy machine guns still intact after the bombard-
> ment were constantly employed on the flanks, so that there
> were but two useful light machine guns emplaced along the
> [Medeah Farm road] at the time the Americans appeared
> there too.[32]

Approaching the crest of the ridge, the 79th Company ran into this
stubborn pocket of Germans along the road. The defenders unleashed heavy machine-gun fire, but the combined firepower of the
company's rifles blanketed the enemy trench, pinning the Germans
below ground level. The 2/74 diary continues:

> But already the enemy, unmindful of the heavy losses suffered,
> had approached within a very short distance of our lines. The

battalion commander put into lines the men of the sub-staff under the command of Lieutenant van der Kammert, the machine-gun officer. They fired free-hand from the parapet of the trench. Despite all this, the Americans came forward until they were at a hand-grenade throw's distance, and also appeared again suddenly, this time greatly outnumbering our own men, on the right and left flanks where the trenches had been completely leveled by the artillery bombardment. They appeared also even in the rear. Further resistance was out of the question, most of the light machine guns having fired their last round, and the half-battalion being surrounded on both flanks. Only a few men succeeded in escaping unharmed, closely pursued by airplanes that fired at random from a height of fifty meters, and their escape was made possible only by the dense shrubbery and by utilization of the changing range of the box barrage. The enemy had appeared at the Sommepy-Saint Etienne road, cunningly utilizing the depressions, in extraordinarily superior numbers, according to some reports outnumbering our troops by twenty to one. Here, finally, our men, retreating at last, were forced to fight through the ring of enemies that gradually enveloped them.[33]

West's marines swarmed over the Germans, bagging fifty prisoners, twenty-five machine guns, and five artillery pieces. A few more yards and the marines had crossed the Medeah Farm road. West arrayed his men to defend the objective. Paradis, who had participated with the 79th Company, pitied the young German prisoners. "They were so scared their knees actually knocked together."[34]

To West's left, as the 96th and 78th Companies had skirted the summit of Blanc Mont, the slope of the ground combined with enemy fire had caused the left-hand companies to drift to the right. Powers and much of the 80th Company could not be found. The 78th linked up with the 79th Company on its right. Williams's lieutenants began organizing the line to repel counterattacks, with the 96th bending back to face the high ground of Blanc Mont. The 81st Machine Gun Company arrayed its Hotchkiss guns among the four rifle companies, but the regiment's Stokes mortars and all but one of the one-pounders had not kept up with the rapid advance and were nowhere to be seen.

Williams sent a courier back to Lee with the following message, an innocuous miscommunication that would severely mislead the

4th Brigade's leadership: "Objective reached at 8:30 A.M. Position now being consolidated. From first information casualties appear to have been light and the bag of prisoners was good. Spirits of all very high. Barrage was beautiful. Williams." The battalion had *reached* the Medeah Farm road but had not *taken* Blanc Mont. Lejeune's order had identified 2/6's objective as the Medeah Farm road, from the Saint-Étienne road on the right to the division's left boundary. Lejeune's order specifically *included* the summit of Blanc Mont. But Williams had not received this order until ten minutes before going over the top.[35]

Some of Williams's marines had worked their way close to the summit. In fact, German artillery observers and headquarters troops had all fled or surrendered their dugouts by 8:30, and a determined effort might have secured the crest. This was certainly the perspective of the defending 2/74: "The Americans must have designated the Medeah Ferme-Blanc Mont Hill crest as their attack objective because, had they pushed ahead regardlessly. [*sic*] Not one man of our battalion would have been able to escape capture, not even by flight." Williams did not recognize his error and so did not assault and secure Blanc Mont. The French had failed to advance on the 2nd Division's left, and 2/6 began to take a pummeling from machine guns and one-pounders on its left flank and 88-mm artillery to its front. Among those killed by this fire was the 78th Company's dynamo, Corporal Pruitt. This oversight left the summit itself unoccupied and its western slope a covered avenue of approach for German counterattacks.[36]

Just before noon the 51st Division managed to work the 149th Infantry around the left flank of 2/6. Williams detected what he described as seven hundred to eight hundred troops trying to encircle him to the west. He sent a runner to 3/6, eight hundred yards to the rear, for support. But before any assistance arrived, Cates's marines and the 81st Company's machine gunners opened up a withering fire against the counterattack. Cates sprinted over to grab four French tanks he spotted trundling up the hill, part of the unit that should have accompanied the attack. The tanks obligingly crawled over and blasted apart the counterattack at point-blank range. "You should have heard the boche yell," Cates delightedly wrote home.[37]

The lieutenant's quick action stopped the German envelopment. But elements of the 159th now burrowed into the dense woods on the battalion's left flank. Direct fire from these flanking positions and from others to the front continued to whittle away at 2/6's numbers. Far worse, Lee and his superiors had misinterpreted Williams's "objective reached" message to mean that 2/6 held the summit of Blanc Mont. This miscommunication would contribute materially to a disastrous attack by the 5th Marines on October 4.[38]

An Accusation of Cowardice

Individual squads and platoons of the 80th Company had reached the summit intermingled with the other companies. But as the battalion consolidated its defense, Williams and others began to wonder what had become of the 80th in general and of Captain Powers in particular. Powers's own lieutenants accused him of lagging far to the rear.[39] When The Bull assembled his company commanders for a conference, Powers "had a lot to say," recalled Sellers. Sellers thought his story did not ring true, but the whole truth would not come out until after 2/6 had pulled back from Blanc Mont. In a startling case of bald-faced dereliction, Powers had issued hardly any instructions to his platoon commanders before the attack and lagged well to the rear throughout the assault.

Relieved by Williams after the battle, Powers submitted a detailed rebuttal. "The undersigned commanded the company as he understands the term," the former lawyer protested. He claimed that he had not abandoned his company during the advance but had run over to direct French tanks against a particularly stout machine-gun position, then supervised the collection of prisoners from some nearby dugouts. The fact that the barrage was still advancing up the hill, or that Powers had lost track of all but fifteen men of his company, appears not to have dissuaded him from his belief that he commanded the company "as he understood the term." Except for occasional peeks outside, Powers would keep deep underground in a captured bunker for the next two days.[40]

In Support on Blanc Mont, October 4–5

The battalion held onto the position it had seized the morning of October 3, leaving the German 149th Infantry in control of the summit. Early on October 4, the 5th Marines passed through 2/6 to continue the assault. For obscure reasons, the 5th Marines attacked without artillery support. Striking toward Saint-Étienne, the regiment took heavy fire from multiple directions, including from the 159th Infantry on top of Blanc Mont. The Germans stopped this attack cold, and the 5th Marines retreated in disorder.[41]

Still under the impression that Blanc Mont was secure, General

Neville ordered the 6th Marines to resume the offensive. Lee accordingly directed an attack for 2:30 P.M. It was only this order that prompted Williams to finally clarify the situation on the summit. At around 2:00 P.M. the major reported that his left flank rested 450 yards farther east than he had previously admitted. "The enemy consequently holds a good portion of Blanc Mont," he wrote.[42] Williams's error had misled the 4th Brigade into ordering the costly 5th Marines attack on October 4 under the false perception that the summit was secure.

Williams now reported that the enemy position on Blanc Mont was "heavily held with machine guns" and that any exposure within 2/6's positions immediately drew rifle and machine-gun fire. Having witnessed the slaughter of the 5th Marines, he cautioned Lee that an attack against Blanc Mont without artillery support and an advance by the French on the left could not succeed.[43]

The Bull concluded the report with a revealing tabulation of his effective strength: "78th Company: 95, 80th Company: 60, 79th Company: 85, 96th Company: 65." Even accounting for the 20 percent cadre left behind, these figures indicate losses of nearly five hundred of the eight hundred marines who had begun the attack, a startling casualty rate of 62 percent. As the *Muster Roll* records a total of only three hundred casualties for 2/6 during the entire Blanc Mont fight, Williams's figures suggest his companies had lost track of a large number of able-bodied men. This does not necessarily indicate that two hundred marines had shirked away from the front line; no doubt many had merely become cut off from their chain of command amid the fog of battle. Certainly the enfilading fire pinning 2/6's marines to their foxholes made an accurate count difficult to obtain. Nonetheless, the fact that a very large number of 2/6's marines had lost contact with their companies indicates a substantial breakdown in unit cohesion.[44]

The battalion's hospital corpsmen and litter bearers made heroic efforts to keep up with the many wounded. Under Lieutenant Mueller's leadership, the battalion aid station rapidly assessed, bandaged, and rushed casualties to the field hospital downhill by litter or ambulance. From its relatively covered location directly behind 2/6's position, Mueller's corpsmen were able to work unmolested. In a dramatic improvement from the debacle at Soissons, no casualty remained at the aid station longer than thirty minutes before evacuation.[45]

At 2:40 Williams reported by telephone that the machine-gun fire from his left made an advance impossible. On the basis of this, Lee attempted to reorient 3/6 against Blanc Mont. Once again the artillery could not respond as quickly to changing events as the infantry required. Maj. George Shuler, commanding 3/6, reported that incoming German artillery was far heavier than the destructive fires he had requested against Blanc Mont, which he described as "feeble." The division could not get its artillery and infantry to coordinate their actions before nightfall and thus postponed the attack.

One More Attack: October 5

Early on the morning of October 5, after a furious barrage, 3/6's marines swarmed over the summit of Blanc Mont. The artillery made a decisive difference; 3/6 reported the capture of 275 prisoners and eighty machine guns without losing a man. With Blanc Mont now securely in American hands and the French more or less closed up on the 2nd Division's left flank, Lejeune ordered the 4th Brigade to resume the attack toward Saint-Étienne. At 8:45, seventy minutes after receiving word that 3/6 had seized the crest, Lee issued the following order: "This regiment will be organized at once and be prepared to pass through the 5th Marines when ordered. Order of battalions, front to rear, Williams [2nd], Shuler [3rd], Barker [1st]."[46]

Lee issued the order to execute the attack at 12:50 P.M.: "The 6th Regiment advances at once. Advance to Saint Etienne, keeping liaison with French on our left and the 3rd Brigade on our right. French have already advanced. Halt at Saint Etienne and await orders." Lieutenant Colonel Holcomb came to Williams's command post before the attack began and modified the order, directing Williams to halt when he reached a ridge southeast of Saint-Étienne. The attack did not commence till 3:00.[47]

In a dumbfounding repeat of the previous day's mistake, the infantry would again strike without a rolling barrage. Down to less than three hundred effectives, 2/6 led the attack on a fifteen-hundred-yard front, with the 78th and 79th Companies leading and the 80th and 96th Companies in support. With strength greatly reduced, each company formed in a single wave to cover the wide front.[48]

On the left flank, the lack of artillery support did not materially hinder the advance. Lieutenant Sellers reported that the 78th Company reached its objective, an east-west ridge fifteen hundred yards southeast of Saint-Étienne, without encountering opposition. Powers creditably advanced at the head of his company on this occasion.[49]

On the right, however, a machine-gun position concealed in heavy

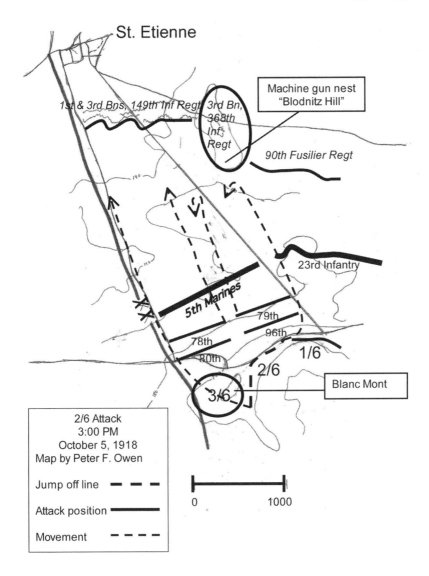

St. Etienne

Machine gun nest
"Blodnitz Hill"

1st & 3rd Bns, 149th Inf Regt   3rd Bn,
368th
Inf
Regt

90th Fusilier Regt

23rd Infantry

5th Marines

79th

78th   96th

80th   1/6

2/6

3/6   Blanc Mont

2/6 Attack
3:00 PM
October 5, 1918
Map by Peter F. Owen

Jump off line

Attack position

Movement

0   1000

woods on Blodnitz Hill ripped apart the 79th Company. Cates called this fortification "the largest machine gun nest that I have ever seen." A battalion commander in the 23rd Infantry watched with horror as Lieutenant West's marines advanced toward the position, which had annihilated his own command on October 4. The army major dispatched a runner to West *ordering* the marine to stop. West sent the runner back with the tactful reply, "My orders were to take a position in the woods, and any further word from him would find me in the woods."[50]

The company managed to overcome a few outposts, but by the time West reached the tree line, the few marines with him could not make any further headway. Trying to reorganize his thin line, West received a severe wound in the head. Lt. Maurice Barnett took charge of the company, had West carried out of the woods, and pulled his tiny command back to link up with Lieutenant Cates, who had established a supporting position with his 96th Company.[51]

The battalion held this ragged line until early on October 6, when Shuler's 3/6 relieved it. No longer capable of offensive action, 2/6 straggled back to its previous position on Blanc Mont. The 6th Marines continued the advance after an hour's artillery preparation. Shuler's battalion attacked behind a rolling barrage across the very ground vacated by the 79th Company, piercing the German line of trenches between Blodnitz Hill and Saint-Étienne. Williams's 2/6 sat out this fight as well as the last three days of the battle on Blanc Mont until the U.S. 36th Division relieved the 2nd Division on October 9. Captain Powers remained deep underground for almost this entire period. When relief finally came, he merely sent runners to his platoons with instructions to pull out and meet him at the foot of the hill.[52]

The Essence of Combat

The night attack on October 2 and the assault up the slope of Blanc Mont on October 3 were spectacular successes, marred only by the confusion over the seizure of the summit. The intrepid lieutenants of 2/6, especially Cates, Sellers, and West, once again led from the front. Of particular note, the rifle companies had maintained the momentum of the attack and reduced casualties by aggressively exploiting covering terrain and by assaulting with fire and movement. Sellers neatly captured the essence of combat in a letter home: "We start over in a pretty formation but the fight soon degenerates into a sort of free for all, every man for himself and everybody right up behind the line of the barrage, which is proper."[53] The tactical renaissance of late August and September paid unmistakable dividends at Blanc Mont in October. At the company level, the esprit de corps, training, experience, leadership, and self-confidence within 2/6 combined in the assault on October 3 to make Blanc Mont its finest hour.

Even Major Williams deserves high accolades for his leadership. As the commander, he bore the responsibility for the decision to attack at H-Hour behind the barrage instead of awaiting the French tanks. Whether through his own judgment, explicit guidance from Lee, or by his willingness to listen to his lieutenants, Williams ensured that his battalion did not repeat the mistake of Soissons. Aggressiveness and courage were required on October 3, and The Bull delivered.

On the crest of Blanc Mont, though, Williams failed to recognize the need to secure the summit on his left flank, for he believed that 2/6 had attained the objective. This wooded hillock posed a severe threat to his position and to the security of other battalions passing through 2/6. Even after fighting off the enveloping counterattack to his left, Williams failed to understand his vulnerability and neither attempted to clear the wood himself nor advised other commanders of the danger. He was mistakenly convinced that he had carried out his explicit instructions and simply waited for the French to join up on his left. This failure subsequently exposed both 2/6 and the 5th Marines to crippling fire from their left flank, which consequently rendered both nearly combat ineffective.

For this blunder, Lee, Neville, and even Lejeune must shoulder their share of the blame, for higher echelons had failed to deliver Williams a copy of the order until minutes before the attack. Consequently, The Bull had only an approximate idea of the plan. With 2/6 leading the main assault of an entire army, one wonders why neither Lee nor Holcomb came forward to brief Williams face to face, either before the assault or on the summit. Such active leadership at higher echelons might have alleviated an important miscommunication and its consequent loss of life.

Several other external factors created conditions that optimized 2/6's performance. The "beautiful" preplanned barrage provided the fire superiority and obscuration that 2/6 had been denied at Bouresches and Soissons. The tanks, though late in arriving, helped devastate the German counterattack against the 96th Company on October 3. Even Allied aircraft added their firepower against the beleaguered defenders. Conversely, it was the lack of supporting artillery that doomed the 79th Company's assault on October 5.

This latter oversight cannot be explained away as a well-intentioned mistake through inexperience at higher echelons of command. Lejeune, Neville, and Lee had all seen first hand the dramatic results artillery support had provided to attacking infantry on October 3. They and their staffs had witnessed only that morning the difference preplanned artillery made in 3/6's assault on the summit of

Blanc Mont and arranged a rolling barrage in support of another successful attack by 3/6 on October 6. The inability of the 2nd Division to support 2/6's attack on October 5 suggests that the division's command-and-control system was manifestly incapable of maintaining an operational tempo higher than a single coordinated assault per day.[54]

The 2nd Battalion had conducted the attack on October 5 with fewer than three hundred effectives. Even had the division coordinated adequate artillery, the battalion had been whittled down to little more than company strength. Such a small force likely could not have overwhelmed the defenders of "the largest machine gun strong point [Cates] had ever seen." But many missing marines were not battle casualties, rather having come adrift from their companies in the confusion of battle. Combined with heavy attrition, these losses rendered 2/6 combat ineffective in the aftermath of a single *successful* assault. This breakdown suggests a marked change in the character of the battalion. While 2/6 could now achieve spectacular results in the attack, its ranks could no longer so easily absorb the high cost of such assaults and maintain its esprit and cohesion.

8   The Meuse-Argonne

CAPT. KIRT GREEN HAD HIS WORK CUT OUT FOR HIM. His predecessor, Captain Powers, had let down the tired young men of the 80th Company assembled around him. The rank and file disdained two key leaders, Lieutenant Skoda and First Sergeant Dean, as cronies of the battalion commander and members of a cabal of prewar regulars. Even as Green looked into the expectant faces of his men, Powers was engaged in finger-pointing correspondence with Lieutenants Hopke and Ehrhart, two decorated platoon commanders who had risen from the ranks. The 80th was not a happy company.

This was Green's first command, and it had been a long time coming. Green had enlisted in 1905, and his lengthy record was far from spotless. A summary court-martial had convicted him of being AWOL for six days. In Panama he had incurred more infractions for fighting, neglecting duties, and missing class at NCO school. Nonetheless, someone recognized leadership potential in him, for he had been promoted to sergeant in 1908 (the same year he married a young Irish girl from County Mayo) and three years later was accepted into Marine Officer School at Parris Island. Green was a keen student of military history and the American Civil War in particular, but when it came to his routine duties, he apparently had trouble meeting the school's strict standards. He incurred two minor infractions in as many months and was consequently dropped from the officer course. Over the next six years, Green bounced from marine barracks to sea duty. Despite his past difficulties, his innate leadership ability helped him ascend the ranks to sergeant major. When the declaration of war brought a scramble to expand the officer ranks, the Marine Corps dusted off Green's file, concluded that the thirty-year-old sergeant major was not such a bad fellow after all, and commissioned him a second lieutenant in April 1917.[1] Now, a year and a half later, Green was undeniably a lifer, untested in battle, and standing in front of a company of battle-weary veterans who had come to regard career men with suspicion and even scorn.

If the new captain was intimidated by the situation, he hid it well.

Green's brief remarks were upbeat, to the point, and well received by the rank and file. He told the men that he had never before been at the front, but he was proud to be in the 80th Company and would try his best to give the men proper leadership—and by the way, General Lejeune had authorized furloughs to the nearby town of Chalons for a few men each day.

The bit about furloughs won over the "lads." There were still a lot of miseries a private in the 80th Company could wallow in if he chose, but now there was the prospect of getting away from it all for a day and a night; this new Captain Green did not seem like a bad sort. The men began to bounce back. It was not long before "everyone in the company loved Captain Green," recalled Sergeant Paradis.[2]

Green was not the only untested regular officer joining the battalion. Maj. Clyde Metcalf relieved Captain Collier as the battalion second in command. Thus far the major's wartime experience was limited to guarding enemy prisoners and training replacements. Thin, studious, and acerbic looking, Metcalf would later become chief historian of the Marine Corps. Collier took command of the 79th Company.[3]

Sellers and Cates, both now captains despite less than eighteen months of service, retained their companies. Most NCOs in 2/6 now had just as little time in uniform as these new captains. Small-unit leadership heretofore had been a consistent hallmark of the battalion's successes. Thus far, 2/6 had plucked standout wartime volunteers from the ranks to fill its NCO vacancies. The quality of marine replacements restocking Lejeune's battalions immediately after Blanc Mont portended that fewer natural leaders would emerge in the months to come. Many of the newcomers who joined 2/6 seemed to lack the spirit and physical constitution of their predecessors. "They are naturally green and inexperienced," Cates wrote home. "But they will soon learn, as they will be mixed up with old men."[4]

Some of these "old men" were returning NCOs who had recovered from their wounds. Sgts. Victor Sparks and Melvin Krulewitch and Cpl. Carl Brannen returned to leaven the ranks with their battle-wise confidence. Yet Cates's concern was well founded, for the battalion's movements over the next few weeks afforded insufficient time to drill the replacements in tactics. Of even greater concern, these men seemed to lack the physical and mental toughness that constituted the fiber of the battalion. Sergeant Paradis wondered "how [the new replacements] ever passed the examination to get into the marines. They sure must have been scraping the barrel back home. They were still so scared they did not want to leave their foxholes." Like their predecessors who had reached the battalion in the summer, these newcomers were all volunteers who had completed the Marine Corps's uncompromising recruit training. The men joining the 80th Company may have been an anomaly, or Paradis may have exaggerated the deficiencies of a few. But if his observations held true for the majority of replacements, continued heavy casualties would ultimately dilute leadership within the battalion's critical NCO ranks.[5]

"I Prayed I Would be Killed"

After Blanc Mont the battalion had only four days to familiarize the new arrivals with its offensive tactics. The remainder of the intervening three weeks consisted of marching and countermarching in a series of bewildering maneuvers that wore out the men. The 4th Brigade was detached from the 2nd Division on October 19 and dispatched by the French command on a grueling forced march to relieve a French division at the front. The 6th Marines covered twenty-five miles on October 21, slogging across the shell-torn battlefield at Blanc Mont. Many of the men cursed their new, inferior, and painful English boots. Upon reaching their destination, disbelieving leaders learned that they were required to push on immediately that night to reconnoiter the French front line more than seven miles away, adding fifteen miles roundtrip to the day's total. "That was the last straw," wrote Cates. "I was ready to quit then." Sergeant Sparks could barely squeeze his swollen feet into his boots. "I prayed I would be killed and get over doing anything."[6]

Sparks's prayer for a respite was granted, though without his demise. The French Fourth Army cancelled the relief of the French division. After a night's sleep the battalion retraced its route at a more leisurely pace over the next two days, followed by a treasured day of rest and hot meals. The weary riflemen unlaced their hated English boots and aired their sore feet in the sunlight. All the hiking had pushed them to their physical limit. The regiment's official history admitted, "This regiment could not have continued the movement by marching on the 24th of October without its combat efficiency being seriously effected."[7]

In the near term, the poor health of replacements and exhausted veterans alike would increase their vulnerability to illness. Krulewitch discovered that his buddy Victor Sparks had come down with influenza and had the hospital corpsman look him over. Sparks's temperature had risen to 104; he was tagged for evacuation.[8]

The following morning the reason for the reverse of orders was revealed. The dreaded French *camions* pulled into the battalion area to truck the marines to the Meuse-Argonne sector to rejoin the U.S. First Army. The 2nd Division was about to spearhead yet another attack.

The forced marches had exacerbated a bitter mood creeping through 2/6. Veterans who had endured unfathomable hardships in combat found themselves pushed to exhaustion without apparent reason. Veteran and replacement alike felt among strangers in their own battalion, alienated from all but their closest buddies. Leaders within 2/6 and above were unknown to them, distrusted, and suspected of indifference to the men in the line. Cold days and increasingly longer nights heralded the onset of the endless misery of a winter at the front. To the sprinkling of veterans, the stirring days when they had avenged pitiful refugees and when newspaper headlines had extolled their victories around the world were all distant memories. The battalion had also lost the close, almost familial comradeship built through a year of arduous training and trials in combat. Strangers in their own platoons, the veterans huddled in the cold truck beds and bounced painfully toward one more battle.

The Operational Situation

The 2nd Division's spectacular seizure of Blanc Mont had not led to a breakthrough in the Meuse-Argonne as hoped. If one were to gauge the Allied efforts exclusively by the progress of the U.S. First Army in the Meuse-Argonne, it would appear likely that the war might yet proceed into the next year. By late October three separate American attacks had failed to gain more than nine miles. Conversely, British and French armies were now achieving impressive gains that contrasted conspicuously with the American setback. Faced with the threat of collapse, Germany stubbornly fought on while opening a dialogue with President Wilson, seeking an armistice based on his Fourteen Points. Such an end conflicted with the ambitions of French president George Clemenceau, who sought harsher terms and was considering demanding nothing less than unconditional surrender. The U.S. representative to the Allied Supreme War Council, Gen. Tasker Bliss, summarized the imperative to revive the Meuse-Argonne offensive: "[The French and British will] attempt to minimize the American effort as much as possible. They think they have got the Germans on the run and they do not need as much help as they were crying for a little while ago."[9]

With such political issues hanging overhead and his army's reputation in the balance, Pershing felt considerable pressure to resusci-
tate his sluggish campaign. Resolved to succeed, the general ordered
a fourth attack in the Meuse-Argonne for November 1, with the dependable 2nd Division spearheading its main effort.[10]

The Tactical Situation

Upon arriving in the First Army's sector, the 2nd Division reported
to Gen. Charles Summerall's V Corps to take its position in line for
the attack. The 2nd Division would relieve the U.S. National Guard's
42nd "Rainbow" Division. The 42nd Division faced a series of three
east-west ridges, each heavily fortified. The slopes and valleys in this
sector lay open and devoid of cover, much like Blanc Mont. The V
Corps's ambitious plan intended for the 2nd Division to seize all
three ridges the first day, an unprecedented advance of six miles.

The First Army's disappointing progress to date hung heavily over
a V Corps planning conference in late October. Summerall pointedly
asked Lejeune how far the 2nd Division could realistically advance on
the first day of the offensive. Lejeune was surprisingly optimistic: "I
didn't believe any force could withstand the vigor, power and speed
of its initial attack when backed up by well-directed artillery fire; and
that I also was of the opinion that it would be able to take and hold
the final objective of the day provided one of its flanks was protected
by an adjacent division."[11]

Lejeune's confidence infected Summerall and his staff. On October 26 the men of 2/6 assembled around a barn, upon which some
V Corps headquarters soldiers had tacked a huge map of the Meuse-
Argonne sector. General Summerall hopped up on a large stump to
personally address the battalion. He was on a crusade to ensure that
every doughboy and leatherneck in his corps understood the purpose
of the offensive and his role in it. Sergeant Paradis recalled: "It was
the only pep talk I had ever heard on any front and the only time we
actually knew before we went in what our main purpose was outside
of stopping the Heinies or pushing them back. It sure had its effect
on the morale of the men. It was the first really good news they had
heard for months."[12]

Later that day Summerall addressed the officers of the 6th Marines separately. Describing the offensive in more detail, he told them
that theirs was a place of honor in the impending drive. "Then he
spoiled it all," recalled a disgusted Sellers. According to Lt. Gerald C.
Thomas, a platoon commander in 1/6, Summerall "lashed out at us

Ground Gained by First Army, November 1–11, 1918

as though we were raw, erring recruits. If we failed to take a single objective, he said, he would relieve and send to the rear our regimental commander, our brigade commander, and even our deeply-admired and respected division commander. It was a strange performance and one resented by all. Afterward, General Lejeune's call of 'three cheers for General Summerall' was met with stony silence."[13]

On that sour note, the officers of the 6th Marines returned to their commands to study Summerall's plan and the information available on the enemy defenses facing them. Six regiments of the German 41st and 52nd Divisions defended the Kriemhilde Line opposite the 2nd Division's zone. Each German regiment fielded only eight hundred infantrymen, giving the 2nd Division better than a three-to-one advantage. The line ran through the twin towns of Landres–Saint George, about a mile beyond the division jump-off position. The

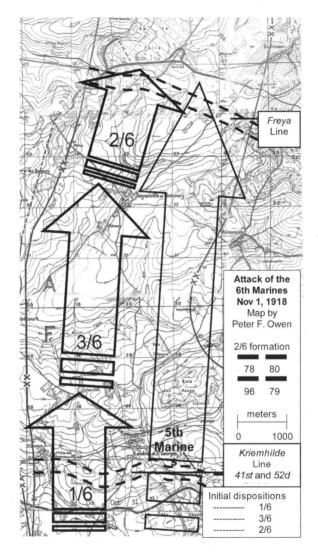

Attack of the
6th Marines
Nov 1, 1918
Map by
Peter F. Owen

2/6 formation

78   80

96   79

meters
0   1000

Kriemhilde
Line
41st and 52d

Initial dispositions
----------   1/6
----------   3/6
----------   2/6

Freya Line ran along the Barricourt Heights, five miles farther. The defenses were well-constructed and bolstered with sufficient automatic weapons and artillery, but with rumors of an impending armistice rampant in both armies, the defending Germans were already a beaten enemy.[14]

The 2nd Division would attack with the 6th Marines on the left and the 5th Marines on the right. The 3rd Brigade would follow in support. To maintain momentum, the lead battalion would halt after seizing the first ridge and let the two supporting battalions pass through. After the next battalion seized the second ridge, 2/6, as the trail battalion, would pass to the front and seize the final ridge, a partly wooded piece of terrain known as Barricourt Heights. Patterned after the successful assaults conducted on September 12 at Saint-Mihiel and on October 3 at Blanc Mont, the plan sought to maximize the fleeting destructive power that could be achieved by synchronizing preplanned artillery fires with the assault of fresh infantry. To maintain liaison with the 80th Division on its left, the 6th Marines formed a special task force under Maj. George Stowell consisting of a company from 3/6, a company from the 80th Division, and a Hotchkiss platoon from the regimental machine-gun company.[15]

With three hundred guns, artillery support would exceed what the division had enjoyed at Blanc Mont. Lavishly supplied with ammunition, the rolling barrage would advance at a leisurely pace of one hundred yards every eight minutes, a rate intended to simplify the infantry's ability to keep up. The division fire plan also had an additional measure of flexibility inserted to limit the damage that would result from one of the more common problems in previous American offensives. The attack order stated, "should the infantry at any time be unable to keep up with the barrage, the barrage may be recalled to some well established line, to rest there until the infantry lines are adjusted." Three hundred machine guns would fire a massed barrage, and a company of fifteen light Renault tanks, driven by American crews this time, would support the assault. The marines had never before gone into battle with such generous and responsive support.[16]

In contrast to rushed efforts in the past, commanders at every level were afforded plenty of time to familiarize themselves with plans and orders and to conduct their own preparations. Officers down to the platoon level entered the 42nd Division's lines to reconnoiter the ground over which they would attack.[17]

In another bright development, the battalion received around eight Browning Automatic Rifles (BAR). A superb weapon, the BAR would have made good the deficiency in organic firepower that had plagued the rifle companies since they had lost their Lewis guns. Unfortunately, the BARs arrived too late and in insufficient numbers to have a decisive influence on the battlefield. To offset this lack of firepower, the 78th Company was toting around two captured German machine guns, confident that the men would capture the needed ammunition during the assault.[18]

The evening after the battalion arrived at its assembly area, Captain Green summoned Sergeant Paradis to his hole. Paradis found the captain sitting cross-legged in front of his pup tent. Green had strewn maps around himself and was studying every inch of terrain he would fight over by candlelight. He expressed concern over Paradis's health and the difficulty he had encountered on the rough hike to Leffincourt. The sergeant assured him that he was fit to fight. Green then asked him how long he had been in the 80th Company. After Paradis replied that he was one of the last original members and had fought in all four engagements thus far, Green said: "Well sergeant, I've got some good news for you. I'm going to put you in the twenty percent reserve of the company who are to be left behind. You won't have to enter the lines with us this time." Having received this unexpected reprieve, Paradis slept more soundly that night than he had in months.[19]

To the Barricourt Heights

At 3:30 A.M. on November 1, American artillery erupted in a two-hour barrage. As the intense shelling deafened frontline troops on both sides, the 2nd Division pulled its forward companies back five hundred yards. The First Army had noted that prior to previous American attacks, German machine gunners had eased closer to the doughboys' forward positions to evade the rolling barrage. In a clever refinement, a ten-minute standing barrage crashed among the vacated American holes at 5:20, obliterating any German who had dared to slip forward. While this barrage pummeled enemy advanced outposts, the 4th Brigade's leading battalions, 1/6 and 1/5, assembled into attack formation and leaned forward tightly against the barrage line. At 5:30 the barrage began to creep forward. Five thousand marines followed in its wake. Among them was Victor Sparks, who went over the top with the 78th Company, medical tag and all.[20]

The lead battalions of the 5th and 6th Marines smashed through their objectives against stubborn opposition. By 8:00 A.M. 1/6 had secured the first objective. The rolling barrage remained stationary for an hour to allow 3/6 time to close up and pass through 1/6. Then 3/6 resumed the advance, with 2/6 following in trace. Renault tanks advancing with 3/6 compelled a large number of German artillerymen to surrender with their guns. When the 78th Company passed through the abandoned artillery, the marines realized organized resistance was disintegrating, and an exultant shout rolled down the company line; "The cry for victory," Krulewitch called it. Straining to pass through 3/6 and get at the Germans, Major Williams grew frustrated at the slow advance of the barrage.[21]

Around noon 2/6 at last took the lead, with the 78th and 80th Companies up and the 79th and 96th Companies in support. Three platoons of the 81st Machine Gun Company followed just behind the lead companies. Of the fifteen tanks that had started the attack with 1/6 and 1/5, all but three had broken down by the time 2/6 assumed the lead. These vehicles worked across the front of the brigade in advance of the infantry, helping overcome the remaining German opposition and destroying a solitary machine-gun position on Barricourt Heights.[22]

On the battalion's right, Captain Sellers sent Johnnie Kelly off with a message for Green in the 80th Company. But Kelly was disoriented; for some reason, he overshot the 80th Company. Beyond the 78th Company's left flank, he stumbled upon a group of riflemen he did not recognize.

"Is this the 80th!" he shouted.

"Yes, it's the 80th," they shouted back.

Something seemed out of place. These men did not look like marines. He inquired of a corporal leading a squad. "Is this the 80th?"

"Yes, it's the 80th," The corporal assured Kelly.

Kelly was still suspicious. "80th what?"

"80th Division," responded the corporal.

Kelly had crossed the division boundary and was among the right-flank battalion of the 80th Division. He had little time to reflect on his error. As he watched the green soldiers move forward, a German machine-gun plastered the squad and nearly killed him. His gas mask was cut to ribbons, and he counted sixteen punctures in his uniform, but he was remarkably unscathed. Recognizing that the inexperienced doughboys needed a hand, Kelly shouldered his way behind their Chauchat. He saw a patch of woods that offered a sheltered route forward. "Tell your men to beat it over there," he told the corporal. As the doughboys scurried for cover and their corporal loaded for Kelly, the young leatherneck peppered the German gun with bursts of Chauchat fire. Once the squad was under cover, he and the corporal dashed over to join them. They advanced under cover of the trees up to the hole, where they found the tripod with its gun and crew gone.

The gun had protected a group of underground dugouts. "Bomb all those f——ing holes!" Kelly ordered the doughboys. He tossed a couple of grenades from his own musette bag down the entrance to one dugout. Hearing muffled cries, Kelly eased down the steps to discover six terrified Germans and a badly wounded officer. He snatched up some maps and papers that he knew the intelligence section would want to see, then as the petrified Germans watched, he calmly sat and ate the remains of a meal left at their table. Ignoring the cries of the dying officer, Kelly consumed their horse steak and mashed potatoes, washing it down with a little wine.[23]

Following in trace of the 78th Company, the 79th Company's Captain Collier and his second in command fell wounded. Lt. Lloyd Houchin took over and led the company without a break in stride.[24]

On the left, the 80th Company's advance hesitated in front of a stubborn field gun. The German crew was using its precise accuracy and range in the direct-fire mode, sharp shooting at the Americans as they descended the opposite slope five hundred yards away. The marines dove into shell holes for cover. The men watched as the barrage continued to advance, slipping away from the stalled company.

This was the moment for which Kirt Green had been preparing for thirteen peacetime years of service. It was his first command, his first battle, and his first decision in combat. He summoned his officers to his shell hole while sizing up the situation. The solitary gun threatened to disrupt the 80th Company's attack. Every eight minutes the American barrage would creep another hundred yards forward. Green had time, if he used it well, to organize a coordinated attack that could envelop the gun and conserve lives.

The German gun crew spied the congregation in Green's hole. None of the officers had worn rank insignia, and Green carried a rifle and combat pack so as not to draw fire, but the Germans sensed the significance of the gathering. The gun barked and shot a high-velocity round smack into the middle of the group, blasting the knot of officers to smithereens. The force of the blast sent Green's helmet hurtling fifty feet into the air. Lt. George Ehrhart lost an eye. Shrapnel and concussion severely wounded platoon commanders King and Skoda. John Schneider, the last of the 80th Company's original lieutenants, was mortally wounded. Kirt Green, beloved husband, father, and commander, died instantly.[25]

Before the stunned 80th Company could fall to pieces, Lt. George Hopke, the only officer to escape the devastating round, got the men moving again. Gy. Sgt. James Foley leapt to his feet and took charge of two of the stalled platoons. Despite having lost five of its six officers in a moment, the 80th kept up the assault. There was no opportunity for fancy maneuvers, but all that was required was to follow the barrage when it moved. By standing up, shouting, gesturing, and leading from the front, Hopke and Foley revived the attack. The onslaught was too much for the solitary German gun, which was swept aside by the unstoppable leathernecks. Private McQuain watched as "the wave of men ahead of us almost had to kick the Germans off these guns before they got them stopped."[26]

By 3:15 P.M. 2/6 had seized its objective at the cost of only fifteen killed and sixty-one wounded, a very low casualty rate of less than 10 percent. Officer casualties, though, had been disproportionately heavy at 30 percent, with Green and Schneider killed and five others wounded. Williams consolidated his line, sending contact patrols to the left and right and reconnaissance to the front. As his marines dug in atop the Barricourt Heights, German machine guns continued to fire into their positions from within the Bois de la Folie to their direct front.[27]

Advancing under the umbrella of overwhelming artillery support, 2/6 had brushed aside the halfhearted defenders on November 1 and handily seized its objective with very light losses. Besides the magnificent support of the artillery, the direct support of the 81st Machine Gun Company had once again proved more responsive than it had been when operating under a separate machine-gun-only chain of command. The supporting tanks, though few in number, had worked well with the infantry. Their appearance in small numbers, along with the delivery of a handful of BARs, suggests that 2/6 would have benefited enormously from substantial numbers of these weapons had the war progressed into 1919.

On November 2 Williams pushed his 96th and 79th Companies forward. The 79th advanced to the northeast edge of the Bois de la Folie along the Nouart road without encountering opposition. But on their left a German machine gun and a one-pounder dogged the 96th. Cates's company was able to advance only five hundred yards. As this left the 79th in an exposed position, Lieutenant Houchin pulled back his marines before nightfall almost to their limit of advance of the day before.[28]

The Limits of Endurance, November 2–11

On the night of November 2, a column of soldiers from the 23rd Infantry marched up to 2/6's position along the Nouart road. Williams approached the regimental commander, Col. Edward Stone, to find out what was going on, and Sellers followed to listen. Stone informed the major that division had ordered a bold move: the entire 3rd Brigade would be passing through 2/6's lines along the road, infiltrating through the woods in a column of twos. The audacity of the plan dumbfounded Williams. "What about it?" inquired the infantry colonel. "Well," The Bull replied, possibly recalling his own debacle at Saint-Mihiel. "It's as good a way to commit suicide as any I know of."[29]

This time, however, boldness paid off, and the 23rd and 9th Infantry achieved a stunning success. After passing though the battalion's lines, the doughboys penetrated almost two miles by morning. The 3rd Brigade led the division's advance for the next seven days. Until the armistice on November 11, 2/6 shuttled from one support position to another. During these last nine days of the war, these marines saw very little fighting, losing only three men killed and thirty-six wounded to enemy fire. Nonetheless, casualties from sickness crippled the battalion.[30]

A driving rain began on November 2, and temperatures plummeted. Having left behind their raincoats, overcoats, and shelter tents, most of the men had only a solitary blanket for protection. A member of the 78th Company wrote, "When we would lie down our blankets would soak up water like a burning wick drawing oil."[31]

Compounding the marines' misery, the Germans poisoned many of the wells along their line of march. The Americans could not refill canteens until the battalion surgeon had purified the water with chemicals that left a nauseating taste. As a result, few men drank enough water. Many marines had begun to suffer from dysentery, a condition dehydration would now exacerbate. Carl Brannen recalled, "We were all weak and exhausted."[32]

After five months of combat, Cates referred to this miserable period as "the worst fight of our lives." He continued: "It was not the fighting, but it was the cold, rainy, muddy weather. It rained every day and was bitter cold. We were drenched to the skin and our blankets were soaked. . . . We went for hours and hours without food. No shelter of any kind, and we couldn't have fires. . . . God only knows how we existed. It was truly hell on earth." Sergeant Krulewitch recalled how the grueling marches and abysmal weather combined to bring the battalion to its knees. "Food was hard to get. We would hike to the limit of endurance through mud and rain; you couldn't pull your feet out of the mud. You had to reach down and put two hands around your ankle to pull your foot out of the mud and then take another step. We almost reached the limit of human existence, of human misery."[33]

Just when faced with these appalling conditions, 2/6 was struck a second blow by the great flu pandemic of 1918. Like no enemy action had done, the weather and the flu rendered 2/6 combat ineffective in the last ten days of the war. The muster roll reports 178 men evacuated sick by November 11. Far more actually left the front line; the 6th Marines's official history reports that the effective strength of the entire regiment was reduced by flu from 3,500 to only 1,000 men, an astounding loss of 70 percent of its men. Even in the slaughterhouse at Soissons, the regiment had lost only 50 percent in casualties.[34]

Anecdotal testimony from 2/6 supports this high sickness rate: Cates lost only thirty-two men to enemy fire in November, yet he wrote home that he had less than fifty men still with the 96th Company on November 11.[35] Sellers fell ill briefly, passing command to Lt. Emmons Robb, a mustang who had led a platoon at Blanc Mont. On November 9 The Bull himself fell out sick, and Major Metcalf found himself in command of a rapidly disintegrating battalion.[36]

There was more working against the battalion than the flu and the weather. After passing a grim group of bodies one evening, two marines in the 80th Company urged Private McQuain to fall out with them. "It is foolish to go on up there and just get killed," one explained. McQuain genuinely felt ill but decided to stick with the unit. He thought he might be needed. The two marines snatched evacuation tags off dead Americans and disappeared. McQuain did not see them again until after the Armistice.[37]

Few of the absent men could fairly be labeled malingerers. The influenza sweeping the battalion was a true global epidemic, one that would claim fifty million lives. Nonetheless, one suspects that the characteristic determination and obstinacy of the marines had been undermined by the miserable field conditions, the relatively low spirits of the men before the battle, and the whisper of an impending ceasefire.

The Meuse River Crossing and the Armistice, November 10–11

Sergeant Krulewitch could not sleep the night of November 9–10. Despite a nest made of twigs and boughs on the floor of his hole, his shelter filled with water and he arose soaked, cold, and hungry. His buddy Sparks had relented to illness and left for the hospital days before. Krulewitch was in a sour mood, but dawn brought an unaccustomed delight: hot chow for breakfast. "The rough food was like manna from the gods—hot black coffee and French canned meat with black bread. The revived marines started to chatter animatedly of rumors of an armistice. But the old hands were not so optimistic. 'How come we get it so good?' the veterans muttered."[38]

Two days before, on November 8, Marshall Foch had sat down across the table from a German delegation authorized to negotiate an armistice. Foch refused a temporary ceasefire, declaring, "Hostilities cannot cease before the armistice is signed." While not privy to the ongoing talks, the marines of 2/6 knew a truce might be concluded any day. A false United Press report had unleashed a premature celebration in New York on November 7. Then, Kaiser Wilhelm II had abdicated on November 9.[39] Carl Brannen for one did not believe the rumors. "A few weeks before we had heard that German troops had mutinied and killed the Kaiser." He wrote off the armistice talk as another false rumor.

Notwithstanding Brannen's skepticism, the war was in its final act. Yet the U.S. First Army would vigorously continue its attack in the Meuse-Argonne, affording the German Army no respite. On November 9 Lejeune had reported to V Corps headquarters, where he learned that his division would be ordered to cross the Meuse. Rather than force an opposed crossing in the face of the enemy, Lejeune wanted the American divisions on the east bank of the river to push forward, uncovering the crossing points. "I stated that our reconnaissances clearly indicated that the east bank of the Meuse was strongly held, many machine guns being in place and the enemy artillery being very active." To Lejeune's dismay, upon returning to his division, he was notified that his proposal had been disapproved. The 2nd Division would have to fight its way across the Meuse on the night of November 10–11.[40]

Lejeune's estimate of enemy strength was accurate. Along the riverbank, remnants of the 31st Division, with a total strength of 850 men and twenty-five machine guns, and the 353rd Regiment of the 88th Division, with 380 men and eleven machine guns, had established a thin outpost line stretching more than six miles along the east bank of the Meuse. The main line of resistance ran along the high ground above the river, where the Germans had insufficient infantry to organize a cohesive defense. About 1,000 infantry had been scraped together from the 52nd Division at Vigneron Farm and the 236th Division between Autreville and Moulins. While the Germans could not hope to hold the river line indefinitely, they could expect to make the marines and doughboys pay dearly to cross. Their artillery was still strong, lethal, and hidden from American reconnaissance planes due to stubborn and capable German pilots flying overhead.

Without precise locations of the enemy artillery, American counter-battery fire could not silence the guns.[41]

With the American regiments at 30 percent strength, the 2nd Division held merely a three-to-two advantage. Despite the desperate condition of its battalions, the 2nd Division ordered the 4th Brigade to cross the Meuse on what would be the last night of the war. The 5th Marines would cross at Letanne, and the 6th Marines, reinforced with 3/5, were ordered to conduct the main attack farther north at Mouzon. Both towns lay on the opposite bank, affording cover and concealment to the defenders. Open flat fields ran along the bank on the American side. Steep hills on the German side towered nearly five hundred feet above the river, dominating the crossing sites.

For obscure reasons, Colonel Lee did not exercise command of his regiment at the Mouzon crossing, instead placing all four battalions under the tactical control of Major Shuler, the commander of 3/6. The 12th Field Artillery, reinforced with four batteries of 155-mm howitzers from the 17th Field Artillery, would fire in support of the 6th Marines. The 15th Field Artillery, reinforced with two batteries from the 17th Field Artillery, would support the 5th Marines. This was roughly one-fourth of the fire support the 4th Brigade had enjoyed on November 1. In General Neville's estimate, the American artillery was insufficient to support his brigade, and he requested massing all of his fires in support of a single crossing point. Nevertheless, he was directed to proceed with two separate crossings.[42] With the possibility of an armistice increasing by the hour, the marines would attempt to cross the icy Meuse River despite the misgivings of both their division and brigade commanding generals and their regimental commander's abrogation of direct authority.

The Last Night of the War

On the afternoon of November 9, Williams led 2/6 on one last march to a wooded bivouac area not far from the river before allowing his own medical evacuation. Metcalf found himself facing the daunting prospect of a night river crossing as his first tactical operation, with no more than three hundred soggy, hungry, and mostly ill leathernecks to lead across. He likely felt very much alone. Metcalf was as much a stranger to his men as he was to the front. He and his new command stood by all November 10 in the wet forest, awaiting orders.[43]

The 78th Company veterans had grown openly suspicious of the sudden improvement in their treatment. The men had just finished their second hot meal of the day: steak, potatoes, and white bread. Lieutenant Robb, commanding the handful of marines still present for duty, waited until they had finished eating before dropping the ax: "Every man draw four grenades, two extra bandoliers of ammunition and stand by." The marines were about to learn why they had "had it so good today."[44]

In the 80th Company the stalwarts who had stuck it out questioned the need for the attack so close to the end of the war. Private McQuain later wrote: "We had begun to believe the Armistice rumors by now. We could not see the advantage of trying to cross the Meuse tonight. Why not wait and see what happened to the Armistice the next day, and then attack, if necessary? Such were the thoughts of a majority of the men. Again, we were to find that we were not getting paid for thinking."[45]

Shortly after dark, guides led Metcalf and his tiny battalion to the railroad yard about two hundred yards from the crossing site opposite Mouzon. The time of attack had been set for 9:30 P.M., but German artillery was already dropping high-explosive rounds on the roads leading to the crossing site. Metcalf detoured to avoid the shelling and did not reach his attack position until 10:15. Major Schuler arrived shortly thereafter with 3/6.

At 10:30 Schuler learned from an engineer lieutenant named James Slade that the 2nd Engineers had constructed one bridge in the relative shelter of the railroad yard before carrying it down to the riverbank at 9:00. Slade was waiting to hear from another engineer officer at the river if he was ready to throw it across. The lieutenant also told Schuler that when the engineers had carried the span down to the riverbank, the Germans on the opposite bank had detected the activity and opened the artillery and machine-gun fire that continued to harass them. Slade suggested throwing the first bridge across now and forcing their way across, following with the second bridge as soon as the engineers had it constructed.

Schuler had no intention of sending his marines across the Meuse over a single flimsy footbridge into the face of obviously alert defenders. Enemy machine gunners would be able to concentrate all their fire against the lone span. If the bridge failed, marines would be trapped on the far bank with no means of retreat or reinforcement. The major said that he would not cross until two bridges were ready and detailed forty marines to assist the engineers. He summarized the situation in a report to Lee just after midnight. A note of pessimism and perhaps resignation crept into his note. Once the second bridge was ready, Schuler avowed, "We will go across and do our best."[46]

Construction proceeded at an excruciatingly lethargic pace. The engineers had carried the first bridge down to the river at 9:00, but it was not reported ready until 12:05 A.M. At that same time, Slade told Schuler that the second bridge was ready to be carried down to the river. Gauging by the time it took to prepare the first pontoon, the major expected it would be another three hours before he crossed. While the forty marines assisted Slade's engineers in carrying the wooden bridge to the river, Schuler sent his scout officer along to monitor progress. He returned two hours later and reported that the bridges would not be ready until 4:00.

As his doughboys and leathernecks battled to cross the Meuse, Lejeune agonized, knowing full well that an armistice might be signed at any hour. "The night of this last battle of the war was the most trying night I have ever experienced. The knowledge that in all probability the Armistice was about to be signed caused the mental anguish, which I always felt because of the loss of life in battle, to be greatly accentuated, and I longed for the tidings of the cessation of hostilities to arrive before the engagement was initiated; but it was not to be, and many a brave man made the supreme sacrifice for his country in the last hours of the war."[47]

Along the railroad bank, the 78th Company huddled, ready to provide covering fire across the river or to charge across the flimsy footbridge. In the distance the bonfires of burning supplies illuminated the fog. Machine-gun and rifle fire occasionally cracked through the night, and high-explosive rounds crashed intermittently along the river. The return fire was lethal, but compared to previous actions, it seemed comparatively light and caused little anxiety.

As the engineers and marines assembled the clumsy bridges, artillery shells exploded around them with greater frequency. Taking in the scene, the 78th Company riflemen began to feel decidedly exposed as they lay on the railroad embankment overlooking the crossing. Sergeant Krulewitch described what happened next:

> Suddenly there came a new note in the approach of a whiz-bang—and every marine froze to the spot. Each knew from experience that this particular high explosive had his name on it. Even if cover had been available, none could have been reached in time. Fascinated, immobile, they could only await the end.

The shell landed squarely in the middle of the company.
And in that fraction of a second between hit and explosion,
there was no thought as to past and future. Each soldier
braced himself for the terrific impact of the next moment
when the fuse would detonate the charge.

Nothing happened. For that little group of men came the
war's greatest thrill—and my best birthday present. The fuse
was a dud.[48]

At the Mouzon crossing site, the weight of decision now came to
rest upon the shoulders of the four battalion commanders. Schuler,
Metcalf, Stowall (now commanding 1/6), and the commander of 3/5,
Henry Larsen, huddled together at 4:00 A.M. to determine if a crossing could still be attempted—although telephones had been wired
between Mouzon and the regimental command post, Colonel Lee
played no part in the decision. Schuler stated that the determining
factor was that no word had come from the river as to the condition
of the second bridge. With only an hour to go before daylight, he
believed that the conditions had not been established for a successful
attack. As the officer in tactical command and a seasoned veteran of
five campaigns, his opinion met no opposition from the other three
majors. The four commanders determined on their own authority to
abort the assault.[49]

This decision strikes one as especially significant because the official and eyewitness reports conflict on important details of the
crossing. Schuler's messages indicate that the crossing was never
attempted purely due to the slow construction of the bridges. Conversely, the commanding officer of the 2nd Engineers stated in his
after-action report, "Two other footbridges were assembled at the
riverbank north of Mouzon and the Infantry notified that they were
ready, but they notified the 2nd Engineers that the plan to cross there
had been abandoned."[50]

Williams's after-action report, obviously based on others' observations since he was not present, states that the engineers put one
bridge across but a direct hit by artillery swept it downstream. Sellers states in his memoir, "Fortunately, the Germans had blown up
both the bridges the 6th Marines were supposed to use, so we never
crossed."[51]

Sergeant Krulewitch's memoir supports this account, but he goes
on to say that marines actually crossed the Meuse: "The first bridge,
a precarious, two plank affair made fast to the opposite bank by the

tenacious efforts of the 2nd Engineers, had been swept away by the swift current and well-directed artillery fire. The second bridge, held in place for a time by the desperate efforts of men up to their shoulders in flood water and weighed down by heavy marching gear, was thrown across in the face of withering machine-gun fire, and a desperate counter-attack was successfully beaten off by the first companies across. The bridgehead was now secure."[52]

Carl Brannen's account likewise suggests at least one bridge was emplaced at Mouzon and that some marines crossed it: "The boats were tied side by side and a plank laid across them to walk on. When this bridge was made long enough to reach across the stream, the lower end was tied to our side and a soldier took the other end, swimming the cold treacherous river, and fastened it to the other side. The troops carried their equipment, ammunition, and rifles in their hands so as to have a better chance to get out if they made a wrong step in the darkness."[53]

To further muddle what really happened, Lee sent Schuler the following message by runner at 2:30: "Had message from Larsen [3/5] that Stowell [1/6] had crossed and he was about to cross. Advise anything further about this." Lee's message was likely based on an erroneous report, considering the roundabout path it took to reach him and the absence of any mention of marines crossing at Mouzon in the official operations reports and unit histories. Krulewitch and Brannen likely confused some details with the 5th Marines crossing downstream. There, three battalions, including one on loan from the 89th Division, had battled their way across the Meuse at Letanne. They secured the heights above the crossing by dawn, though at a cost of 435 men.[54]

None of the four battalion commanders at Mouzon had demonstrated exceptional vigor or enthusiasm for the operation. There is no indication that any of them walked the short distance from the railyard to the crossing to personally assess conditions there before concluding that the thing could not be done. Schuler in particular seemed content to let the futile construction effort run its course.

These four majors could not have known that even as they conferred, German and Allied negotiators were concluding final terms for an armistice that would cease hostilities at 11:00 A.M. Nonetheless, they were aware an abrupt end to the war might come at any time. They may have known of Lejeune's reservations about the operation. Schuler certainly shared Neville's assessment that artillery support was inadequate. At four o'clock in the morning on the cold banks of the Meuse River, pushing their haggard marines across the rickety bridges promised the possibility of failure, the probability of heavy losses, and the almost certain achievement of nothing of strategic value. Their decision to cancel the attack must be judged as tactically inescapable and an act of commendable moral courage.

The decision was met by unanimous relief among the marines. "I was very glad not to cross the river, I can tell you that," admitted Cates. By sunrise 2/6 had pulled back to the relative safety of its bivouac in the Bois de Fond de Limon. As the men shivered and wondered what would come next, the following message reached Metcalf: "8:30 A.M. Fifth Corps—Armistice signed and takes effect at 11:00 A.M. this morning."[55]

At 11:00 a final German shell crashed defiantly into the battalion's position, fortunately killing no one. Cates wrote: "Then there was a death like stillness along the whole front. Could it be that it was all over? We could not believe it possible. Each man would look at the others in doubt. Finally, word came that the armistice had been signed. Not a cheer did I hear, but there was not a man in the regiment that did not thank God that rainy, muddy, cold morning that it was all over and that he was safe."[56]

Sergeant Krulewitch described the 78th Company's reaction. "Still weary from the morning's attack, cold, tired, and wet, the men looked at each other without comment. The first man to speak said, 'I'm going to build me a fire,' and started digging into the waterlogged deadfalls for some dry wood. Others followed suit and soon groups of men were standing around in the open, enjoying the warmth of an open fire for the first time in months."[57]

Epilogue

THE BATTALION THAT HUDDLED ABOUT ITS BONFIRES on November 11 along the Meuse scarcely resembled the one that had climbed off the French trucks behind the Triangle Farm five and a half months earlier. Owing to the flood tides of attrition and replacement, few of the faces were the same. Having shed their forest greens long ago for olive drab, the marines revealed little in their appearance to distinguish them from the multitude of army battalions throughout the Meuse-Argonne. Debilitating losses due to weather and influenza had reduced 2/6 to a shivering huddle of very sick men. The familial comradeship born in Quantico had washed away, leaving behind an effective, albeit impersonal machine. Wet, weary, and often unknown to each other, these ragged survivors had endured their final fight through individual determination and the ingrained habits of discipline.

A six-day rest restored the marines' health and the battalion's numbers. Although still camping out each night, the men stoked immense bonfires, thawing themselves out and drying their uniforms, blankets, and equipment. The field kitchens caught up with the companies, and the leathernecks gorged themselves on hot chow and coffee. Many influenza victims recovered and returned from the field hospitals while replacements added their numbers to the ranks.

On November 17 the 2nd Division commenced a hard march through France and Luxembourg for occupation duty in the Rhineland. The AEF had reassigned the division to the III Corps as one of the American Army of Occupation's nine divisions. While hostilities had ceased, Allied leadership remained on guard against a resumption of fighting. Battalion commanders were expected to maintain strict march discipline, prevent fraternization, and maintain security.

Gen. John L. Hines, III Corps commander, popped in to inspect 2/6 one evening shortly after the conclusion of another hard day of marching. His first impression of the battalion fell far short of his standards. Expecting to find a tactical command post busy arranging security and billeting, Hines instead found Major Williams and his officers lounging in the hotel bar. Hines dressed down The Bull in front of his subordinates and then dragged him in tow on an inspection of the battalion areas. The major had posted sentries to provide security, but the general nonetheless loudly decried shortcomings in everything from the galley to the mules. Hines had Williams relieved within the month. Maj. Franklin B. Garrett, who had first commanded the 80th Company at Quantico, returned to take over the battalion.

After crossing the Rhine on December 13, 2/6 entered the small town of Rheinbrohl, where for the first time in months, the marines enjoyed the luxury of sleeping indoors. The Allied Army of Occupation remained poised to resume fighting should Germany deviate from the armistice terms. Hard training, inspections, athletic contests, and a liberal leave policy buoyed morale through the winter and spring as the men waited their turn to return home. National Guard and National Army divisions with far less overseas service sailed for home quickly, but as a regular organization the 2nd Division remained in Europe until Allied and German leaders signed the Treaty of Versailles in June 1919. Not until August 5, 1919, would the marines return to New York. After a few celebratory parades, 2/6 mustered out at Quantico on August 13, having been on active service for just over two years.[1]

Conclusions

Despite this battalion's trying ordeal, statistical factors collected by the AEF on each division after the war support the argument that 2/6 may represent as near a thing to an ideal battalion as the United States fielded in 1918. Of the twenty-four divisions that participated in active combat, the 2nd Division ranked second in time spent in active combat, second in distance advanced against fire, highest in casualties suffered, highest in prisoners taken, and highest in the AEF G1's "consolidation of performance factors." The report indicates that the unit received as much training, probably fought in more heavy combat, and acquitted itself as well as any other division, at least according to the AEF's metrics.[2] In a more qualitative measurement, four members of 2/6 received the Medal of Honor (Gy. Sgt. Fred Stockham, Hospitalman Apprentice 1st Class David Hayden, Pvt. John Kelly, and Cpl. Henry Pruitt). When the superior quality of its enlisted marines is considered along with these factors, one can conclude that this battalion probably came as close to any at performing in accordance with the expectations of the AEF and the Marine Corps. The lessons of this book may then support broader conclusions about American infantry in the First World War.

This study has sought to analyze the factors influencing 2/6's unpreparedness and subsequent transformation during the Great War. At the outset, several questions arose regarding the battalion's experience in combat. How good were the leadership, discipline, and morale in 2/6? Were its doctrine, training, organization, and equipment well-suited to the Western Front? Which factors determined the battalion's performance and casualties in each combat operation? How did 2/6 adapt to its experiences?

Leadership, Discipline, and Morale

The battalion had begun the war with superb leadership. Its core of seventy regular officers and NCOs inculcated the volunteers with the steady discipline upon which the Marine Corps had built its reputation. The battalion had also begun its service with splendid discipline and morale. The original members of 2/6 were volunteers who had been selected by the recruiting sergeants in the wave of enthusiasm following the declaration of war. The Marine Corps's uncompromising drill sergeants instilled a profound level of discipline among its recruits. The battalion's leaders fostered this high spirit and maintained these exacting standards of discipline, preserving the core strengths that sustained unit cohesion through the relentless meat grinder at Belleau Wood.

The two combat commanders of 2/6 defied conventional wisdom. Thomas Holcomb was a politically savvy general's aide who had never seen action before 1918. Ernest Williams was a highly decorated and proven veteran. Yet it was Holcomb who proved the more capable leader. His tireless efforts at Quantico and Bourmont built his marines into a tough, well-organized, and highly spirited team. His rock-steady leadership through Belleau Wood and Soissons helped prevent the precious bonds of esprit de corps and discipline from unraveling. Conversely, Williams's arrogance and alcoholism undermined the confidence of the rank and file, threatening to accelerate plummeting morale. Nonetheless, The Bull's decisiveness and example of personal bravery at Blanc Mont ensured success during the attack on October 3. He had also learned to value the counsel of his battle-wise lieutenants and placed his experienced junior officers in command of his companies.

The Bull's decision to fill his key billets with proven combat leaders rather than untested regulars was consistent with practices throughout the Marine Corps during the First World War. Grappling with rapid expansion and heavy attrition, the Corps had to forego peacetime processes such as promotion boards and lineal lists. Instead it had recruited the best men it could find and had then relied on its commanders to screen and promote the cream of these green volunteers to fill their NCO vacancies. Likewise, the Corps had commissioned hundreds of distinguished university graduates virtually sight unseen and had then culled the best and brightest of these to command the platoons in the 6th Marines. After Belleau Wood it commissioned replacement officers almost exclusively from the best NCOs within the brigade's ranks. Throughout the First World War, the Marine Corps had relied upon the subjective judgment of trusted leaders to identify the most capable candidates for advancement. The experience of 2/6 suggests that these methods of selection and promotion succeeded in providing its marines with highly satisfactory small-unit leaders.

Doctrine, Training, Organization, Equipment, and the Realities of the Western Front

The experience of 2/6 sharply focuses the profound effects inadequate doctrine had upon performance in combat and exorbitant casualties. In 1917 the Marine Corps had provided only an outdated doctrine of machine-like musketry. Recruit training at Parris and Mare Islands succeeded in instilling a superb level of discipline while toughening marines and training them to a seldom-matched level of rifle marksmanship. At Quantico Holcomb's efforts to train his men were undermined by the absence of a relevant doctrine.

The AEF had preached open warfare but had organized divisions to absorb punishment in a war of attrition. Lacking any other suitable method of attack, the 2nd Division seized upon the French Army's trench-fighting doctrine. With its service roots as a well-drilled and centrally controlled organization, 2/6 had been predisposed to master the form but not the substance of these tactics. The month at Bourmont had brought the battalion to a reasonable level of readiness for trench warfare, though the singular benefit of this period was the physical toughening of the individual marines.

These French tactics were in any case asymmetrical to 2/6's initial engagements at Belleau Wood and Soissons. The 2nd Division attempted to modify these methods to the AEF's concept of open warfare. In a gross over-reliance on rifle superiority, the division admonished its commanders to abandon the principle that "the way to the front must be 'blasted' by the Field Artillery." Furthermore, the AEF had stripped the battalion of its excellent Lewis guns, then isolated the battalion commander from his supporting arms. These misconceptions directly resulted in the excessively high casualties suffered by 2/6 on June 6 and July 19.

The Ability to Adapt

In his comparative study of four AEF divisions, historian Mark Grotelueschen concludes, "The history of the 2nd Division provides one of the finest examples of doctrinal and operational development in the AEF." The experience of 2/6 supports this statement. After the tactical renaissance before Saint-Mihiel, the combat-wise lieutenants and sergeants adapted their inappropriate French trench-warfare doctrine to meet the conditions they now faced. The two or three weeks of intense retraining in August and early September 1918 did more to improve the battalion's effectiveness than any other measure. The practical utility of the doctrine and method for this training contrasts sharply with the squandered months of drilling and digging at Quantico. Possibly the determining factor in the greater effectiveness of this revitalization was neither the doctrine nor the method of instruction but rather the training audience. The battalion's small-unit leaders had seen mortal combat firsthand and could more readily grasp the intricacies of coordinated fire and movement. These savvy veterans possessed the wisdom and experience to adapt their training to the true conditions on the battlefield.[3]

Likewise, the officers and NCOs themselves began to take advantage of opportunities presented by terrain. With machine guns, tanks, trench mortars, and 37-mm guns now under the battalion commander's control, the riflemen were no longer expected to assault fortified defenses without close, continuous fire support.

The battalion's responses to its high attrition deserve emphasis. After the devastating experience at Soissons, 2/6 began leaving 20 percent of its combat strength out of each major engagement. This drastic measure mitigated the long-term effects of attrition on the unit. But by sidelining experienced leaders, this policy also risked higher losses and jeopardized mission accomplishment. Still, if not done, the loss of experienced marines would have continued unabated.

Factors Determining 2/6's Performance and Casualties in Combat

Consistently, the most influential factors in the first engagements were morale and discipline, small-unit leadership, and the inexperience at higher echelons of command. In later battles the elevated experience level of the 2nd Division and 4th Brigade headquarters proved demonstrably positive. Concurrently, improved tactics and doctrine had a pronounced effect on the battalion's performance. The undeniable erosion of German morale during this same period multiplied the effects of these advantages.

While its officers and the 2nd Division leadership learned to fight by fighting, 2/6 suffered staggeringly high casualties. Although grim, this tragedy was not altogether surprising. Yet a review of how the battalion incurred these losses affords some notable revelations. Notwithstanding the devilish lethality of machine guns and artillery, neither of these weapons ever devastated 2/6 so abruptly as two other trials: chemical warfare and the influenza outbreak. On June 14 it was the gas attack that inflicted almost 100 percent casualties among two companies. This calamity prevented 2/6 from relieving 2/5 and resuming the offensive in Belleau Wood. In nine days in November, influenza brought the battalion to its knees, rendering it incapable of vigorous, sustained attacks, much less forcing its way across a heavily defended river.

It is important to note that in each of these cases, the precipitant cause of the battalion's crushing losses was accompanied by a corresponding condition that created an unforeseen vulnerability. In the case of the gas attack, it was an unprecedented high-explosive barrage that prevented the companies from escaping the clouds of mustard. In the Meuse-Argonne, the combined effects of the weather and combat conditions lowered the marines' resistance to disease. These dramatic shifts in the severity of known threats exceeded the battalion's ability to respond, adapt, and persevere.

The odyssey of 2/6 during the First World War reinforces several obvious axioms that military professionals and scholars will not find particularly astounding: that organizations often begin conflicts with outdated doctrine; that frontline troops who survive their first combat swiftly adapt their tactics to conditions as they find them; that success at lower echelons is as dependent upon higher headquarters learning their trade as it is on mastering its own fight. From these observations one realizes that a military unit would be well served to enter its first action *expecting* to change its doctrine. This is not a highly controversial idea, but one that is not often emphasized during peacetime training and education.

In the context of a more savage future scenario, some of this battalion's lessons offer points worthy of further consideration. Infantry training today is extraordinarily complex. Private soldiers can be instructed and integrated into a team in about six months, but it takes at least that long to develop the individuals into a team and can take years to develop platoon and company leaders. Consider the challenge of tomorrow's infantry if thrust into a high-intensity battlefield: Biological and chemical weapons, recalling the flu in the Meuse-Argonne and the mustard barrage at Belleau Wood, rip apart the battalion's strength, eliminating entire companies. Should the war drag on for months, or longer, the battalion may pass through its critical threshold, a culminating point of experienced manpower beyond which it begins a perilous spiral of deteriorating combat efficiency. It is then that the unit will discover the limit of endurance.

Sacred manpower practices may require suspension in the face of such crushing attrition. Commanders in combat must be trusted to promote proven combat leaders on a scale unimagined under peacetime constraints. If the best-trained leaders are learning to fight while fighting, services may need to resurrect the practice of holding back a cadre of officers and NCOs prior to each engagement. This cadre will preserve both the cohesion of the old battalion and absorb the lessons learned in its engagements. Likewise, the rapid promotion and transfer of a portion of these proven small-unit leaders should be exploited to provide green organizations with a leavening of experience.

No organization can write doctrine for every contingency, equip for every type of combat, or train for the disparate characteristics of every possible scenario. Considering the experience of 2/6 in the First World War, recall that its tactical renaissance could come only after the battalion's lieutenants and sergeants had already "seen the elephant." Despite Holcomb's emphasis on training and the enthusiasm of his men, 2/6 could not master innovative tactics because their service had predisposed them to tactical precision and centralized control. Only after fire and shell had stripped away their pretensions did the surviving marines grasp the intent of the doctrine they had read. How best to preserve and exploit these critical, experienced small-unit leaders will be a difficult problem for any organization.

The archives of the 2nd Battalion, 6th Marine Regiment, in the First World War reveal a determined band of young men struggling to adapt to a devastating and unprecedented type of combat. The most enduring record these leathernecks have left for future generations is their legacy of sacrifice and resilience. Despite the tragic missteps of an organization struggling to adapt to an unfamiliar war, the battalion's marines persevered and triumphed, atoning for the unpreparedness of their country's military. Few chapters in American military history match the severe, sustained tribulations overcome by the men of the 4th Marine Brigade. Their deeds leave behind an astonishing example of what American infantry can endure.

APPENDIX A
Recapitulation of 2/6 Casualties

Table 1. Bouresches and Belleau Wood

	Triangle Farm and Bouresches June 1–11	Belleau Wood June 14–18	Belleau Wood June 25–July 2	Total	Percent*
Killed and died of wounds	60	48	9	117	11.7
Wounded, gassed, and missing	190	434	23	647	64.7
Total	250	482	32	764	76.4

*Percent of authorized strength of 1,000 marines.

Table 2. Soissons

	July 19	Percent*
Killed and died of wounds	87	8.7
Wounded, gassed, and missing	316	31.6
Total	403	40

*Percent of authorized strength of 1,000 marines.

Table 3. Saint-Mihiel

	September 12–15	Percent*
Killed and died of wounds	56	7
Wounded, gassed, and missing	169	21.1
Total	215	26.9

*Percent of the 800 marines who entered the line on September 12; 20 percent cadre not included.

Table 4. Blanc Mont

	October 1–3	October 4–10	Total	Percent*
Killed and died of wounds	55	23	78	9.8
Wounded, gassed, and missing	126	92	218	27.2
Total	181	115	296	37

*Percent of the 800 marines who entered the line on October 1; 20 percent cadre not included.

Table 5. Meuse-Argonne

	November 1–11	Percent*
Killed and died of wounds	20	2.5
Wounded, gassed, and missing	101	12.6
Total battle casualties	121	15.1
Sick	450 (est.)	56.2
Total losses	571 (est.)	71.4

*Percent of the 800 marines who entered the line on November 1; 20 percent cadre not included.

Table 6. Summary of 2/6 Combat Losses

	June 1–November 11, 1918	Percent*
Killed and died of wounds	358	35.8
Wounded, gassed, and missing**	1,451	145.1
Total battle casualties**	1,809	180.9

*Percent of authorized strength of 1,000 marines.
**Sick not included.

2/6 Marines after the Great War

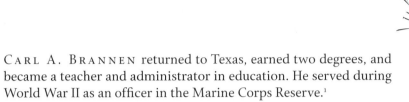

CARL A. BRANNEN returned to Texas, earned two degrees, and became a teacher and administrator in education. He served during World War II as an officer in the Marine Corps Reserve.[1]

CLIFTON B. CATES commanded the 1st Marine Regiment at Guadalcanal and the 4th Marine Division in the Marianas and at Iwo Jima. He served from 1948 to 1952 as the nineteenth commandant of the Marine Corps. After his tour as commandant, he took the unusual step of remaining on active duty, serving as commandant of Marine Corps Schools at Quantico until his retirement in 1954.[2]

After leaving 2/6, ROBERT L. DENIG commanded the 3rd Battalion, 9th Infantry until seriously wounded at Blanc Mont. Between the world wars he served in Santo Domingo and Nicaragua. During World War II, Denig directed Marine Corps Public Affairs. He retired as a brigadier general.[3]

GRAVES B. ERSKINE sufficiently recovered from his Saint-Mihiel wound to remain on active duty. He commanded the 3rd Marine Division at Iwo Jima and retired as a lieutenant general. He served as the undersecretary of defense for special operations during the Eisenhower administration.[4]

BERNARD L. FRITZ lost his left hand after Soissons. He retired as a first lieutenant and later married.[5]

THOMAS HOLCOMB served from 1936 to 1944 as the seventeenth commandant of the Marine Corps. After retirement, he was appointed as U.S. minister to South Africa.[6]

In 1920 JOHN J. KELLY drifted down to Mexico, where he worked for a time as a cowhand. He returned by freight car to the United States to booze and carouse away an entire summer with other veterans at a lakeside cottage. Diagnosed with terminal tuberculosis, Kelly determined to drink himself to death over the next two years. Failing in the attempt, he revisited his doctor, who pronounced him cured. Kelly made an abrupt about face and entered Chicago politics in the late 1920s.[7]

MELVIN L KRULEWITCH returned to study law at Colombia University and worked as a New York public-utilities attorney. In 1927 he was commissioned a second lieutenant in the Marine Corps Reserve. Krulewitch served under General Cates in the 4th Marine Division in the Marianas and at Iwo Jima. He returned to active duty once more to serve in Korea with the 1st Marine Division. Krulewitch retired from the reserves as a major general in 1956.[8]

DON V. PARADIS returned to his job with the Detroit gas works and later retired to Florida. During the 1970s, he accompanied Gen. Louis Wilson, commandant of the Marine Corps, on a visit to Belleau Wood.[9]

JAMES MCB. SELLERS served for decades as the superintendent of Wentworth Military Academy in Lexington, Missouri. He retired from the reserves as a colonel.[10]

LUCIAN H. VANDOREN became an assistant U.S. attorney for the District of Colombia, a member of the bar of the U.S. Supreme Court, and a professor of law. He attained the rank of major in the reserves and served as president of the Second Division Association. He suffered an untimely death in 1935.[11]

ERNEST C. WILLIAMS narrowly escaped a court-martial in Haiti for appearing drunk on duty. He received a medical discharge for complications from an old leg injury and transferred to the retired list as a lieutenant colonel.[12]

WILLIAM A. WORTON recovered from his Belleau Wood wound and remained in the Marine Corps. He spent fifteen of the interwar years overseas, thirteen of those in China. He commanded 2/6 at the outset of World War II in Iceland and served on various staffs in the Pacific. After retiring as a major general in 1949, Worton became chief of the Los Angeles Police Department.

Notes

Abbreviations

2nd Div. Records: U.S. Army, *Records of the Second Division (Regular)*, 9 vols. (Washington, D.C.: Army War College, 1927)

BF: Biographic Files, Historical Reference Branch, U.S. Marine Corps History Division, Quantico, Va.

CG: Commanding General

CO: Commanding Officer

German War Diaries: U.S. Army, *Translations of War Diaries of German Units Opposed to the 2nd Division (Regular)*, 4 vols. (Washington, D.C.: Army War College, 1918)

HQ: Headquarters

HRB: Historical Reference Branch, U.S. Marine Corps History Division, Quantico, Va.

MCPPC: Marine Corps Personal Papers Collection, Archives and Special Collections, U.S. Marine Corps University, Quantico, Va.

OHC: Oral History Collection, Historical Reference Branch, U.S. Marine Corps History Division, Quantico, Va.

OMPF: Official Military Personnel Files, National Personnel Records Center, St. Louis, Mo.

RG 117.4.2: Correspondence with Officers of the 2nd Division, AEF, Records Relating to World War I Frontline Maps and Accompanying "Summaries of Operations," Records of the American Battlefield Monuments Commission, RG 117.4.2, National Archives

RG 127: Records Relating to Marine Participation in World War I, RG 127, A1, Entry 240, National Archives

Preface

1. See Braim, *Test of Battle;* Coffman, *War to End All Wars;* Grotelueschen, "AEF Way of War"; Johnson, "Few Squads Left"; Lofgren, "Unready for War," 11–19; Millett and Murray, *Military Effectiveness;* Paschall, *Defeat of Imperial Germany;* Rainey, "Questionable Training of the AEF"; Smythe, *Pershing;* and Trask, *AEF and Coalition Warmaking.*

2. "Final Report of Assistant Chief of Staff G-1 to Commander-in-Chief, American Expeditionary Forces, 22 April 1919," cited in Braim, *Test of Battle,* App. 2, 176. For an excellent comparative study of the 1st and 2nd Divisions, the 26th National Guard Division, and the 77th National Army Division, see Grotelueschen, "AEF Way of War."

Chapter 1

1. Millett, *Semper Fidelis,* 287–88. Influential officers such as Eli Cole, Earl H. "Pete" Ellis, and John H. Russell were already thinking about seizing naval

bases in an amphibious assault. For Earl H. "Pete" Ellis's work, see Lt. Col. John J. Reber, "Pete Ellis, Amphibious Warfare Prophet," *U.S. Naval Institute Proceedings* (Nov. 1977): 53–64; and David H. Wagner, "The Destiny of Pete Ellis," *Marine Corps Gazette*, June 1976, 50–55.

2. For a discussion of the Advance Base Force, see ibid., 267–86. See also Thomas, "Marine Corps Prepares for War."

3. Described in Lejeune, *Reminiscences*, 237–39. For a battalion commander's perspective, see Wise, *A Marine Tells It to You*, 157–60. See also Millett, *Semper Fidelis*, 289–90; and Thomas, "Marine Corps Prepares for War."

4. U.S. Department of Commerce, *Historical Statistics of the United States*, 383. Figures are for 1916. The regimental commander insisted that 60 percent of the 6th Marines came from college campuses. Catlin, *With the Help of God and a Few Marines*, 19.

5. Silverthorn interview, OHC, 4–5.

6. Hamburger, *Learning Lessons*, 20.

7. Brannen, *Over There*, 1.

8. Hemrick, *Once a Marine*, 4–5.

9. Krulewitch interview, OHC, 11–12.

10. Paradis memoir, MCPPC, 3.

11. The Marine Corps accepted 60,189 men from among 239,274 applicants. Edwin N. McClellan quoted in Millett, *Semper Fidelis*, 289. Parris Island was spelled "Paris Island" in 1918.

12. Paradis memoir, MCPPC, 10; Hemrick, *Once a Marine*, 10. "Drill sergeant" was the term in vogue in 1917. "Drill instructor" became popular years later.

13. Recruits also trained at Mare Island, California; Norfolk, Virginia; and Philadelphia, Pennsylvania. W. R. Coyle, "Parris Island in the War," *Marine Corps Gazette*, Dec. 1925, 187–91.

14. Brannen, *Over There*, 6.

15. Krulewitch interview, OHC, 19.

16. Capt. William C. Harlee, *U.S. Marine Corps Score Book and Rifleman's Instructor* (Philadelphia: International Printing, 1916).

17. Paradis memoir, MCPPC, 8–9.

18. Krulewitch interview, OHC, 19; Jaffe letter in Cowing, *Dear Folks at Home*, 5, 8.

19. Hemrick, *Once a Marine*, 22; Johnson, "Few Squads Left," v.

20. The Marine Corps commissioned only seven Naval Academy graduates between the declaration of war and October 1917. During this period, 211 warrant officers, paymaster's clerks, and NCOs received commissions. McClellan, *Marine Corps in the World War*, 21.

21. Ibid., 21. Of these, 284 had attended military colleges.

22. Sellers, memoir, copy in author's possession, 1.

23. McClellan, *Marine Corps in the World War*, 22; Sellers, memoir, 2. The "navy" qualification course refers to the Navy Department, to which the Marine Corps belonged. It was used by both sailors and marines.

24. Cates interview, OHC, v–vi.

25. Yale annual (1917), 253–54.

26. Worton interview, OHC, 8, 10. Captain Delano had raised the Stars and Stripes over Veracruz, Mexico, on April 27, 1914. Jack Sweetman, *The Landing at Veracruz: 1914* (Annapolis: Naval Institute Press, 1968), 149.

27. Cates interview, OHC, 8.

28. Sellers, memoir, 3.

29. Holcomb BF; Erskine interview, OHC, 45. Erskine is likely exaggerating, but his assertion indicates how highly he perceived Holcomb to value marksmanship.

30. Edwin Simmons, interview by author; "Brief History of the Second Battalion, Sixth Regiment, U.S. Marine Corps," Box 36, 2/6 File, RG 127.

31. Worton interview, OHC, 57; Cates, interview by Robert B. Asprey, June 25, 1963, Folder 9a, Box 1, Asprey Notes, Records, and Correspondence [hereafter Asprey NRC], MCPPC, 2.

32. Erskine interview, OHC, 18.

33. Sellers, letter, Oct. 23, 1917, copy in author's possession.

34. Sellers, letter, July 22, 1917, copy in author's possession.

35. Spaulding and Wright, *Second Division*, 6.

36. Worton interview, OHC, 42; Messersmith BF.

37. Sellers, memoir, 4; Worton interview, OHC, 42.

38. Sellers, memoir, 4.

39. Catlin, *With the Help of God and a Few Marines*, 19; Donaldson, *Seventy-Eighth Company*.

40. Donaldson, *Seventy-Eighth Company*, 18; Sellers memoir, 7.

41. Erskine interview, OHC, 20, 36; Worton interview, OHC, 42; Hill to G. N. Neufeld, Jan. 17, 1979, HRB, 5 [emphasis in original].

42. Worton interview, OHC, 43. West was from Cincinnati, Ohio.

43. Erskine interview, OHC, 40–41; Worton interview, OHC, 43.

44. Erskine interview, OHC, 39.

45. Capt. Graves Erskine to ABMC, n.d., RG 117.4.2; Hill to Neufeld, Jan. 17, 1979, 1; Muster Roll of the United States Marine Corps, June 1918, HRB [hereafter Muster Roll, by month]. Submitted monthly by each company, the muster rolls provide detail on personnel assignments and casualties.

46. Paradis memoir, MCPPC, 7, 18; MacGillivray and Clark, *80th Company*; Hartman, "From Culver's Corps to the Marine Corps."

47. "In Memoriam—Capt. Donald F. Duncan," *St. Joseph Gazette*, June 8, 1919, Duncan BF; Capt. Donald F. Duncan official biography, ibid.; Hartman, "From Culver's Corps to the Marine Corps"; Cates interview, OHC, 14.

48. Stockham, Biographic File, Medal of Honor Society, Patriot's Point, S.C.

49. Sgt. Aloysius Sheridan to Mrs. Cox [Duncan's mother], Aug. 14, 1918, Folder 22, Box 1, Asprey NRC, MCPPC.

50. Worton interview, OHC, 16–18. Holcomb eventually had Spaulding transferred out of 2/6.

51. *History of the Sixth Regiment United States Marines*, 3.

52. Lee, "Some Notes on Musketry Training."

53. Lee used the term "section" vice "platoon."

54. Lee, "Some Notes on Musketry Training."

55. Johnson, "Few Squads Left," 79, 84; War Department, *Infantry Drill Regulations, 1911* (Washington, D.C.: Government Printing Office, 1911), para. 355, cited in ibid., 81.

56. For a critical analysis, see Gudmundsson, *Stormtroop Tactics*.

57. For discussions of open warfare, see Braim, *Test of Battle*, 50–53; and Paschall, *Defeat of Imperial Germany*, 169.

58. Erskine Service Record, Erskine Personal Papers, MCPPC. Cates jotted down the schedule of a typical Quantico training day in September 1917: an hour of bayonet exercise; an hour of close-order drill, skirmishing, signaling, and bomb throwing; an hour of battalion parade or drill; and after the noon meal, two hours of close-order drill. The next week they would start spending two days a week digging trenches and erecting barbed-wire obstacles in the woods. Cates, letter, Sept. 19, 1917, MCPPC.

59. *History of the Sixth Regiment United States Marines*, 3; Paradis memoir, MCPPC, 18–20.

60. Paradis memoir, MCPPC, 19–20; Sellers memoir, 4; Worton interview, OHC, 39–40.

61. Sellers, letter, Sept. 28, 1917, copy in author's possession.

62. Cates interview, Asprey NRC, 2.

63. Holcomb BF, HRB; *History of the Sixth Regiment United States Marines*, 5; Sellers, letter, Jan. 15, 1918, copy in author's possession. Some of the manuals Holcomb read from included discussions of the French doctrine 2/6 would employ in Europe (discussed later in this chapter).

64. Redesignated the 6th Machine Gun Battalion upon arrival in France.

65. Sellers, letter, Aug. 26, 1917, copy in author's possession.

66. Sellers memoir, 4–5. See also Waller, "Machine Guns of the Fourth Brigade," 3–4; and *History of the Sixth Machine Gun Battalion*, 5–7. Curtis was the 6th Machine Gun Battalion's adjutant. The battalion kept its Lewis guns until arriving in France, whereupon they were exchanged for the heavier, longer-ranged Hotchkiss guns.

67. Worton interview, OHC, 18.

68. Ibid., 51.

69. Sellers memoir, 9; Erskine interview, OHC, 22; *History of the Sixth Regiment United States Marines*, 5.

70. Worton interview, OHC, 19–20; Erskine interview, OHC, 22–23.

Chapter 2

1. Braim, *Test of Battle*, 60–61.

2. Paschall, *Defeat of Imperial Germany*, 168–69.

3. Johnson, "Few Squads Left," 116; U.S. Army, *Field Service Regulations*, 3, 73–111 passim.

4. 6th Marines HQ, Special Order 67, Mar. 6, 1918, Box 33, RG 127; *History of the Sixth Regiment United States Marines*, 8.

5. Worton interview, OHC, 23–24. Officers wore collar devices, but enlisted marines would not begin wearing Marine Corps collar discs until the end of the war.

6. U.S. Army, *Field Service Regulations*, 58.

7. Hyatt, "U.S. Defensive Grenades in WWI."

8. Donovan, "Viven-Bessiere Rifle Grenade and Launchers."

9. Sellers memoir, copy in author's possession, 6; Cates, interview by Robert B. Asprey, June 25, 1963, Folder 9a, Box 1, Asprey NRC, 3.

10. Worton interview, OHC, 25.

11. Hemrick, *Once a Marine*, 66–69; Paradis, memoir, 29; Sellers, letter, Apr. 3, 1918, copy in author's possession.

12. Hemrick, *Once a Marine*, 51–56.

13. 2nd Division HQ, memorandum, "Revised Program of Training for the Second Division, AEF," Feb. 6, 1918, Box 52, RG 127.

14. MacGillivray and Clark, *80th Company*, 1–2; 2nd Division HQ, General Order 8, Jan. 24, 1918, Box 33, 2nd Division Files, RG 127. See also Paradis, memoir, MCPPC, 53. A "mustang" is an officer commissioned from the enlisted ranks. The table of organization differentiated between "scouts" and "observers" and included two snipers. "Brief History of the Second Battalion, Sixth Regiment, U.S. Marine Corps," Box 36, 2/6 File, RG 127, 3.

15. "Brief History of the Second Battalion," 1; 6th Marines HQ, Special Order 111, May 24, 1918, Box 33, 6th Regiment Files, RG 127; Paradis memoir, MCPPC, 33. Each company detailed one NCO and two privates as battalion runners. The battalion in turn detailed one NCO and four privates as regimental runners. 6th Marines HQ, Special Order 111.

16. Muster Roll, July 1918; U.S. Navy, *Medical Department*, 23. Naval officers in the AEF were referred to by their equivalent army rank (e.g., a lieutenant commander was called "major"). The original surgeon of 2/6 was Lt. Sydney Walker. At some point he was replaced by Lts. Gordon Grimland and George White.

17. 2nd Division HQ, memorandum, Feb. 8, 1918, Box 16, 6th Marines File, RG 127.

18. Four companies were assigned to the 6th Machine Gun Battalion and one each to the 5th and 6th Marine Regiments. *History of the Sixth Machine Gun Battalion*, 5–6; Waller, "Machine Guns of the Fourth Brigade," 2.

19. Denig, "Diary," MCPPC, 61.

20. 4th Brigade HQ, General Order 3, May 1, 1918, Box 14, 4th Brigade File, RG 127.

21. Lupfer, *Dynamics of Doctrine*, 11–19.

22. Paradis memoir, MCPPC, 28; Erskine interview, OHC, 29; Sellers memoir, 12; "Brief History of the Second Battalion," 3; Paradis memoir, MCPPC, 26–27. See also 6th Marines HQ, General Order 1, Jan. 14, 1918, Box 36, 2/6 File, RG 127 (marked "2nd Battin Hqdrs," for health and sanitation instructions, with special emphasis on foot care).

23. Cates, letter, Feb. 20, 1918, MCPPC; Cates, letter, Mar. 10, 1918, ibid.

24. Paradis memoir, MCPPC, 30–31.

25. Ibid., 26–29; Erskine interview, OHC, 27–29; Cates, letter, Feb. 20, 1918, MCPPC.

26. U.S. Army, *Instructions for the Offensive Combat of Small Units*; U.S. Army, *Manual for Commanders of Infantry Platoons*. The French doctrine articulated in these two publications bears striking similarities to German stormtrooper tactics. The Germans achieved considerably greater success for a number of reasons. Probably the most important of these were superior artillery tactics, more mobile machine guns, the ability to draw upon significant numbers of motivated volunteers, and—especially—an officer corps predisposed to implement new doctrine. For an excellent treatment of the subject, see Gudmundsson, *Stormtroop Tactics*, 172–79, 193–95.

27. U.S. Army, *Instructions for the Offensive Combat of Small Units*, 16–19; U.S. Army, *Manual for Commanders of Infantry Platoons*, 395–96. Standard operating procedure in the 2nd Division was proscribed in 2nd Division HQ, Memorandum 52, May 13, 1918, Box 9, 2nd Division Files, RG 127.

28. U.S. Army, *Instructions for the Offensive Combat of Small Units*, 18–19. Compare this to current USMC doctrine: "an entrenched enemy should

discover that if he stays hunkered down in fighting holes, marine artillery and air will blast him out. If he comes out to attack, marine infantry will cut him down." Also, "The firepower from the automatic weapons keeps the enemy in their fighting holes while grenades make their holes untenable." U.S. Marine Corps, *Marine Corps Doctrinal Publication 1: Tactics*, 40.

29. U.S. Army, *Instructions for the Offensive Combat of Small Units*, 10–15, 19; U.S. Army, *Manual for Commanders of Infantry Platoons*, 384–91.

30. U.S. Army, *Manual for Commanders of Infantry Platoons*, 391.

31. Ibid., 381–414. Scheduled fires are planned for a predetermined location and time. On-call fires are preplanned for a particular location but are executed only upon request of the infantry. During World War I, on-call fires during the assault were usually requested by colored flares; such missions provided very little flexibility and were fraught with opportunities for miscommunication.

32. 2nd Division HQ, Memorandum 52, May 13, 1918.

33. U.S. Army, *Manual for Commanders of Infantry Platoons*, 386.

34. 2/6 HQ, Field Order 2 (Drill), Mar. 6, 1918, Box 36, 2/6 File, RG 127.

35. Cates interview, Asprey NRC, 2.

36. Worton interview, OHC, 57; "Brief History of the Second Battalion," 3; MacGillivray and Clark, *80th Company*, 2.

37. Worton interview, OHC, 27, 58.

38. Ibid., 27, 39–40.

39. The term *poilu*, literally "hairy one," referred to French frontline soldiers of World War I.

40. Worton interview, OHC, 28.

41. For a classic account of the mutiny, see Richard M. Watt, *Dare Call It Treason* (New York: Simon & Shuster, 1962).

42. For an insightful account of the German offensive, see Paschall, *Defeat of Imperial Germany*, 128–62. For a study of German tactics, see Gudmundsson, *Stormtroop Tactics*. For an equally superb study of German artillery innovation, see Zabecki, *Steel Wind*.

43. *History of the Sixth Regiment United States Marines*, 8; "Brief History of the Second Battalion," 4; "Brief History of the 79th Company, Sixth Marines," n.d., Box 36, RG 127, 1; Donaldson, *Seventy-Eighth Company*, 1.

44. *History of the Sixth Regiment United States Marines*, 9; "Brief History of the 79th Company," 1; Donaldson, *Seventy-Eighth Company*, 1.

45. Catlin, *With the Help of God and a Few Marines*, 34–35.

46. Cates interview, Asprey NRC, 2; Cates, letter, Apr. 17, 1918, MCPPC. The "Austrian 88" was an artillery piece.

47. Catlin, *With the Help of God and a Few Marines*, 44; Hemrick, *Once a Marine*, 29–30; Cates interview, Asprey NRC, 2.

48. "Brief History of the Second Battalion," 4; Cates, *96th Company*, 6; "Brief History of the 79th Company," 2; Denig, "Diary," MCPPC, 192; Vandoren, Military Record, Personnel Records, OMPF.

49. Catlin, *With the Help of God and a Few Marines*, 35; 6th Marines HQ, Special Order 90, Apr. 19, 1918, Box 33, RG 127.

50. Catlin, *With the Help of God and a Few Marines*, 37; 33rd Division HQ, Standing Order B (I), Apr. 17, 1918, Box 33, RG 127.

51. Hemrick, *Once a Marine*, 76, 77; MacGillivray and Clark, *80th Company*, app. A.

52. U.S. Navy, *Medical Department*, 32.

53. Ibid., 32–34.

54. Ibid., 35.

55. MacGillivray and Clark, *80th Company*, 2; 6th Marines HQ, Special Order 90, Apr. 19, 1918.

56. Sellers memoir, 14.

57. Erskine to ABMC, n.d.

58. Donaldson, *Seventy-Eighth Company*, 2; Cates, *96th Company*, 6; Cates, letter, Apr. 25, 1918, MCPPC.

59. Cates interview, OHC, 12, 15; Fisch, *Field Equipment*, 162, 172.

60. Sellers memoir, 14–15.

61. 6th Marines Regimental Gas Officer, "Report on Gas Attack," Apr. 27, 1918, Box 31, RG 127. Chandler's recommendations notwithstanding, General Bundy directed Catlin to severely reprimand the lieutenant and two platoon commanders for their inattention to duty. 2nd Division Adj. to Commanding Officer, 6th Marines, May 3, 1918, Box 32, ibid.

62. HQ, 2nd Division General Orders 39, May 28, 1918, RG 127.

63. Reference Section, "Experience with Gas in WWI," HRB, 2.

64. Ibid., 3.

65. "Brief History of the 79th Company," 2; "Brief History of the Second Battalion," 4.

66. Hemrick, *Once a Marine*, 31, 88.

67. *History of the Sixth Regiment United States Marines*, 10; Donaldson, *Seventy-Eighth Company*, 2.

68. Sellers memoir, 16.

69. Worton interview, OHC, 59.

70. Sellers memoir, 15.

71. 6th Marines HQ, Special Order 96, May 10, 1918, Box 33, RG 127.

72. 2nd Division HQ, Memorandum 52, May 13, 1918.

73. "Brief History of the Second Battalion," 5; Paradis memoir, MCPPC, 33.

74. 2nd Division HQ, Memorandum 52, May 13, 1918.

Chapter 3

1. Jean de Pierrefeu, *French Headquarters, 1915–1918*, trans. C. J. C. Street (London, 1924), quoted in Asprey, *German High Command at War*, 417; ibid., 416.

2. Asprey, *At Belleau Wood*, 82–84; Toland, *No Man's Land*, 199–200.

3. Messersmith, "Operations of Company 'E,'" 6–7, copy in author's possession; Paradis memoir, MCPPC, 34.

4. Hemrick, *Once a Marine*, 92–96.

5. Hill to G. N. Neufeld, Jan. 17, 1979, HRB; West, "Belleau Wood," HRB, 3–4.

6. For additional personal accounts by marines of 2/6 that reflect this attitude, see Benjamin, "June, 1918," MCPPC, 1; Cates interview, OHC; Cates, "Personal Observations," MCPPC; Cates, letters, MCPPC; Sellers memoir, copy in author's possession, 16–18; and "Brief History of the Second Battalion, Sixth Regiment, U.S. Marine Corps," Box 36, 2/6 File, RG 127, 5–7.

7. Hill to Neufeld, Jan. 17, 1979, 2.

8. Harbord, *Leaves from a War Diary*, 291; Paradis memoir, MCPPC, 36–37.

9. Catlin, *With the Help of God and a Few Marines*, 85–88.

10. "Brief History of the Second Battalion," 5–7; Messersmith, "Operations of Company 'E.'"

11. 2nd Div. HQ, "G2 Intel Summary," noon June 4 to noon June 5, 1918, *2nd Div. Records*, vol. 9; Hill to Neufeld, Jan. 17, 1979, 3. See also Paradis memoir, MCPPC, 37; and Messersmith, "Operations of Company 'E.'" A French liaison officer assigned to the battalion was wounded on June 3. No mention is made of what tactical advice he may have offered.

12. *History of the Sixth Machine Gun Battalion*, 13–15; Waller, "Machine Guns of the 4th Brigade," 9–10.

13. "Brief History of the Second Battalion," 1; *2nd Div. Records*, vol. 5.

14. Hill to Neufeld, Jan. 17, 1979.

15. *2nd Div. Records*, vol. 5.

16. Muster Roll, June 1918; Otto, "Belleau Woods," 943–44. Three were killed and three wounded in the 79th Company, and another three were wounded in the 96th Company.

17. Asprey, *At Belleau Wood*, 102; *2nd Div. Records*, vol. 5.

18. Hemrick, *Once a Marine*, 113–14.

19. Paradis memoir, MCPPC, 38–43. For casualties, see Muster Roll, June 1918.

20. Hemrick, *Once a Marine*, 113–14.

21. Otto, "Belleau Woods," 944.

22. Asprey, *At Belleau Wood*, 139.

23. Messersmith, "Operations of Company 'E'"; Capt. Graves Erskine to ABMC, n.d., RG 117.4.2; MacGillivray and Clark, *80th Company*, 3; Trumpeter Hugo A. Meyer, letter, *Recruiter's Bulletin*, Oct. 1918; Cates, "Personal Observations."

24. Catlin, *With the Help of God and a Few Marines*, 110–11; 4th Brigade HQ, Field Order 2, 2:05 P.M. on June 6, 1918, *History of the Sixth Regiment United States Marines*, 13–15; Messersmith, "Operations of Company 'E'"; Holcomb to Maj. Edwin McClellan, n.d., cited in Thomason, *Second Division Northwest of Chateau Thierry*, 106.

25. Louis Timmerman, interview by Robert Asprey, Asprey NRC, MCPPC. Timmerman, a lieutenant in 3/6, recalled very specifically that it did not get dark until about 10:00 P.M.

26. Catlin, *With the Help of God and a Few Marines*, 110.

27. 461st Regiment War Diary, June 1918, *German War Diaries*, vol. 4; 398th Regiment War Diary, June 1918, ibid.

28. Otto, "Belleau Woods," 944–48.

29. 4th Brigade HQ, Field Order 2, 2:05 P.M. on June 6, 1918, 13–15; Holcomb to McClellan, n.d.

30. 2nd Field Artillery Brigade HQ, Field Order 3, June 6, 1918, *2nd Div. Records*, vol. 9; 4th Brigade HQ, Field Order 2, 2:05 P.M. on June 6, 1918, 13–15; *History of the Sixth Machine Gun Battalion*, 13–15; Waller, "Machine Guns of the 4th Brigade," 15–16. The three attacking battalions, three thousand strong, were supported by five battalions of 75-mm guns and two battalions of 155-mm guns from the 2nd Field Artillery, plus the French 167th Division's field artillery; roughly 180 guns.

31. Cates interview, OHC; Cates, "Personal Observations"; Cates, letters, MCPPC; Clifton B. Cates, interview by Robert B. Asprey, June 25, 1963, Folder 9a, Box 1, Asprey NRC, MCPPC; Erskine to ABMC, n.d.; Messersmith, "Operations of Company 'E'"; Paradis memoir, MCPPC; West, "Belleau Wood," 5; Holcomb to McClellan, n.d.

32. Cates interview, Asprey NRC.

33. Hill to Neufeld, Jan. 17, 1979; West "Belleau Wood," 5; Erskine to ABMC,

n.d. Two lieutenants in the 96th Company and one in the 80th Company were also army officers. The quality of these leaders appears to have been good to excellent.

34.   Pvt. Charles Vanek, letter, n.d., cited in Cowing, *Dear Folks at Home;* Asprey, *At Belleau Wood,* 182; Otto, "Belleau Woods," 948; Hill to Neufeld, Jan. 17, 1979.

35.   Maj. Frank Evans to Commandant George Barnett, June 29, 1918, in Catlin, *With the Help of God and a Few Marines,* 332. Cole was killed June 10.

36.   Catlin, *With the Help of God and a Few Marines,* 115; Asprey, *At Belleau Wood,* 184; Hill to Neufeld, Jan. 17, 1979; Otto, "Belleau Woods," 948.

37.   Sgt. Aloysius Sheridan, letter, Aug. 14, 1918, Asprey NRC, MCPPC.

38.   Cates interview, OHC; Cates, "Personal Observations"; Cates, letters, MCPPC; Cates interview, Asprey NRC. For additional, vivid eyewitness accounts of the attacks, see Benjamin, "June, 1918," 1–3; Erskine interview, OHC, 35–39; Hill to Neufeld, Jan. 17, 1979; Messersmith, "Operations of Company 'E'"; and Paradis memoir, MCPPC, 44–52.

39.   Sheridan, letter, Aug. 14, 1918. Oddly, of the four men killed by this shell, the Department of the Navy singled out the dentist, Lieutenant Osborne, to receive the Medal of Honor.

40.   Paradis memoir, MCPPC, 47–48; Sheridan, letter, Aug. 14, 1918.

41.   Hill to Neufeld, Jan. 17, 1979; Benjamin, "June, 1918."

42.   Meyer, letter, *Recruiter's Bulletin,* Oct. 1918; Hill to Neufeld, Jan. 17, 1979; Vanek, letter, n.d., cited in Cowing, *Dear Folks at Home;* Benjamin, "June, 1918"; Worton interview, OHC, 29.

43.   Erskine to ABMC, n.d.

44.   Asprey, *At Belleau Wood,* 182–83.

45.   West, "Belleau Wood."

46.   Ibid.

47.   Bailey M. Coffenberg to ABMC, Apr. 18, 1930, Box 190, RG 117.

48.   Otto, "Belleau Woods," 948; Catlin, *With the Help of God and a Few Marines,* 112; *History of the Sixth Machine Gun Battalion,* 15. A total of four companies, or sixty-four Hotchkiss guns, supported the 6th Marines. How many were firing in support of 2/6 is impossible to ascertain.

49.   Messersmith, "Operations of Company 'E.'"

50.   Sellers memoir, 18–19.

51.   Paradis memoir, MCPPC, 48–49.

52.   Clark, *Devildogs,* 116–19; Bellamy, *Third Battalion, Sixth Regiment,* 19.

53.   Cates, "Personal Observations"; Hill to Neufeld, Jan. 17, 1979; Muster Roll, June 1918.

54.   Cates interview, OHC; Cates, "Personal Observations"; Cates, letters, MCPPC; Cates interview, Asprey NRC.

55.   Timmerman interview, Asprey NRC.

56.   Catlin, *With the Help of God and a Few Marines,* 402; Cates, "Personal Observations"; Cates interview, Asprey NRC; Hill to Neufeld, Jan. 17, 1979; 2nd Battalion, 398th Regiment, War Diary, June 6, 1918, *German War Diaries,* vol. 1.

57.   Cates, "Personal Observations"; Cates interview, Asprey NRC; Otto, "Belleau Woods," 948. Why the marine thought it was important to carry a bottle of wine into the attack was never adequately explained.

58.   Cates interview, OHC; Cates, "Personal Observations"; Cates, letters, MCPPC; Cates interview, Asprey NRC.

59. Cates, "Personal Observations"; Cates interview, Asprey NRC; Major Evans to Major General Barnett, June 29, 1918, in Catlin, *With the Help of God and a Few Marines*, 334; Citation of Pvt. Herbert D. Dunlavy, in ibid., 381–82.

60. Paradis memoir, MCPPC, 49.

61. Cates interview, OHC; Cates, "Personal Observations"; Cates, letters, MCPPC; Cates interview, Asprey NRC; Hill to Neufeld, Jan. 17, 1979; Meyer, letter, *Recruiter's Bulletin*, Oct. 1918.

62. Cates interview, OHC; West, "Belleau Wood."

63. Holcomb to Catlin, Field Message, 9:27 P.M. on June 6, 1918, *2nd Div. Records*, vol. 5.

64. Benjamin, "June, 1918"; George Clark, *A List of Officers of the 4th Marine Brigade*, 22; Evans to Barnett, June 29, 1918, in Catlin, *With the Help of God and a Few Marines*, 324. The army's inflexible, impersonal manpower administrators plucked Leonard from a frontline battalion in the thick of combat. One suspects that Holcomb would have delayed releasing Leonard had he held the officer in higher regard.

65. The 79th Company reported sixty wounded and twelve dead for June 6. The 96th Company muster roll for June reports forty-three wounded and eleven dead for June 6 and 7 combined. These figures *must* be low. The rolls list only marines evacuated—those treated at aid stations and returned to duty are not recorded. Likewise, army and navy casualties, as well as those from battalion headquarters, are not reflected in this count. The morning of June 8, after most stragglers had caught up with their companies, Captain Zane reported that he had only ninety marines from the 79th Company and one hundred marines from the 96th Company with him in Bouresches. Even accounting for additional casualties from June 7 and 8, these figures suggest total losses for June 6 exceeding 50 percent.

66. West, "Belleau Wood."

67. 6th Marines to 23rd Infantry, Field Message, 5:05 A.M. on June 8, 1918, *2nd Div. Records*, vol. 5.

68. Erskine to ABMC, n.d.

69. *History of the Sixth Regiment United States Marines*, 16; *History of the Sixth Machine Gun Battalion*, 15–16; Cates interview, Asprey NRC; Cates interview, OHC.

70. CO 2/6 to CO 6th Marines and CG 4th Brig, 11:30 P.M. on June 6, 1918, *2nd Div. Records*, vol. 4; West, "Belleau Wood."

71. Paradis memoir, MCPPC, 50.

72. Erskine to ABMC, n.d.; Paradis memoir, MCPPC, 51; 4th Marine Brigade telephone log, June 8, 1918, *2nd Div. Records*, vol. 5.

73. Bellamy, *Third Battalion, Sixth Regiment*, 21–22.

74. Hemrick, *Once a Marine*, 106–107.

75. Timmerman interview, Asprey NRC; 461st Regiment War Diary, June 8, 1918, *German War Diaries*, vol. 4; Bellamy, *Third Battalion, Sixth Regiment*, 21–22; *History of the Sixth Regiment United States Marines*, 17. For graphic accounts of the attack by 3/6, see David Bellamy, diary, MCPPC; and Gen. Alfred H. Noble, USMC (Ret.), interview by Maj. L. E. Tatem, 1973, OHC.

76. Hemrick, *Once a Marine*, 109–10; Paradis to Mom and Dad, July 15, 1918; Paradis to Maj. Gen. Thomas Holcomb, Dec. 1937, Paradis Personal Papers Collection, MCPPC.

77. MacGillivray and Clark, 80th *Company*, 3.

78. Muster Roll, June 1918; McClellan, *Marine Corps in the World War*, 34.

79. Lee's letter is quoted in Asprey, *At Belleau Wood,* 236–37.

80. Brannen, *Over There,* 17–20; Krulewitch, *Now That You Mention It,* 45–46.

81. Harbord to Holcomb, Field Message, 9:15 P.M. on June 8, 1918, *2nd Div. Records,* vol. 5.

82. *History of the Sixth Regiment United States Marines,* 18; Muster Roll, June 1918. As indicated previously, this figure is certainly low. The casualty figures for the 78th and 96th Companies are underreported due to near complete annihilation of these units on June 14. If the 78th and 96th suffered casualties comparable to the 79th and 80th Companies, they lost an additional one hundred men combined.

83. Grotelueschen, "AEF Way of War," 58–59.

84. Catlin, *With the Help of God and a Few Marines,* 340–417 passim.

Chapter 4

1. *History of the Sixth Regiment United States Marines,* 18; Messersmith, "Operations of Company 'E,'" copy in author's possession; Muster Roll, June 1918. The YMCA filled the role of the post exchange during the First World War with the encouragement and approval of General Pershing, yet the perception among combat soldiers that the association was exploiting their situation was commonplace. Replacements were distributed as follows: the 78th Company received eleven; the 79th received seventy-nine; the 80th received seventy; and the 96th—which had suffered grievously—received only five. The newcomers were distributed unevenly between the companies, with little effort to preserve unit cohesion from the replacement organizations, probably because the men arrived at different intervals. It is likely that the 96th Company received so few replacements because it was the only one with a lieutenant (Robertson) commanding, and Holcomb did not want to overburden the company leadership.

2. "Rockport Man Wins Promotion in Marine Corps," *Rockport Pilot,* n.d.; Simon David Barber funeral card (provided by Jeanette Barber); Erskine interview, OHC, 43.

3. Spaulding and Wright, *Second Division,* 57–59; Asprey, *At Belleau Wood,* chaps. 16–17; Otto, "Belleau Woods," 953–54; Clark, *Devildogs,* 134–38, 139–60.

4. Hemrick, *Once a Marine,* 105.

5. West, "Belleau Wood," HRB.

6. Messersmith, "Operations of Company 'E.'"

7. CO 2/6 to CO 6th Marines, 10:05 P.M. on June 13, 1918, *2nd Div. Records,* vol. 5.

8. Messersmith, "Operations of Company 'E'"; Paradis memoir, MCPPC, 59–61; "Brief History of the Second Battalion, Sixth Regiment, U.S. Marine Corps," Box 36, 2/6 File, RG 127.

9. *German War Diaries,* vol. 4.

10. Messersmith, "Operations of Company 'E'"; Paradis memoir, MCPPC, 59–61; *History of the Sixth Regiment United States Marines,* 19.

11. Cates interview, Asprey NRC.

12. Clifton B. Cates, "The Bravest Man I Ever Knew," *Saga,* Mar. 1952, 45. Stockham was posthumously awarded the Medal of Honor.

13. Paradis memoir, MCPPC, 61.

14. Cates interview, Asprey NRC.

15. Benjamin, "June, 1918," MCPPC; West, "Belleau Wood."

16. 2nd Div. HQ, "G2 Intel Summary," noon June 13 to noon June 14, 1918, *2nd Div. Records*, vol. 9; Muster Roll, June 1918; Cates interview, Asprey NRC; Hopper, *Medals of Honor*, 124.

17. Paradis memoir, MCPPC, 61. Maj. Fritz Wise, commanding 2/5, later wrote that Holcomb had 325 marines with him when he arrived at Wise's headquarters but nonetheless offered to go ahead with the relief. Wise, *A Marine Tells It to You*, 230–31.

18. Wise, *A Marine Tells It to You*, 230–35; Cates interview, Asprey NRC; Clark, *Devildogs*, 176–77; Otto, "Belleau Woods," 956.

19. 9th Co., 461st Regiment, War Diary, June 12, 1918, *German War Diaries*, vol. 4; Lieutenant Breil, diary, quoted in Otto, "Belleau Woods," 957.

20. Benjamin, "June, 1918," 4; 461st Regiment War Diary, June 14–18, 1918, *German War Diaries*, vol. 4; 2nd Div. HQ, "G2 Intel Summaries," noon June 14 to noon June 16, 1918, *2nd Div. Records*, vol. 4; Cates, letter, June 18, 1918, MCPPC.

21. West, "Belleau Wood," 13; Muster Roll, June 1918.

22. Hemrick, *Once a Marine*, 106; Paradis memoir, MCPPC, 64; Muster Roll, June 1918.

23. Brannen, *Over There*, 21–22; Cates to Mother, June 14–16, 1918, letters, MCPPC. The paper Cates wrote this letter on had been punctured by shrapnel.

24. Benjamin, "June, 1918."

25. West, "Belleau Wood," 14.

26. Maj. J. C. Montgomery to CG 2nd Div., "Report of Inspection of 2/6," June 19, 1918, *2nd Div. Records*, vol. 7. Montgomery's casualty figures are far higher than those reported in the Muster Roll, probably for reasons discussed earlier.

27. Wethered Woodworth, Personnel Records, OMPF; Cates, June 26, 1918, letters, MCPPC; Muster Roll, June 1918; Montgomery, "Report of Inspection of 2/6"; Capt. Egbert T. Lloyd, Memorandum, Aug. 28, 1918, Box 36, 80th Company File, RG 127.

28. These commissions became effective June 27. Muster Roll, June 1918. By the end of the war, 164 second lieutenants had come from the ranks of the 4th Brigade. McClellan, *Marine Corps in the World War*, 23.

29. Summary of promotions: 78th Company—ten corporals, one sergeant; 79th Company—three gunnery sergeants, seven sergeants, twenty-one corporals; 80th Company—none recorded; 96th Company—five corporals. Muster Roll, June 1918; Erskine interview, OHC, 43.

30. Muster Roll, June 1918; Erskine interview, OHC, 43. In 1918 first sergeant was not a permanent rank a marine carried from one unit to the next but a temporary post held only so long as the marine filled the billet.

31. Muster Roll, June 1918. Missing marines whose status was changed to "presumed killed" are so indicated in the rolls. The conclusion is that most or all of these men went AWOL.

32. Spaulding and Wright, *Second Division*, 66–70.

33. Benjamin, "June, 1918."

34. West, "Belleau Wood," 7. Zane died from his wounds on October 24, 1918. Zane BF.

35. Erskine interview, OHC, 43.

36. Ibid., 44; West "Belleau Wood"; Muster Roll, June 1918; Benjamin, "June, 1918."

37. *History of the Sixth Regiment United States Marines*, 20.

38. Paradis memoir, MCPPC, 70–74.

39. West, "Belleau Wood."

40. Cates to Mother and Sister, July 13, 1918, MCPPC.

41. Ibid.; Cates interview, Asprey NRC.

42. *History of the Sixth Regiment United States Marines*, 20; Muster Roll, June 1918; West, "Belleau Wood."

43. Muster Roll, June 1918.

44. West, "Belleau Wood."

Chapter 5

1. Paradis memoir, MCPPC, 80; Muster Roll, July 1918.

2. Denig BF; Muster Roll, July 1918; Denig, "Diary," MCPPC, 210.

3. Hopper, *Medals of Honor*, 125–26. The muster roll for July neither confirms nor disproves Kelly's account.

4. Muster Roll, July 1918. Dean would be accidentally killed while on Rhine River patrol on May 18, 1919.

5. Ibid.

6. Ibid.; Cates, *96th Company;* Cates interview, Asprey NRC.

7. Asprey, *German High Command at War*, 427–28; Toland, *No Man's Land*, 238–40; Spaulding and Wright, *Second Division*, 96–104.

8. Spaulding and Wright, *Second Division*, 99–101, 103–104.

9. Ibid., 107; Denig, "Diary," 193; Muster Roll, July 1918.

10. Denig, "Diary," 196–97.

11. Van Haften, "Attack and Capture of Bouresches," Box 36, RG 127. The section of Van Haften's manuscript found in the National Archives appears to be an extract from a longer memoir, dealing only with the period July 16–19.

12. Ibid.

13. Denig, "Diary," 196–98. The Viller-Cotterets Forest is also known as the Forest of Retz.

14. Denig, "Diary," 197–98; Van Haften, "Attack and Capture of Bouresches"; Paradis memoir, MCPPC, 82; "Brief History of the Second Battalion, Sixth Regiment, U.S. Marine Corps," Box 36, 2/6 File, RG 127.

15. Paradis memoir, MCPPC, 83. Neither side enjoyed air superiority at Soissons, thus observation balloons rarely appeared in the sky.

16. Denig, "Diary," 198–201.

17. Spaulding and Wright, *Second Division*, 115–21; Harbord, *American Army in France*, 334.

18. Denig, "Diary," 202; Spaulding and Wright, *Second Division*, 126; Thomas Holcomb, "Report of Operations of the 2nd Battalion, 6th Marines, July 18–20, 1918," *2nd Div. Records*, vol. 4; Derby, *Wade In*, 90.

19. Denig, "Diary," 202; *History of the Sixth Regiment United States Marines*, 21; Holcomb, "Report of Operations."

20. *German War Diaries*, vol. 5. German units were greatly understrength. The 14th Reserve Infantry Division exercised tactical control of remnants of regiments from three different divisions.

21. 2nd Div. HQ, Field Order 16, reprinted in McClellan, "Aisne-Marne Offensive" (June 1921), 204. This document states that the artillery pre-

paration would begin at 6:00 A.M. according to orders approved by the commanding general, 2nd Field Artillery Brigade. These orders have not been located. Mark Grotelueschen writes that the 2nd Division planned no rolling barrage for July 19 and that the preparatory barrage lasted one hour. *Doctrine under Trial*, 67–68, 70.

22. *History of the Sixth Machine Gun Battalion*, 27; *History of the Sixth Regiment United States Marines*, 21. The 2nd Engineers and 4th Machine Gun Battalion constituted the division reserve.

23. Holcomb, "Report of Operations."

24. *History of the Sixth Regiment United States Marines*, 21; Hillman and Johnson, *Soissons*, 105; *German War Diaries*, vol. 5.

25. Cates to Mother and Sister, Aug. 1, 1918, letters, MCPPC; Paradis memoir, MCPPC, 85, 86. See also Cates interview, OHC, 32.

26. Sparks, Diary, MCPPC, 16; Capt. Clifton B. Cates, "Description of the Attack of the 2nd Batt. 6th Marines, July 19, 1918," RG 117.4.2; Denig, "Diary," 203. Thomas in 1/6 later recalled that the attack was held up while awaiting the French tanks. Thomas, "Soissons," *Marine Corps Gazette*, Nov. 1965, 43.

27. Bellamy, *Third Battalion, Sixth Regiment*, 32–33; Paradis memoir, MCPPC, 85.

28. Sparks interview, MCPPC, 16; *History of the Sixth Regiment United States Marines*, 21; Holcomb, "Report of Operations."

29. Denig, "Diary," 204; Cates interview, OHC, 33.

30. Cates, "Attack of the 2nd Batt. 6th Marines." Paradis recalled that the 80th Company formed in two waves. Memoir, MCPPC, 86. Major Denig, Corporal Sparks, and Private Van Haften all stated four waves. Sparks interview, 15; Denig, "Diary," 203; Van Haften, "Attack and Capture of Bouresches." Cates's account concurs: "It was a pretty sight to look out at that bunch of men in eight waves, moving across the open wheat fields." Eight waves would describe four ranks in the front companies and four in the supporting companies. Cates to Mother and Sister, Aug. 1, 1918.

31. The battalion covered no more than fifteen hundred yards between 8:25 and 9:00 A.M.

32. Cates to Mother and Sister, Aug. 1, 1918; Cates, "Attack of the 2nd Batt. 6th Marines"; *History of the Sixth Regiment United States Marines*, 21; Paradis memoir, MCPPC, 86–87; Denig, "Diary," 204; Muster Roll, July 1918; Sparks, Diary, MCPPC, 16.

33. Cates to Mother and Sister, Aug. 1, 1918; Denig, "Diary," 205.

34. Cates to Mother and Sister, Aug. 1, 1918; Cates interview, OHC. Details on Fritz's wound are from Fritz, Personnel Records, OMPF.

35. Paradis memoir, MCPPC, 87; Brannen, *Over There*, 31.

36. U.S. Navy, *Medical Department*, 32; Muster Roll, July 1918.

37. Brannen, *Over There*, 31.

38. CO 80th Company to Regimental Commander, Aug. 10, 1918, Box 36, 80th Company File, RG 127. Yohner was given the benefit of the doubt, for he kept his stripes and transferred to the 79th Company at his own request.

39. Paradis memoir, MCPPC, 87.

40. Denig, "Diary," 204.

41. Cates to Mother and Sister, Aug. 1, 1918; Denig, "Diary," 205; 2nd Battalion, 16th Reserve Infantry, "Report of Operations," *German War Diaries*, vol. 5. The sugar-beet mill is referred to as "la Raperie" in many accounts.

42. Cates interview, OHC; Cates, "Attack of the 2nd Batt. 6th Marines"; Cates to Mother and Sister, Aug. 1, 1918.

43. Brannen, *Over There*, 31–32.

44. Paradis memoir, MCPPC, 87; Denig, "Diary," 207.

45. *2nd Div. Records*, vol. 5; Maj. Robert L. Denig to ABMC, July 10, 1930, RG 117.4.2.

46. *2nd Div. Records*, vol. 5; Denig, "Diary," 206.

47. 14th Reserve Division War Diary, *German War Diaries*, vol. 5; 16th Reserve Infantry War Diary, ibid.

48. *2nd Div. Records*, vol. 5.

49. Denig, "Diary," 206.

50. *2nd Div. Records*, vol. 5.

51. Sparks, Diary, 16.

52. *2nd Div. Records*, vol. 5.

53. Ibid., vol. 7; Muster Roll. As the muster roll was submitted at the end of July, those listed as "missing" were all true casualties; marines separated from their companies on July 19 who subsequently rejoined were not carried as missing.

54. Denig, "Diary," 209; Cates to Mother and Sister, Aug. 1, 1918.

55. Cates to Mother and Sister, Aug. 1, 1918.

56. Brannen, *Over There*, 36.

57. *2nd Div. Records*, vol. 5.

58. Derby, *Wade In*, 88–95; U.S. Navy, *Medical Department*, 64–65.

59. Denig, "Diary," 208.

60. Spaulding and Wright, *Second Division*, 130; Asprey, *German High Command at War*, 441; Brannen, *Over There*, 33.

61. Paradis memoir, MCPPC, 89–90.

62. Spaulding and Wright, *Second Division*, 130.

63. Cates to Mother and Sister, Aug. 1, 1918.

64. Paradis memoir, MCPPC, 89–90.

65. Cates to Mother and Sister, Aug. 1, 1918.

66. Muster Roll, July 1918.

67. Brannen, *Over There*, 33–34.

68. Grotelueschen, "AEF Way of War," 72–74.

Chapter 6

1. Lejeune, *Reminiscences*, 307.

2. 6th Marines, General Order 38, Aug. 11, 1918, *2nd Div. Records*, vol. 9; Sellers memoir, copy in author's possession, 25; Cates interview, OHC, 49; Erskine interview, OHC, 62; Paradis memoir, MCPPC, 93.

3. Maddox, "Medal of Honor Recipient"; Williams, Personnel Records, OMPF. For accounts of the action at San Francisco de Macoris, see 1st Lt. Ernest C. Williams, "Report Concerning the Operations Resulting in the Seizure of Fortalenza, November 29, 1916," Dec. 1, 1916, in Williams, Personnel Records, OMPF. Second-hand accounts of this incident include Bob Considine, "One-Man Task Force," *American Weekly*, Oct. 5, 1958; Hoyte Evans, "Who's Knocking at My Door?" *Phoenix Exchange*, Spring 1988; and Musicant, *Banana Wars*, 269–71.

4. Williams, Personnel Records, OMPF.

5. *History of the Sixth Regiment United States Marines*, 22–23; Paradis memoir, MCPPC, 95–97.

6. *History of the Sixth Regiment United States Marines*, 23; "General Principles Governing the Training of Units of the 2nd U.S. Division (Regular)," Box 16, 6th Marines File, RG 127 [hereafter cited as "2nd Division Training"]. This document is undated, but as it is signed by Col. J. C. Rhea, AC/S G-3, by order of General Lejeune, it undoubtedly was issued for this August training period.

7. First Army HQ, "Combat Instructions for the Troops of First Army," Aug. 29, 1918, quoted in Grotelueschen, "AEF Way of War," 29–30; John J. Pershing (AEF HQ), "Combat Instructions," Sept. 5, 1918, 3, quoted in ibid., 32.

8. "2nd Division Training"; Grotelueschen, "AEF Way of War," 194. The marines learned at least one technique that would not prove as effective. In the 80th Company, a new lieutenant named David Kilduff taught his platoon to advance with "marching fire"—firing their bolt-action Springfields from the waist or shoulder to suppress the enemy while advancing. The inaccurate fire of such a technique could hardly threaten a machine gunner, while the marine utilizing it would have to slowly walk erect toward the enemy. Kilduff probably learned the technique at one of the AEF's schools. Brannen, *Over There*, 142–43.

9. Brannen, *Over There*, 40–41.

10. Lejeune, *Reminiscences*, 306; Braim, *Test of Battle*, 58; Muster Roll, Aug.–Sept. 1918; *History of the Sixth Regiment United States Marines*, 23.

11. Muster Roll, Aug.–Sept. 1918; McClellan, *Marine Corps in the World War*, 34. Four battalions of marine replacements arrived in France August 26–27, the 3rd, 4th, 5th, and 6th Separate Battalions. Most of 2/6's replacements arriving September 11 joined from the 5th Separate Battalion.

12. Muster Roll, Sept. 1918; Brannen, *Over There*, 36. Brannen says Coffenburg, who was shot in the hand and evacuated on September 13, took over from Lloyd. Paradis says Kilduff relieved Lloyd. The muster roll for September records Coffenburg's wounding but does not indicate who commanded. Most likely Coffenburg, as the "old" company commander, relieved Lloyd, and Kilduff took over upon Coffenburg's evacuation. Just as army lieutenants occasionally served with the marine brigade, marine officers such as Minnis often served in army units. Major Denig was now commanding 3rd Battalion, 9th Infantry.

13. McClellan, *Marine Corps in the World War*, 21–23; George Clark, e-mail message to author, Sept. 20, 2005.

14. Muster Roll, Sept. 1918; MacGillivray and Clark, *80th Company*, v. Wilmer had been transferred to Paris; he would return to work for Holcomb at regimental headquarters. Lloyd must have been transferred; he does not appear on the muster roll for September. The roll is unclear about who commanded the 80th Company. Paradis states that Kilduff relieved Lloyd. Memoir, MCPPC, 111. Brannen writes that "Captain Woodall" commanded the 80th (probably he confused this for Woodworth in the 78th Company) and that Kilduff was his platoon commander. *Over There*, 42.

15. Capt. John A. Minnis to CO 6th Marines, "Report on Tank Maneuvers, September 7, 1918," Sept. 8, 1918, Box 30, RG 127.

16. Ibid.

17. *History of the Sixth Regiment United States Marines*, 42; Clifton B. Cates to Mother and Sister, Sept. 22, 1918, letters, MCPPC; Brannen, *Over There*, 40.

18. Cates to Mother and Sister, Sept. 22, 1918.

19. Pershing, *My Experiences*, 2:243–55.

20. Ibid., 266, 270–71; Smythe, *Pershing*, 179–80; Spaulding and Wright, *Second Division*, 152.

21. Smythe, *Pershing*, 180; American Battlefield Monuments Commission, "2nd Division Limey Sector, September 9–11, 1918, Saint Mihiel Offensive, September 12–16, 1918," *American Armies and Battlefields in Europe*, map (1937). This ratio determined by U.S. infantry battalions having one thousand men each versus three German battalions and one Landsturm battalion with less than five hundred men each.

22. Spaulding and Wright, *Second Division*, 149.

23. Ibid., 147.

24. Brannen, *Over There*, 42; Spaulding and Wright, *Second Division*, 152–58.

25. Maj. Ernest C. Williams, "Operation Report Covering Period from September 12 to September 15, 1918," *2nd Div. Records*, vol. 7 [hereafter cited as Williams, "Saint-Mihiel Report"]; Erskine scrapbook, Erskine Personal Papers, MCPPC; Erskine interview, OHC, 62–63; 2nd Division AC/S G-2, "Summary of Intelligence," Sept. 13–14, 14–15, 1918, *2nd Div. Records*, vol. 9.

26. 3rd Battalion, 398th Regiment, War Diary, Sept. 13–16, 1918, *German War Diaries*, vol. 7; 2nd Division AC/S G-2, "Summary of Intelligence," Sept. 14–15, 1918, *2nd Div. Records*, vol. 9.

27. At least 2,400 men in the 6th Marines versus about 360 in the 3/398th Battalion.

28. Brannen, *Over There*, 42. Marines in World War I frequently referred to themselves as "soldiers."

29. *History of the Sixth Regiment United States Marines*, 28–29.

30. Bellamy, *Third Battalion, Sixth Regiment*, 63; Maj. Francis Barker, "1/6 Report of Operations," Sept. 17, 1918, *2nd Div. Records*, vol. 7; *German War Diaries*, vol. 6.

31. *History of the Sixth Regiment United States Marines*, 30; CO 6th Marines to CO 2/6, 2:12 A.M. on Sept. 15, 1918, *2nd Div. Records*, vol. 5.

32. Erskine interview, OHC, 63; Williams, "Saint-Mihiel Report."

33. Erskine interview, OHC, 63; Williams, "Saint-Mihiel Report."

34. Paradis memoir, MCPPC, 116–17.

35. Brannen, *Over There*, 42; Erskine interview, OHC, 63. Erskine also states: "We had a little advance guard, we didn't have much. We had mostly guides from the other battalion. Why the guides let these people go there, I don't know." If 1/6 had managed to send guides all the way back to Williams, link up with him, and bring him forward, they nonetheless were not following Barker's route and would have offered little assistance on navigation or enemy positions.

36. Erskine interview, OHC, 63.

37. Williams, "Saint-Mihiel Report"; Erskine interview, OHC, 64–65.

38. Paradis memoir, MCPPC, 117; *History of the Sixth Machine Gun Battalion*, 37.

39. Erskine interview, OHC, 63; Paradis memoir, MCPPC, 117.

40. Brannen, *Over There*, 42; Paradis memoir, MCPPC, 117.

41. For eyewitness accounts from the 80th Company, see Brannen, *Over There*, 42; and Paradis memoir, MCPPC, 116–18.

42. Cates to Mother and Sister, Sept. 22, 1918; Muster Roll, Sept. 1918. Minnis volunteered after the war for flight training at Pensacola, where he died in a tragic crash.

43. CO 78th Co. to 6th Marines, 7:15 A.M. on Sept. 15, 1918, *2nd Div. Records*,

vol. 5; 2nd Lt. James Adams, "Report of Operations, September 15th, 1918," Sept. 17, 1918, *2nd Div. Records,* vol. 7; Hopper, *Medals of Honor,* 127.

44.   Erskine interview, OHC, 63; Williams, "Saint-Mihiel Report."

45.   Hayden, Biographic File, Medal of Honor Society, Patriot's Point, S.C. Hayden received the Medal of Honor.

46.   Adams, "Report of Operations"; *History of the Sixth Machine Gun Battalion,* 37; Sparks, Diary, MCPPC, 20.

47.   *History of the Sixth Machine Gun Battalion,* 37.

48.   Sparks, Diary, 21.

49.   Adams, "Report of Operations."

50.   Ibid.; Maj. G. A. Stowall to ABMC, June 7, 1929, Box 192, RG 117.4.2; *German War Diaries,* vol. 6. Stowall reported: "On arriving at the south edge of these woods, two companies of the 2nd Battalion of the 6th Marines, were found in position. . . . The senior officer of these two organizations stated that they had advanced to the north edge of the woods but had been driven back by heavy machine gun and rifle fire coming from the woods . . . and also from the North East. They also stated that about 100 dead and wounded had been left in the woods, which were very open." This senior officer was likely Martin.

51.   *2nd Div. Records,* vol. 5.

52.   CO 2/6 to CO 6th Marines, 7:35 A.M. on Sept. 15, 1918, *2nd Div. Records,* vol. 5; 3rd Battalion, 398th Regiment, War Diary, Sept. 13–16, 1918, *German War Diaries,* vol. 7.

53.   Woodworth to Holcomb, 8:00 A.M. on Sept. 15, 1918, *2nd Div. Records,* vol. 5 [emphasis added].

54.   *2nd Div. Records,* vol. 4.

55.   Bellamy, *Third Battalion, Sixth Regiment,* 64.

56.   *2nd Div. Records,* vol. 4; *History of the Sixth Machine Gun Battalion,* 37; Stowall to ABMC, June 7, 1929; Adams, "Report of Operations"; Barker, "1/6 Report of Operations."

57.   Hopper, *Medals of Honor,* 128–29; Adams, "Report of Operations."

58.   Paradis memoir, MCPPC, 117.

59.   Brannen, *Over There,* 42; Paradis memoir, MCPPC, 118.

60.   Adams, "Report of Operations;" Williams, "Saint-Mihiel Report."

61.   Stowall to ABMC, June 7, 1929; Barker, "1/6 Report of Operations."

62.   Curiously, The Bull addressed this to Lieutenants Adams, Hawkins, Denham, and Goode. Adams had taken over the 78th when Woodworth took his three bullets. Most likely, Denham and Goode commanded the 80th and 96th Companies respectively after Kilduff and Minnis fell. Lieutenant Hawkins was a 79th Company officer—and Captain Martin was unscathed and presumably very much in command. Martin may have been incommunicado or rumored to be a casualty. *2nd Div. Records,* vol. 4.

63.   Stowall to ABMC, June 7, 1929. The senior officer was likely Martin but might have been Adams or Williams.

64.   *2nd Div. Records,* vol. 5; Stowall to ABMC, June 7, 1929; Paradis memoir, MCPPC, 119.

65.   Bellamy, *Third Battalion, Sixth Regiment,* 65.

66.   Lejeune, *Reminiscences,* 332–33; *2nd Div. Records,* vol. 4; *History of the Sixth Machine Gun Battalion,* 37; Williams, "Saint-Mihiel Report."

67.   Stowall to ABMC, June 7, 1929.

68.   Muster Roll, Sept. 1918.

69. Erskine scrapbook, MCPPC. Erskine mentions that he brought Williams a German helmet filled with beer after one patrol into Xammes. This patrol could have taken place on the night of September 13 or 14.

70. *2nd Div. Records*, vol. 4.

71. Grotelueschen, *Doctrine under Trial*, 91.

72. Muster Roll, Sept. 1918; Smythe, *Pershing*, 217–18.

73. Muster Roll, Sept. 1918; Paradis memoir, MCPPC, 125.

Chapter 7

1. *History of the Sixth Regiment United States Marines*, 31; Paradis memoir, MCPPC, 127.

2. Sellers memoir, copy in author's possession, 25. The five captains are not listed on the rolls, so this cannot be confirmed. Muster Roll, Oct. 1918.

3. Sellers memoir, 31; Clark, *Devildogs*, 4, 24n, 263; Williams Personnel Records, OMPF; Capt. Walter A. Powers to Regimental Commander, Oct. 15, 1918, Box 36, 80th Company File, RG 127; Paradis memoir, MCPPC, 125.

4. Muster Roll, Oct. 1918; Sellers memoir, 27.

5. Toland, *No Man's Land*, 316–18.

6. Lejeune, *Reminiscences*, 342–43.

7. "2nd Division, Meuse-Argonne (Champagne) Offensive, September 29–October 14, 1918" (Washington: American Battlefield Monuments Commission, 1936), map; personal reconnaissance of battlefield by author, 1992; Brannen, *Over There*, 47.

8. Otto, *Blanc Mont*, 14–20.

9. Ibid., 28–48, passim. German strength is very difficult to estimate. This calculation is based on an estimate of 225 men for the 2/235th, 250 each for the 18th Jaeger Battalion and 2/74, 50 in the 2nd Landsturm Company, 100 in the 10th Field Artillery Battalion, and up to 300 (total) for the various headquarters units.

10. Spaulding and Wright, *Second Division*, 170–71; 2nd Div. HQ, Field Order 35, Oct. 2, 1918, in McClellan, "Battle at Blanc Mont Ridge" (June 1922), 206–209; Grotelueschen, *Doctrine under Trial*, 103.

11. Maj. Ernest C. Williams, "Operation Report Covering Period from September 29 to October 10th, 1918," Oct. 17, 1918, Box 36, RG 127 [hereafter cited as Williams, "Blanc Mont Report"]; Paradis memoir, MCPPC, 126.

12. Paradis memoir, MCPPC, 127; Williams, "Blanc Mont Report"; *History of the Sixth Machine Gun Battalion*, 41.

13. Hopper, *Medals of Honor*, 132.

14. Clifton B. Cates to Mother and Sister, Oct. 13, 1918, letters, MCPPC; Cates, *96th Company*, 10; *History of the Sixth Regiment United States Marines*, 32–33.

15. Capt. James McB. Sellers, "Report of Operations from October 2nd to October 10th Inclusive," Box 36, RG 127; Sellers memoir, 27; *History of the Sixth Regiment United States Marines*, 33.

16. Williams, "Blanc Mont Report"; Paradis memoir, MCPPC, 129.

17. *History of the Sixth Regiment United States Marines*, 33; *History of the Sixth Machine Gun Battalion*, 42; Cates to Mother and Sister, Oct. 13, 1918. The 96th suffered ten wounded by Cates's count.

18. Williams, "Blanc Mont Report."

19. West's Medal of Honor recommendation cited in Muster Roll, Oct. 1918. West received the Distinguished Service Cross.

20. Williams, "Blanc Mont Report"; *History of the Sixth Regiment United States Marines*, 33 (capitalization and misspelling are Lee's).

21. *History of the Sixth Regiment United States Marines*, 33; Williams, "Blanc Mont Report."

22. Sellers memoir, 27.

23. Brannen, *Over There*, 47.

24. Williams, "Blanc Mont Report"; Sellers, "Report of Operations"; Sellers memoir, 27; Cates, *96th Company*, 10; Powers to Regimental Commander, Oct. 15, 1918.

25. Paradis memoir, MCPPC, 129; Brannen, *Over There*, 47.

26. Williams, "Blanc Mont Report"; Sellers memoir, 27–29; Hopper, *Medals of Honor*, 137–39. Kelly received the Medal of Honor for this action.

27. Otto, *Blanc Mont*, 32.

28. John Henry Pruitt, Medal of Honor citation, Pruitt BF.

29. Brannen, *Over There*, 48.

30. Ibid., 49–50.

31. Williams, "Blanc Mont Report"; Cates to Mother and Sister, Oct. 13, 1918.

32. Otto, *Blanc Mont*, 33.

33. Ibid.

34. John A. West to Maj. Charles D. Barrett, ABMC, Sept. 10, 1926, RG 117.4.2; 2nd Lt. Lloyd Houchin, "Report of Operations, 79th Company," Oct. 12, 1918, Box 36, RG 127; Paradis memoir, MCPPC, 130. Paradis writes that he was among Cates's 96th Company. But as the sergeant was on the right flank of the 80th Company formation, he must be mistaken.

35. Williams, "Blanc Mont Report"; 2nd Div. HQ, Field Order 35, 11:00 P.M. on Oct. 2, 1918, quoted by George B. Clark, *The Marine Brigade at Blanc Mont*, rev. ed. (Pike, N.H.: Brass Hat, 1994), 6.

36. Otto, *Blanc Mont*, 33, 48–50; *History of the Sixth Regiment United States Marines*, 37; Williams, "Blanc Mont Report." Williams corrected the error on October 4, as discussed below. In this instance his mistake is understandable. The author walked the battleground in 1992 and experienced the same difficulty distinguishing the summit of Blanc Mont from a slightly lower feature just to the east, upon which Williams's flank rested.

37. Otto, *Blanc Mont*, 50; Williams, "Blanc Mont Report"; Cates to Mother and Sister, Oct. 13, 1918.

38. Otto, *Blanc Mont*, 50; Williams, "Blanc Mont Report"; *History of the Sixth Regiment United States Marines*, 37.

39. 2nd Lt. George W. Hopke to CO 2/6, Oct. 12, 1918, cosigned by 2nd Lt. George Ehrhart, Box 36, 80th Company File, RG 127.

40. Powers to Regimental Commander, Oct. 15, 1918; Sellers memoir, 29–31. Powers turned the prisoners over to Gunnery Sergeant Yohner, who was now with the 79th Company after Lloyd had relieved him following Soissons. Yohner was setting a pattern by locating himself so far to the rear once again. Statements from other officers of the 80th Company to Williams are found in the 80th Company file, RG 127. Another eyewitness account of the bizarre case of Captain Powers is found in Paradis memoir, MCPPC, 131, 143–44.

41. Clark, *Marine Brigade at Blanc Mont*, 14–24.

42. *History of the Sixth Regiment United States Marines*, 37.

43. Ibid.

44. Ibid.; Muster Roll, Oct. 1918.

45. Williams, "Blanc Mont Report."

46. Bellamy, *Third Battalion, Sixth Regiment,* 78–81; *History of the Sixth Regiment United States Marines,* 39.

47. *History of the Sixth Regiment United States Marines,* 39; Williams, "Blanc Mont Report."

48. Cates to Mother and Sister, Oct. 13, 1918; Williams, "Blanc Mont Report"; Paradis memoir, MCPPC, 137.

49. Sellers, "Report of Operations." Statements from other officers of the 80th Company are found in Box 36, 80th Company File, RG 127.

50. West to Barrett, ABMC, Sept. 10, 1926.

51. Cates to Mother and Sister, Oct. 13, 1918; West to Barrett, ABMC, Sept. 10, 1926; Muster Roll, Oct. 1918.

52. *History of the Sixth Regiment United States Marines,* 42; Hopke to CO 2/6, Oct. 12, 1918; Paradis memoir, MCPPC, 143.

53. Sellers to sister-in-law, Oct. 17, 1918, copy in author's possession.

54. At the Meuse-Argonne, the 1st Division was able to restart a rolling barrage amid an attack. Grotelueschen, "AEF Way of War," 103.

Chapter 8

1. Green, Personnel Records, OMPF; John C. Green, correspondence with author, Feb. 4, 1996.

2. Paradis memoir, MCPPC, 172.

3. Col. Rolfe Hillman to Brig. Gen. Edwin Simmons, June 2, 1988, in author's possession; Muster Roll, Oct. 1918.

4. Clifton B. Cates to Mother and Sister, Oct. 13, 1918.

5. Lejeune, *Reminiscences,* 367; Cates to Mother and Sister, Oct. 13, 1918; Paradis memoir, MCPPC, 156–57.

6. Clifton B. Cates to ?, Dec. 16, 1918, letters, MCPPC; Sparks, Diary, 22.

7. *History of the Sixth Marines,* 43.

8. Sparks, Diary, 22.

9. American Battlefield Monuments Commission, "The Meuse-Argonne Offensive of the American First Army, September 26–November 11, 1918," *American Armies and Battlefields in Europe,* map; Paschall, *Defeat of Imperial Germany,* 473; Tasker quoted in Braim, *Test of Battle,* 130.

10. Lejeune, *Reminiscences,* 377–79.

11. Ibid., 378.

12. Paradis memoir, MCPPC, 150–51.

13. Sellers memoir, copy in author's possession, 37; Thomas, memoir, MCPPC, 52. Thomas retired as a general after commanding the 1st Marine Division in Korea and serving as assistant commandant.

14. Spaulding and Wright, *Second Division,* 196–97, 201–203.

15. *History of the Sixth Marine Regiment,* 45.

16. Grotelueschen, *Doctrine under Trial,* 120; Spaulding and Wright, *Second Division,* 199–201.

17. Lejeune, *Reminiscences,* 379.

18. *History of the Sixth Regiment United States Marines,* 45; Sellers to "Haze," Oct. 14, 1918, copy in author's possession.

19. Paradis memoir, MCPPC, 149–50.

20. Spaulding and Wright, *Second Division,* 200–203; Sparks, Diary, 22.

21.   *History of the Sixth Marines*, 46.

22.   Krulewitch interview, OHC, 44; Maj. Ernest C. Williams, "Operation Report Covering the Period November 1 to 11, 1918," Box 36, RG 127 [hereafter cited as Williams, "Meuse-Argonne Report"]; *History of the Sixth Machine Gun Battalion*, 52; *History of the Sixth Regiment United States Marines*, 46–47; Wilson, *Treat 'Em Rough*, 179–81.

23.   Hopper, *Medals of Honor*, 141–48.

24.   *History of the Seventy-Ninth Company*, 3.

25.   Paradis memoir, MCPPC, 160–61; Muster Roll, Nov. 1918.

26.   Paradis memoir, MCPPC, 160–61; CO 80th Co. to Regimental Commander, Dec. 11, 1918 (recommendation for Distinguished Service Cross for Gunnery Sergeant Foley), 80th Company File, RG 127; Muster Roll, Nov. 1918. Foley received the Silver Star. Spaulding and Wright, *Second Division*, 326.

27.   *History of the Sixth Marines*, 47; Muster Roll, Nov. 1918.

28.   *History of the Sixth Marines*, 47; "Brief History of the 79th Company, Sixth Marines," n.d., Box 36, RG 127; Cates, *96th Company*.

29.   Sellers memoir, 38.

30.   Spaulding and Wright, *Second Division*, 207–208; Muster Roll, Nov. 1918.

31.   Donaldson, *Seventy-Eighth Company*, 7.

32.   Brannen, *Over There*, 55.

33.   Clifton B. Cates to Mother and Sister, Nov. 27, 1918, letters, MCPPC; Krulewitch interview, OHC, 45.

34.   Muster Roll, Nov. 1918; *History of the Sixth Regiment United States Marines*, 22; Sparks, Diary, 22.

35.   Cates to Mother and Sister, Nov. 27, 1918. The muster roll records only 63 evacuated sick for the 96th Company during November 1–11. Cates's figures indicate that he lost more like 118 out of 200 marines to illness. With less than 50 men—a loss rate of over 75 percent—this more closely matches the regiment's estimate.

36.   *2nd Div. Records*, vol. 5. Krulewitch states unequivocally that Robb commanded the 78th Company for the Meuse crossing on November 10–11. The muster roll reports Sellers commanding the company throughout November. Sellers's memoir is uncharacteristically short on details of the Meuse crossing. He wrote home on November 14 that "many of us were a little under the weather. I was glad it didn't get me till all the scrapping was over though." The reasonable interpretation is that Sellers fell ill between November 2 and 10 but rejoined the company by November 14.

37.   McQuain, *To the Front and Back*, 102.

38.   Krulewitch, *Now That You Mention It*, 55–56.

39.   Toland, *No Man's Land*, 417–19, 426.

40.   Lejeune, *Reminiscences*, 399.

41.   Spaulding and Wright, *Second Division*, 218–19.

42.   Ibid., 219; Grotelueschen, *Doctrine under Trial*, 127; Hillman, "Crossing the Meuse."

43.   *History of the Sixth Marines*, 48.

44.   Krulewitch, *Now That You Mention It*, 56.

45.   McQuain, *To the Front and Back*, 107.

46.   Williams, "Meuse-Argonne Report," 49; *History of the Third Battalion, Sixth Marines*, 110.

47.   Lejeune, *Reminiscences*, 401.

48.   Krulewitch, *Now That You Mention It*, 57–58. Krulewitch turned twenty-three on November 11, 1918.

49.   Hillman, "Crossing the Meuse," 71–73; Metcalf, *History of the U.S. Marine Corps*, 518.

50.   CO 2nd Engineers, after-action report, n.d., quoted in Hillman, "Crossing the Meuse," 73.

51.   Sellers memoir, 39. As noted previously, Sellers appears to have been evacuated sick and almost certainly was not present for duty the night of November 10–11.

52.   Krulewitch, *Now That You Mention It*, 57. Krulewitch did not publish his memoir until 1973, fifty-five years after the event. He repeats this account of the crossing in Krulewitch interview, OHC, 45–46.

53.   Brannen, *Over There*, 55, 147. Brannen wrote his memoir in the 1930s.

54.   *2nd Div. Records*, vol. 5; Hillman, "Crossing the Meuse," 71–73.

55.   Cates interview, OHC, 44; Williams, "Meuse-Argonne Report"; *2nd Div. Records*, vol. 5.

56.   Cates to Mother and Sister, Nov. 27, 1918.

57.   Krulewitch, *Now That You Mention It*, 58–59.

Epilogue

1.   Spaulding and Wright, *Second Division*, 223–24; *History of the Sixth Regiment United States Marines*, 50–55; Sellers memoir, copy in author's possession, 42–43.

2.   "Final Report of Assistant Chief of Staff G-1 to Commander-in-Chief, American Expeditionary Forces, 22 April 1919," cited in Braim, *Test of Battle*, 176–83.

3.   Grotelueschen, "AEF Way of War," 217; Mark Grotelueschen comes to the same conclusion about the AEF in general. "Most AEF units simply did not have the training, experience, or weaponry required to carry out the tactics in *Combat Instructions*." "AEF Way of War," 31.

Appendix B

1.   Brannan, *Over There*, flyleaf.

2.   Cates BF.

3.   Denig BF.

4.   Erskine BF.

5.   Fritz, Personnel Records, OMPF.

6.   Holcomb BF.

7.   Clark, "John Joseph Kelly," 47; Hopper, *Medals of Honor*, 149–50.

8.   Krulewitch BF.

9.   Paradis memoir, MCPPC.

10.   "Announcement to the Supreme Court of the District of Colombia of the Death of Lucian H. Vandoren," *Journal of the District of Colombia Bar Association*, Aug. 1935.

11.   "Brief History of the Second Battalion, Sixth Regiment, U.S. Marine Corps," Box 36, 2/6 File, RG 127.

12.   Sellers memoir, copy in author's possession, 42; Williams, Personnel Records, OMPF.

Bibliography

MANUSCRIPTS AND COLLECTIONS

AUTHOR'S COLLECTION

Green, John C. Letter and questionnaire regarding Capt. Kirt Green, February 15, 1996.

Messersmith, Robert E. "Operations of Company 'E' (78th Company), Sixth Regiment Marines (2nd Division) at Belleau Woods, June 1 to June 13, 1918," a personal experience submitted to the U.S. Army Infantry Advanced Course, Fort Benning, Ga., 1928–29. Copy.

Sellers, James McB. Unpublished memoir and letters (furnished by William W. Sellers).

Simmons, Edwin H., director emeritus, Marine Corps Historical Center. Interview by the author, September 30, 1998.

Swan, Philip G., Bentley Historical Library, University of Michigan, Ann Arbor. Letter to the author, June 28, 1996.

Vandoren, Lucien Hall, J.D. Letter and questionnaire, July 17, 1996.

HISTORICAL REFERENCE BRANCH, U.S. MARINE CORPS HISTORY DIVISION, QUANTICO, VA.

Biographic Files: Clifton B. Cates; Bailee M. Coffenburg; Robert L. Denig; Donald F. Duncan; Graves B. Erskine; Thomas Holcomb; John Joseph Kelly; Egbert T. Lloyd; Robert E. Messersmith; John Henry Pruitt; Ernest C. Williams; Randolph T. Zane.

Casualty List of the American Expeditionary Forces.

Cates, Clifton B. Papers.

Hill, Glenn G., to G. M. Neufeld, head, Reference Section, Marine Corps History and Museums Division, January 17, 1979.

Muster Roll of the United States Marine Corps.

Oral History Collection, interviews by Benis M. Frank, Oral History Unit, Historical Division, HQMC: Clifton B. Cates, 1973, transcript; Graves B. Erskine, 1973, transcript; Melvin L. Krulewitch, 1974, transcript; Merwin H. Silverthorn, 1973, transcript; William Arthur Worton, n.d., transcript.

Reference Section. "Marine Corps Experience with Gas in WWI," 1984.

West, John A. "Belleau Wood."

MARINE CORPS PERSONAL PAPERS COLLECTION, ARCHIVES AND SPECIAL COLLECTIONS, U.S. MARINE CORPS UNIVERSITY, QUANTICO, VA.

Asprey, Robert B. Notes, Records, and Correspondence.

Benjamin, Romeyn P. "June, 1918."

Cates, Clifton B. Letters.

————. "Personal Observations of the Taking of Bouresches."

Denig, Robert. "Diary of a Marine Officer during the World War."

Erskine, Graves B. Personal Papers.

Paradis, Don V. Unpublished memoir.

Sparks, Victor. Interview by J. Michael Miller, n.d. Transcript.

————. Diary.

Thomas, Gerald C. Memoir.

MEDAL OF HONOR SOCIETY, PATRIOT'S POINT, S.C.

Hayden, David. Biographic File.

Stockham, Fred. Biographic File.

OFFICIAL MILITARY PERSONNEL FILES, NATIONAL
PERSONNEL RECORDS CENTER, ST. LOUIS, MO.

Adams, James P., Personnel Records.

Brannen, Carl A., Personnel Records.

Fritz, Bernard L., Personnel Records.

Grayson, Joseph Charles, Personnel Records.

Green, Kirt, Personnel Records.

Holcomb, Thomas, Personnel Records.

Kilduff, David R., Personnel Records.

Paradis, Don V., Personnel Records.

Powers, Walter A., Personnel Records.

Robb, Emmons J., Personnel Records.

Sellers, James McB., Personnel Records.

Skoda, Stephan, Personnel Records.

Ulrich, William, Personnel Records.

Vandoren, Lucien, Personnel Records.

Williams, Ernest C., Personnel Records.

Woodworth, Wethered, Personnel Records.

Zane, Randolph T., Personnel Records.

NATIONAL ARCHIVES, WASHINGTON, D.C.

Correspondence with Officers of the 2nd Division, AEF. Records Relating to
World War I Frontline Maps and Accompanying "Summaries of Opera-
tions," Records of the American Battlefield Monuments Commission,
RG 117.4.2.

Records Relating to Marine Participation in World War I, RG 127, A1, Entry 240.

BOOKS, ARTICLES, AND DISSERTATIONS

American Battlefield Monuments Commission. *American Armies and Battlefields
in Europe*. Washington, D.C.: American Battlefield Monuments Commission, 1938.

Asprey, Robert B. *At Belleau Wood.* New York: G. P. Putnam's Sons, 1965.

———. *The German High Command at War.* New York: William Morrow, 1991.

Bellamy, David. *History of the Third Battalion, Sixth Regiment, U.S. Marines.* Hillsdale, Mich.: Akers, MacRitchie, and Hurlbut, 1919.

Braim, Paul F. *The Test of Battle: The American Expeditionary Forces in the Meuse-Argonne Campaign.* Newark: University of Delaware Press, 1987.

Brannen, Carl Andrew. *Over There! A Marine in the Great War.* Edited by Rolfe L. Hillman Jr., Peter F. Owen, and J. P. Brannen. College Station: Texas A&M University Press, 1996.

Cates, Clifton B. *History of the 96th Company.* Washington, D.C.: HQMC, 1935.

Catlin, Albertus W. *With the Help of God and a Few Marines.* New York: Doubleday, Page, 1919.

Clark, George B. *Devildogs: Fighting Marines of World War I.* Novato, Calif.: Presidio, 1999.

———. "John Joseph Kelly." *Leatherneck,* November 1998, 40–47.

———. *A List of Officers of the 4th Marine Brigade.* Pike, N.H.: Brass Hat, n.d.

———. *Major Awards to U.S. Marines in World War One.* Pike, N.H.: Brass Hat, n.d.

Cochrane, Rexmond C. *Gas Warfare at Belleau Wood, June 1918.* Washington, D.C.: U.S. Army Chemical Corps Historical Office, 1957.

Coffman, Edward M. *The War to End All Wars.* Madison: University of Wisconsin Press, 1986.

Cowing, Kemper F. *Dear Folks at Home. . . .* New York: Houghton Mifflin, 1919.

Department of the Army. *The Writing of American Military History: A Guide.* DA Pamphlet 20–200. Washington, D.C.: Department of the Army, 1956.

Derby, Richard. *Wade In, Sanitary!* New York: Putnam's Sons, 1919.

Donaldson, G. H. *History of the Seventy-Eighth Company, Sixth Marines.* Neuwied, Ger.: W. Jenkins, 1919.

Donovan, John. "Viven-Bessiere Rifle Grenade and Launchers." *Arrghh! The Home of Two of Jonah's Military Guys.* http://www.thedonovan.com/archives/002234.html (accessed May 25, 2005).

Fisch, Robert. *Field Equipment of the Infantry, 1914–1945.* Sykesville, Md.: Greenberg, 1989.

Grotelueschen, Mark E. "The AEF Way of War: The American Army and Combat in the First World War." Ph.D. diss., Texas A&M University, 2003.

———. *Doctrine under Trial: American Artillery Employment in World War I.* Westport, Conn.: Greenwood, 2001.

Gudmundsson, Bruce I. *Stormtroop Tactics.* New York: Praeger, 1989.

Hamburger, Kenneth E. *Learning Lessons in the American Expeditionary Forces.* Washington, D.C.: U.S. Army Center for Military History, n.d.

Harbord, James G. *The American Army in France 1917–1918.* Boston: Little, Brown, 1936.

———. *Leaves from a War Diary.* New York: Dodd, Mead, 1925.

Harlee, William C. *U.S. Marine Corps Score Book and Rifleman's Instructor.* Philadelphia: International Printing, 1916.

Hartman, Robert B. D. "From Culver's Corps to the Marine Corps." Culver Academies. http://www.culver.org/alumni/hartmanonhistory/ decmarines/marinecorps.htm (accessed May 2005).

Hemrick, Levi E. *Once a Marine*. New York: Carlton, 1968.

Hopper, James. *Medals of Honor*. New York: John Day, 1929.

Hillman, Rolfe L. "Crossing the Meuse." *Marine Corps Gazette*, November 1988, 68–73.

Hillman, Rolfe L., Jr. and Douglas V. Johnson. *Soissons 1918*. College Station: Texas A&M University Press, 1999.

History of the Sixth Machine Gun Battalion. Neufeld on the Rhine, Ger.: 1919. Reprint, Pike, N.H.: Brass Hat, 1993.

History of the Sixth Regiment United States Marines. Tientsin, China: Tientsin Press, 1929.

Hyatt, Glenn. "U.S. Defensive Grenades in WWI." Trenches on the Web, Special Feature. http://www.worldwar1.com/sfusdg.htm (accessed May 25, 2005).

"In Memoriam—Capt. Donald F. Duncan." *St. Joseph Gazette*, June 8, 1919.

Johnson, Douglas V., II. "A Few Squads Left and Off to France: Training the American Army in the U.S. for WWI." PhD diss., Temple University, 1992.

Krulewitch, Melvin L. *Now That You Mention It*. New York: Quadrangle, 1973.

Lee, Harry. "Some Notes on Musketry Training and Field Exercises." *Marine Corps Gazette*, December 1917, 295–304.

Lejeune, John A. *The Reminiscences of a Marine*. Philadelphia: Dorrance, 1930.

Lofgren, Stephen J. "Unready for War: The Army in World War I." *Army History* 22 (Spring 1922): 11–19.

Lupfer, Timothy T. *The Dynamics of Doctrine: The Changes in German Tactical Doctrine During the First World War*. Fort Leavenworth, Kans.: U.S. Army Command and General Staff College, 1981.

MacGillivray, George C., and George B. Clark. *A History of the 80th Company, Sixth Marines*. Pike, N.H.: Brass Hat, n.d.

Maddox, Rinda. "Medal of Honor Recipient Draws Visitor." *The Sidell Reporter*, May 22, 2002.

McClellan, Edwin N. "The Aisne Marne Offensive." *Marine Corps Gazette*, March 1921, 66–84; June 1921, 188–227.

———. "The Battle at Blanc Mont Ridge." *Marine Corps Gazette*, March 1922, 1–21; June 1922, 206–211; September 1922, 287–88.

———. "Capture of Hill 142, Battle of Belleau Wood, and Capture of Bouresches." *Marine Corps Gazette*, September 1920, 277–313; December 1920, 371–405.

———. "The Fourth Brigade of Marines in the Training Areas and the Operations in the Verdun Sector." *Marine Corps Gazette*, March 1920, 81–110.

———. "In the Marbache Sector." *Marine Corps Gazette*, September 1921, 253–68.

———. "Operations of the Fourth Brigade of Marines in the Aisne Defense." *Marine Corps Gazette*, June 1920, 182–215.

———. "St. Mihiel." *Marine Corps Gazette*, December 1921, 375–97.

———. *The United States Marine Corps in the World War.* Washington, D.C.: Government Printing Office, 1920. Reprint, Nashville, Tenn.: Battery, 1997.

McQuain, Thomas Bryan. *To the Front and Back: A West Virginia Marine Fights World War I.* Westminster, Md.: Heritage Books, 2005.

Metcalf, Clyde. *History of the U.S. Marine Corps.* New York: G. P. Putnam's Sons, 1939.

Millett, Alan R. *Semper Fidelis: The History of the United States Marine Corps.* New York: Macmillan 1980.

Millett, Alan R., and Williamson Murray, eds. *Military Effectiveness.* Vol. 1, *The First World War.* Boston: Allen & Unwin, 1988.

Musicant, Ivan. *The Banana Wars.* New York: Macmillan, 1990.

Otto, Ernst. *The Battle at Blanc Mont.* Translated by Martin Lichtenburg. Annapolis: U.S. Naval Institute, 1930.

———. "The Battles for the Possession of Belleau Woods, June 1918." *U.S. Naval Institute Proceedings* 54, no. 11 (November 1928): 941–62.

Paschall, Rod. *The Defeat of Imperial Germany, 1917–1918.* Chapel Hill: Algonquin Books, 1989.

Pershing, John J. *My Experiences in the World War.* New York: Frederick A. Stokes, 1931.

Rainey, James W. "The Questionable Training of the AEF in World War I." *Parameters* 22 (Winter 1992–93): 89–103.

Simmons, Edwin K. "The Second Day at Soissons" *Fortitudine* 22 (Summer-Fall 1993).

Smythe, Donald. *Pershing: General of the Armies.* Bloomington: Indiana University Press, 1986.

Spaulding, Oliver L., and John W. Wright. *The Second Division, American Expeditionary Force in France, 1917–1919.* New York: Hillman, 1937. Reprint, Nashville: Battery, 1989.

Thomas, Gerald C., Jr. "The Marine Corps Prepares for War." *Marine Corps Gazette,* June 1993, 66–71.

Thomason, John W., Jr. *The United States Second Division Northwest of Chateau Thierry in World War I.* Edited by George Clark. Jefferson, N.C.: McFarland, 2006.

Toland, John. *No Man's Land: 1918—The Last Year of the Great War.* New York: Ballentine, 1980.

Trask, David F. *The AEF and Coalition Warmaking, 1917–1918.* Lawrence: University Press of Kansas, 1993.

U.S. Army. *Field Service Regulations 1914, corrected to April 1917.* Washington, D.C.: War Department, 1917.

———. *Instructions for the Offensive Combat of Small Units.* Adapted from the French Edition. Headquarters, American Expeditionary Forces, France, 1918.

———. *Manual for Commanders of Infantry Platoons.* Translated from the French. Washington, D.C.: Army War College, 1917.

————. *Records of the 2nd Division (Regular).* 9 vols. Washington, D.C.: Army War College, 1927.

————. *Translations of War Diaries of German Units Opposed to the 2nd Division (Regular).* 9 vols. Washington, D.C.: Army War College, 1918.

U.S. Department of Commerce. *Historical Statistics of the United States, Colonial Times to 1970.* Part 1, Series H-706. Washington, D.C.: Government Printing Office, 1975.

U.S. Marine Corps. *Marine Corps Doctrinal Publication 1: Tactics.* Washington D.C.: Government Printing Office, 1997.

U.S. Navy. *The Medical Department of the United States Navy with the Army and Marine Corps in France in World War I.* Washington, D.C.: U.S. Navy Department, 1947.

Waller, L. W. T., Jr. "Machine Guns of the Fourth Brigade." *Marine Corps Gazette,* March 1920, 1–31.

Wilson, Dale E. *Treat 'Em Rough: The Birth of American Armor, 1917–20.* Novato, Calif.: Presidio, 1991.

Wise, Frederic M., as told to Meigs O. Frost. *A Marine Tells It to You.* New York: J. H. Sears, 1929. Reprint, Quantico, Va.: Marine Corps Association, 1981.

Zabecki, David T. *Steel Wind: Colonel Georg Bruchmuller and the Birth of Modern Artillery.* Westport, Conn.: Praeger, 1994.

Index

ISBN-13: 978-1-58544-599-8
ISBN-10: 1-58544-599-1

53250

9 781585 445998